HOW *to* USE

Dreamweaver® 4 and Fireworks® 4

SAMS

Sams Publishing
201 West 103rd Street
Indianapolis, Indiana 46290

Lon Coley

Visually in Full Color

How to Use Dreamweaver®4 and Fireworks®4

Copyright © 2001 by Sams Publishing

International Standard Book Number: 0-672-32041-X

Library of Congress Catalog Card Number: 00-111606

Printed in the United States of America

First Printing: February 2001

04   03   02   01   4   3   2   1

Trademarks

All terms mentioned in this book that are known to be trademarks or service marks have been appropriately capitalized. Sams Publishing cannot attest to the accuracy of this information. Use of a term in this book should not be regarded as affecting the validity of any trademark or service mark.

Warning and Disclaimer

Executive Editor
Jeff Schultz

Development Editor
Alice Martina Smith

Managing Editor
Charlotte Clapp

Project Editor
Elizabeth Finney

Indexer
Greg Pearson

Proofreader
Katherin Bidwell

Technical Editor
Susannah Hall

Team Coordinator
Amy Patton

Interior Designer
Nathan Clement

Cover Designers
Nathan Clement
Aren Howell

Page Layout
Gloria Schurick

Contents at a Glance

Contents

About the Author

Lon Coley (**LonColey@ariadne-webdesign.co.uk**) is an IT professional, specializing in Office and Internet applications.

Her company site at **http://www.ariadne-webdesign.co.uk** holds far more information than we could put here and is updated as often as time allows.

Her experience and expertise means that as well as designing sites for clients, she now acts as a consultant and troubleshooter to companies of all sizes who are looking to improve and develop their Internet presence or who have sites that they feel don't do their organization justice.

A firm believer that anyone can build a Web site with the right tools and training, Lon often works with companies who want to develop their own Web sites but feel they need an expert "to call on" when they are struggling, or need professional guidance about new technologies when developing their existing sites.

An experienced teacher and trainer, Lon writes and develops dedicated customized training courses for business and education. These courses cover the whole spectrum of her expertise and are always prepared with the individual client in mind, thus guaranteeing that the needs of the client are addressed and met in full.

Acknowledgments

Thanks to everyone at Macmillan for their help and skill in getting this book together, but especially to Amy for answering questions and supplying information whenever I needed it, Elizabeth for her encouragement, and Alice for her humor.

Thanks to Jon for letting me work when I needed to and helping when I needed him to.

Dedication

To Jan—for everything.

Tell Us What You Think!

As the reader of this book, *you* are our most important critic and commentator. We value your opinion and want to know what we're doing right, what we could do better, what areas you'd like to see us publish in, and any other words of wisdom you're willing to pass our way.

You can email or write me directly to let me know what you did or didn't like about this book—as well as what we can do to make our books stronger.

Please note that I cannot help you with technical problems related to the topic of this book, and that due to the high volume of mail I receive, I might not be able to reply to every message.

When you write, please be sure to include this book's title and author as well as your name and phone number. I will carefully review your comments and share them with the author and editors who worked on the book.

Email: webdev_sams@mcp.com

Mail: Mark Taber
Associate Publisher
Sams Publishing
201 West 103rd Street
Indianapolis, IN 46290 USA

How to Use This Book

The Complete Visual Reference

Each part of this book consists of a series of short instructional tasks designed to help you understand all the information you need to get the most out of Dreamweaver and Fireworks.

Each task includes a series of easy-to-understand steps designed to guide you through the procedure.

Click: Click the left mouse button once.

Double-click: Click the left mouse button twice in rapid succession.

Right-click: Click the right mouse button once.

Selection: This circle highlights the area that is discussed in the step.

Keyboard: Type information or data into the indicated location.

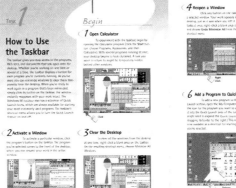

Drag

Drop

Drag & drop: Position the mouse pointer over the object, click and hold the left mouse button, drag the object to its new location, and release the mouse button.

Each step is fully illustrated to show you how it looks onscreen.

Extra hints that tell you how to accomplish a goal are provided in most tasks.

Screen elements (such as menus, icons, windows, and so on), as well as things you enter or select, appear in **boldface** type.

Continues

If you see this symbol, it means that the task you're in continues on the next page.

Introduction

"Anyone can design a Web site."

This is a statement I use often when teaching and training those new to the idea of Internet design. This statement is made all the more accurate by using Dreamweaver—a piece of software that combines the best features of an HTML editor with those of a text editor. You have complete control over what happens and when. Bring in the best dedicated Web graphics application in Fireworks, and you are suddenly in control of one of the best and most powerful software combinations around today.

What Are Dreamweaver and Fireworks?

Both are award-winning software applications recognized within the Internet industry as leaders in their fields. The two applications integrate almost seamlessly, letting you move between them whenever you want to.

Dreamweaver will let you create everything from simple pages to the most complicated ones with a minimum of effort. It isn't just an HTML editor, but a complete application that carries on when most other applications have given up.

Fireworks can create not only simple graphics, but also complex animations, rollovers, imagemaps, and slices. This gives you control not only over the design of your pages but also—and more importantly—the finished result.

Who Should Use the Software?

In reality, the answer to this question could or should be "everyone," but the applications are best suited to those who want to create wonderful Web sites and to control the way their site(s) look.

From the user-friendly interfaces that Macromedia has made even better in the latest release of these titles to the ever-present user control, there is something for everyone in both Dreamweaver and Fireworks 4.

Stunning visuals combined with excellent layout will always make for successful Web pages, and Dreamweaver and Fireworks give you the power to create both simply and easily.

Task

1

Getting Started with Dreamweaver 4

*O*kay, so you have a brand new copy of Dreamweaver 4 and are ready to go. Indeed, you will soon be creating your own pages and sites easily and quickly.

Before you do that, however, you need to know a little about the software. Dreamweaver is an HTML editor, site manager, and authoring program all combined in one easy-to-use interface. The HTML editor is where you can input page content and change the HTML code (the programming language that actually tells the browser how your page is supposed to look); the site manager lets you see all the files in your Web site at a glance; and the authoring side of Dreamweaver allows you to add scripts and animations wherever and whenever you want them.

Being a WYSIWYG (what you see is what you get) editor, Dreamweaver is an extremely powerful application that is also a lot of fun to use. You can use Dreamweaver without ever having to learn any HTML. For total beginners in the world of Web page creation, this is an appealing idea. Still, because most of us like to check what is happening behind the scenes from time to time, Dreamweaver lets you fuss with the HTML code directly if you want to do that, too.

Dreamweaver not only creates your HTML code for you, but it also has the built-in capability to let you create animations, mouseovers, and many other effects to give your Web pages the edge over others in cyberspace. With thousands of new pages appearing on the Net every day, you need to make your pages stand out above the crowd. Dreamweaver can help you do that.

The tasks in this first part of the book are really an introduction to the software; they show you around the application. In this first part, you will do a lot of looking and clicking—all to prepare you for the rest of the book, when you will be doing, doing, doing!

From creating pages and sites from scratch to editing and updating existing sites without fear of your code being changed, Dreamweaver is the most powerful Web creation software available. Enjoy your work with it. ●

How to Open and Exit Dreamweaver 4

This book assumes that you have already installed your Dreamweaver software into its default location on your hard disk. Thankfully, the Dreamweaver program has always been straightforward to open and use. Unlike some other HTML software, Dreamweaver opens quickly and easily into the user interface. For this first task, we will just look around and go in and out of the program.

Begin

1 Open Dreamweaver 4

From the **Start** menu, choose **Programs**, Macromedia Dreamweaver 4, Dreamweaver 4.

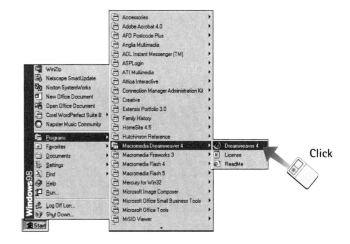

Click

2 Take a Look Around

For now, don't do anything—just look around the screen and familiarize yourself with the display. There is a toolbar across the top of the screen, the **Objects** panel containing a series of buttons, and another window known as the **Properties Inspector**.

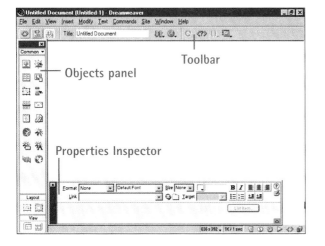

Toolbar

Objects panel

Properties Inspector

3 What Are You Seeing?

The big white area onscreen is the *document window*. Although it might look cluttered at times, you can choose what to show or hide in it. In this example, everything has been closed but the software. The document window is where you work to create your Web pages.

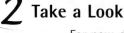

4 Close Dreamweaver

To close the software, choose **File, Exit** (or press Ctrl+Q).

File	
New	Ctrl+N
New from Template...	
Open...	Ctrl+O
Open in Frame...	Ctrl+Shift+O
Close	Ctrl+W
Save	Ctrl+S
Save As...	Ctrl+Shift+S
Save as Template...	
Save All Frames	
Revert	
Import	▶
Export	▶
Convert	▶
Preview in Browser	▶
Debug in Browser	▶
Check Links	Shift+F8
Check Target Browsers...	
Design Notes...	
1 webdesign.htm	
2 index.htm	
3 contact.htm	
4 advice.htm	
Exit	Ctrl+Q

Click

5 Are You Sure?

Dreamweaver prompts you to confirm that you really want to close the application. Click **Yes** to close the software.

Dreamweaver

⚠ Quit Dreamweaver?

☐ Don't warn me again.

[Yes]   [No]

Click

End

How-To Hints

Don't Close by Accident

When you close Dreamweaver, the confirmation dialog box appears. If you enable the **Don't warn me again** check box, Dreamweaver will not confirm your request to shut down the application. Until you are confident with the software, allow it to continue to confirm that you want to close the software each time.

How to Understand the Dreamweaver Interface

The Dreamweaver interface is designed so that you can control most aspects of it. You can make toolbars and panels appear and disappear whenever you want, leaving the main window clear for working; alternatively, you can have as many panels open as you want. After you know what everything does, you will soon realize how flexible Dreamweaver is to work with. Remember that the menus are there to help you, and even if you find the panels confusing at first, everything is named so that the menus will help you find what you are looking for.

Begin

1 The Document Window

The document window is where you do your work in Dreamweaver. As you add page content, the objects and text display here, just as when you use a word processor. In this example, you see the document window after several words have been typed.

Document window

2 The Toolbar

Unlike other applications that have many toolbars, Dreamweaver has only one. You can look at your pages in different ways and access several handy shortcuts from this toolbar.

3 The Launcher and Mini Launcher

The **Launcher** and **mini Launcher** are filled with buttons that give you quick access to inspectors and panels. Display the **Launcher** by choosing **Window, Launcher**. The group of icons on the right end of the status bar constitute the **mini Launcher**, which makes it easy to access panels and inspectors even when the main **Launcher** is not visible.

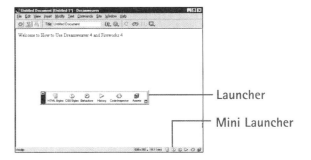

Launcher

Mini Launcher

4 The Properties Inspector

The **Properties Inspector** shows you properties for the elements on your page. For example, if you select an image to make it the current element, the width and height of the image are displayed here. The appearance of the **Properties Inspector** changes depending on the current selection. In this example, an image is selected, and the Properties Inspector shows the properties for that image.

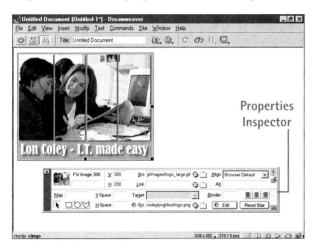

Properties Inspector

5 The Objects Panel

The **Objects** panel might be the single most-used item of Dreamweaver. From this panel you can insert any kind of object, image, or plug-in. The **Objects** panel has six categories, each of which allow you to insert different elements into your page. You also use the **Objects** panel to switch between standard and layout views.

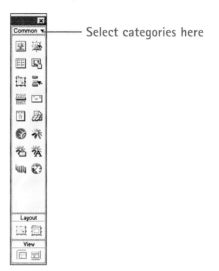

Select categories here

6 The Assets Panel

The **Assets** panel is a great new feature in Dreamweaver 4. In this panel, Dreamweaver categorizes all the different assets used by all the pages in your site. *Assets* are elements such as images, colors, and links. Having all your site's assets displayed by category in the **Assets** panel makes it easy to add them to any new pages that you are creating.

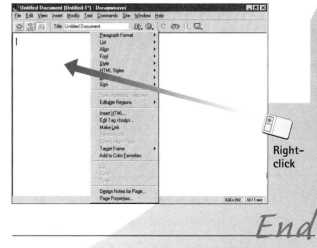

Select asset category here

7 Menus

The menu bar stretches across the top of the Dreamweaver window. These menus give you a direct route to whatever command you want to access. Additional menus, called *context menus*, are available by right-clicking elements on the page (Macintosh users must **Ctrl**+click elements). Context menus offer commands appropriate for the selected item.

Right-click

End

How to Use the Document Window

When you first open Dreamweaver, the document window has no content because you haven't started to create a Web page yet. However, many details in the window provide useful information about your page. Everything in the document window is there for a reason. When you use the document window, you are checking and maintaining the site and determining how long the pages will take to download.

Begin

1 Look at the Status Bar

The status bar appears at the bottom of the document window. It contains all kinds of information and options concerning your page. Nothing that appears there is unnecessary, so let's examine the items in the status bar in order.

Status bar

2 The Tag Selector

The more your page fills with content, the greater the number of HTML tags that will be visible in this area of the status bar. Click any tag in this area to select the corresponding content in the document window.

`<body> <table> <tr> <td> <div> <table> <tr> <td>`

Tag selector

3 Window Size Options

You can use the **Window Size** pop-up menu to display your document window in a variety of different sizes. This feature is useful when you want to see how your Web page will look when viewed on monitors with different resolutions.

```
592w
536 x 196    (640 x 480, Default)
600 x 300    (640 x 480, Maximized)
760 x 420    (800 x 600, Maximized)
795 x 470    (832 x 624, Maximized)
955 x 600    (1024 x 768, Maximized)
544 x 378    (WebTV)

Edit Sizes...
```

Window Size menu

4 Download Time

Next to the **Window Size** menu is an estimate for the time it will take to download your page. The file size displayed here includes not only the HTML file, but also all the image files and other objects included in your page.

`636 x 392 ▾ | 68K / 19 sec | 🖅 ① ⚙ ▷ ◇ 📦`

File size and
download time

5 Mini Launcher

As already mentioned, the icons on the right end of the status bar form the **mini Launcher**. These icons are an always visible version of the main **Launcher**; open and close panels by clicking the buttons on the **Launcher** or in the **mini Launcher** in the status bar.

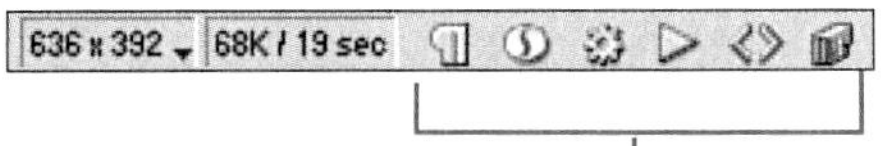

`636 x 392 ▾ | 68K / 19 sec | 🖅 ① ⚙ ▷ ◇ 📦`

Mini Launcher

6 The Title Bar

The Dreamweaver title bar appears at the top of the screen, just above the toolbar and menu bar. The title bar lists the filename, the page title, and, when appropriate, an asterisk indicating that the page has changed since it was last saved.

`Welcome to Lon Coley online (loncoley/index.htm*) - Dreamweaver    _ 🗗 ✕`

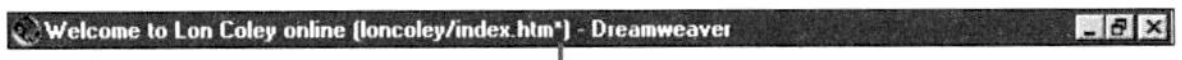

The asterisk indicates that the page
has changed since it was last saved

End

How-To Hints

Snap to It

When you get used to working with the panels in Dreamweaver, you will probably have lots of panels open at once. To keep things neat and tidy onscreen, these panels "snap" to the edge of the document window, giving you the maximum workspace possible. Even when you start a new document, your open panels will stay in place, ready for use.

How to Show and Hide Panels and Windows

You can show or hide windows and panels quickly and easily in Dreamweaver 4. You might want to hide windows or panels to better view the elements on your page. You'll want to display windows and panels to access the controls on these elements. This task explores the options for opening and closing windows and panels in Dreamweaver.

Begin

1 Close All Floating Panels

Everything open onscreen—except for the document itself—is classified as a floating panel. To close all the floating panels with a single command, choose **Window, Hide Panels**. All the panels will disappear at once.

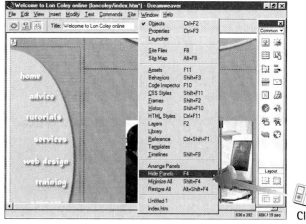

Click

2 Restore All Panels

As easily as you can close all floating panels, you can bring all the panels back just as easily. Choose **Window, Show Panels,** and the panels closed in the previous step will reappear exactly as they were.

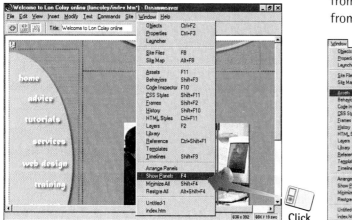

Click

3 Show or Hide Panels Using Menus

You can make each panel in Dreamweaver visible or invisible at any time. The **Window** menu gives you control over all the panels. Simply select the name of the panel that you want to show from the menu, and it will appear. Select the option from the menu again to hide that panel.

Click

4 Close Panels in the Document Window

Each open panel has an × in the top-right corner of its title bar. This button is called the close button or close box. You may have noticed that Dreamweaver sometimes opens several panels into a single window. Clicking the close button will close the open panel or group of panels.

Click

5 Close Panels Using the Launcher

In the same way that clicking buttons on the **Launcher** (or the **mini Launcher** in the status bar) opens panels and inspectors, clicking the button a second time closes the panel again.

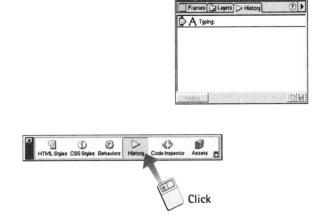

Click

End

How-To Hints

Whatever Feels Good!

After you have been working with Dreamweaver for a while, you will discover an arrangement of panels and inspectors on the screen that is ideal for your work habits. If you arrange the panels as you want and then quit Dreamweaver, the panels will open and be arranged on the screen in exactly the same position the next time you launch the software.

How to Use Dreamweaver Help

Dreamweaver has a great built-in help facility that can answer most—if not all—your questions. The **Help** menus can assist you in working through a tutorial, take you on a guided tour of the program, or simply let you look for whatever information you are trying to find. In addition to the built-in help system installed in the software, the Macromedia Web site (**www.macromedia.com**) has a wealth of help, information, and forums to help ensure that you get the most from the application.

Begin

1 Use the Lessons

For a novice user, the lessons are a good place to start learning about Dreamweaver. To start the tutorial, choose **Help, Lessons**. The **Lessons** screen opens for you to choose the lesson you want to take. Simply click the title that matches what you want to learn about.

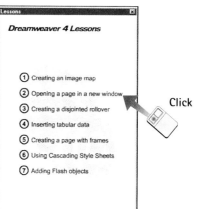

Click

2 Find Out What's New in This Version

Aimed at those who have used previous versions of Dreamweaver, the **What's New** section of the tutorial will help you learn about all the new and updated features of the latest version of Dreamweaver. To learn about new features in Dreamweaver 4, choose **Help, What's New in Dreamweaver 4**.

3 Use the Main Dreamweaver Help Features

To use the main Dreamweaver help features, choose **Help, Using Dreamweaver**. The main Dreamweaver help screen opens in your browser. There are three main sections to the help system: **Contents, Index,** and **Search**.

4 Use the Contents Help

When the main help screen opens in the browser, by default the **Contents** view is enabled. The left frame shows a subject listing; information is displayed in the right frame. To view help topics in a given subject area, click the subject in the left frame. Click a topic heading to expand the contents so that you can move through the files logically.

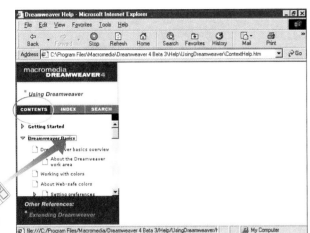

Click

5 Use the Index Help

To use the **Index** help in Dreamweaver, open the main help screen and click the **Index** tab to see an alphabetic listing of topics in the left frame. Scroll up or down to find the topic you're interested in. Click the topic that you want to see information about, and it will open in the right frame.

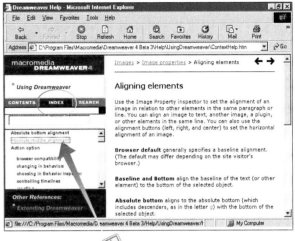

Click

6 Use the Search Help

To search for specific information, open the main help screen and click the **Search** tab to launch a Java applet with a search box. Type the word or words you are looking for and click the **List Topics** button. Matching words appear in the middle box of the screen. Select the one that best suits your search and click the **Display** button to see information about that topic.

Click

How-To Hints

Navigating Help in the Browser

Because all the help files are displayed in your default browser window, you can use the browser's **Forward** and **Back** buttons to return to and from the pages you have already viewed.

End

How to Use the Dreamweaver Support Center

In addition to all the help options you learned about in the preceding task, Macromedia fully supports the Dreamweaver program through its Web site. A direct link from the program to the Web site has been provided for easy access to the information there.

Begin

1 Open the Dreamweaver Support Site

To open the Dreamweaver Support Center Web site, choose **Help, Dreamweaver Support Center**. The Dreamweaver Support Center Web site opens in your browser window.

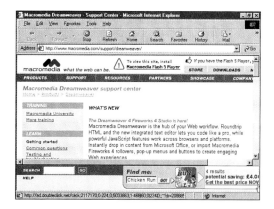

2 Navigate the Support Site

The Support Center is divided into easy-to-use sections and has some great features. Perhaps the most important one of these features is the help facility. Click a link in the **Learn** section to see a list of helpful hints and articles about the selected topic. Alternatively, use the **Search** facility to find references to a specific word.

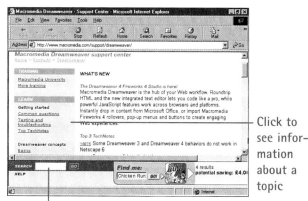

Click to see information about a topic

Search for specific help

3 Keep Up to Date

Click the **Membership** link to subscribe to the Macromedia Membership Center. When you're a member, you'll receive a free email newsletter and keep up to date with new and upcoming products and services from Macromedia.

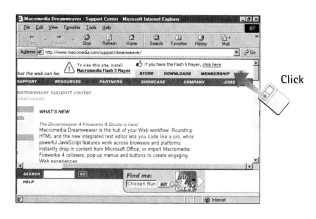

Click

4 Join Online Forums

In addition to its easy-to-follow links, Dreamweaver provides full online support through the **Forums** section of the Support Center. Click the **Online Forums** link in the **Discuss** section of the home page to join discussion groups about various aspects of the Dreamweaver application.

Click

5 Find Out What's New

The main frame of the Support Center Web site opens to a **What's New** section. This information is frequently updated and shows recently released updates and fixes as well as downloadable manuals (in PDF format). Check back often to see what has been added to this area of the Support Center.

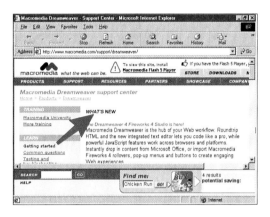

6 The Macromedia Exchange

When you feel that you know the software pretty well, the Dreamweaver **Exchange** will become a regular visiting spot for you. This is the place to get easy-to-install extensions that allow you to add new features to Dreamweaver. You'll look more at extending Dreamweaver in Part 14, "Dreamweaver and Beyond." Choose **Help, Dreamweaver Exchange** to go to the Exchange Web site.

How-To Hints

Take the Tour

When you first use Dreamweaver, choose **Help, Guided Tour** to see what Dreamweaver can do in a series of movies. The "Show Me" movies take you through the main features of Dreamweaver in sequence.

End

Task

2

Using Panels and Windows

In the preceding part of this book, you looked briefly at some of the more common panels used in Dreamweaver. The tasks in this part look in more detail at how to use these panels and examine exactly what they can do to make your work in Dreamweaver easier. One of the great things about Dreamweaver is the way it gives you control not only over the way you create your pages, but also over the area you use to do that work in.

Each area of Dreamweaver has a panel that is named to make it obvious what it is for and when it is used. Some of the panels open in a separate window; others open in groups. When you have a group of panels, simply click the tab for the particular panel you want to use.

If you know that you are going to be working with layers, for example, you can open the **Layers** panel and leave it open onscreen; alternatively, you can open it whenever you want to use it. This is true for all the other panels as well.

The great thing about panels is that you only have to display the ones you want when you want; you can keep you work area clear the rest of the time. Those who have used previous versions of Dreamweaver will be used to the word palette and not panel, but don't worry; the name might have changed, but the functionality is as good as (if not better than) ever.

How to Use the Launcher

As its name implies, the **Launcher** is used to launch things. Specifically, it is a convenient shortcut bar that you can use to open whatever panels, windows, or inspectors you want to use at the time. By default, the **Launcher** shows the most commonly used options. Everything you learn about the **Launcher** in this task also applies to the **mini Launcher**, which is always visible in the status bar. In Task 2, you learn how to customize the **Launcher** to show the panels that you want there.

Begin

1 Show the Launcher

The **Launcher** appears on the screen when you first open Dreamweaver. If you can't see it for some reason, choose **Window, Launcher** to open it on the screen.

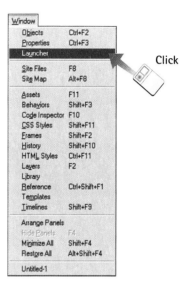

Click

2 Hide the Launcher

To make the **Launcher** disappear, choose **Window, Launcher** again to remove the check mark from the option in the **Window** menu. The **Launcher** disappears from the screen.

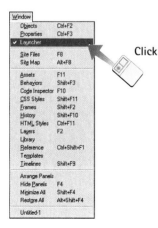

Click

3 Make the Launcher Vertical

By default, the **Launcher** appears as a horizontal bar on the screen and cannot be resized. However, you can change its orientation to vertical by clicking the arrow at the bottom-right corner of the **Launcher** panel.

Click

4 Click a Launchpad

Actually, the elements on the **Launcher** are called buttons, but "launchpad" sounds good! Decide which panel, window, or inspector you want to see on the screen and click the appropriate button on the **Launcher**; that panel or window appears. We will look at all the items you can open from the **Launcher** as we move through the book.

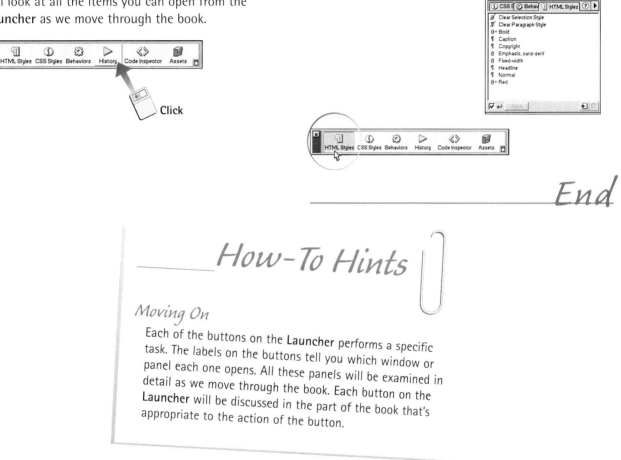

Click

5 Close a Window or Panel

Click the same button on the **Launcher** again to close the panel or window. You can see which panels are open by looking at the "pushed in" buttons on the **Launcher**.

End

How-To Hints

Moving On

Each of the buttons on the **Launcher** performs a specific task. The labels on the buttons tell you which window or panel each one opens. All these panels will be examined in detail as we move through the book. Each button on the **Launcher** will be discussed in the part of the book that's appropriate to the action of the button.

How to Customize the Launcher

The buttons that appear by default on the **Launcher** are the ones most people are likely to use. The Dreamweaver team put them there for a reason! However, you can change the items that appear on the **Launcher** by removing those that you don't use often and adding those that you want.

Begin

1 Open the Preferences Window

Choose **Edit, Preferences**. The main **Preferences** window opens. You can customize many aspects of Dreamweaver—including the options available on the **Launcher**—from this window.

2 Choose Floating Panels

From the options in the **Category** list on the left side of the screen, choose **Panels**. The **Show in Launcher** list box displays all the items currently displayed in both the **mini Launcher** in the status bar and in the **Launcher**.

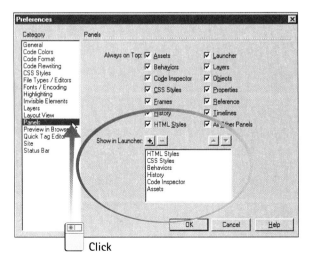

Click

3 Remove an Item from the Launcher

From the **Show in Launcher** list box, select the item you want to remove from the **Launcher** and click the – (minus) button.

Click

$\mathcal{4}$ Add an Item to the Launcher

Click the + (plus) button above the **Show in Launcher** list box to see a list of options you can add to the **Launcher**. Select the item you want to add to the **Launcher**; its name appears in the **Show in Launcher** list box.

$\mathcal{5}$ Change the Order of Items on the Launcher

You can move things around on the **Launcher** into whatever order suits you. To move an item to the left on the horizontal **Launcher** bar, select the item to be moved and click the up arrow. To move the item to the right, click the down arrow.

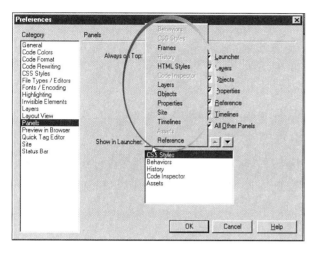

Click

End

How-To Hints

You Can't Have One Without the Other

Whatever changes you make to the main **Launcher** are always reflected in the **mini Launcher** as well. You can't change one and not the other.

Don't Change Just for the Sake of Change

Just because Dreamweaver allows you to make all these changes, it doesn't mean that you have to make any changes. Don't start changing too much right away. Wait until you become familiar with the software and determine what works best before you make many changes.

How to Use the Toolbar

The toolbar is a new feature in Dreamweaver 4. It is designed to make your work in Dreamweaver easier by enabling you to switch between different views at the click of a button. Each view you select from the toolbar has its own set of options that are visible when you click the **View Options** button. You can also use the toolbar to set the page title, manage files (when you have some created), and even check the meaning of HTML tags (using the **Reference** button).

Begin

1 Consider the Default View

By default, Dreamweaver displays the page you're working on in design view. This view shows you no code, only the content of your page as you insert elements on the page. To see the options for this view, click the **Options** button on the toolbar. To return to design view for some other view, click the **Design View** button on the toolbar.

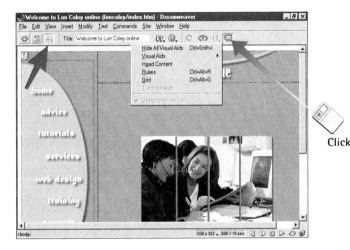

Click

2 Look at Code View

The **Code Only** button on the toolbar shows you all the HTML code in your document and nothing else. Click the **Options** button to see a list of options for this view.

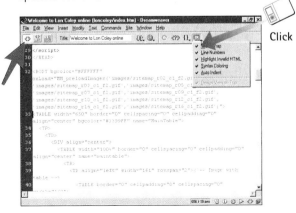

Click

3 Show Both Views at Once

The **Show Code and Design Views** button creates a split-screen effect: The HTML code for your page appears at the top and the design appears at the bottom.

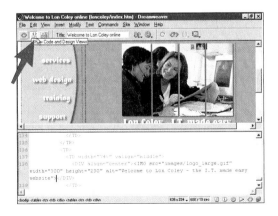

4 Consider Split-Screen Options

To look at the options for the code or design in the split view, simply click the **Options** button. Both sets of options are displayed for you to choose from.

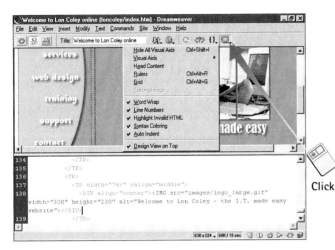

Click

5 Change the Page Title

Dreamweaver automatically gives any new document you create the name **Untitled Document**. This page title appears in the title bar of the document window. Use the **Page Title** text box in the toolbar to specify the title you want the page to have. The title bar updates to reflect the new title.

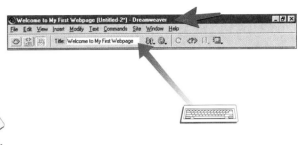

6 Check the File Status

The **File Status** menu in the toolbar gives you, among other things, access to the Document Check In and Out feature, the ability to locate the current page within a site, and the ability to change a file from Read Only status. Click the **File Status** button in the toolbar to see the menu; click an option in the menu to select it.

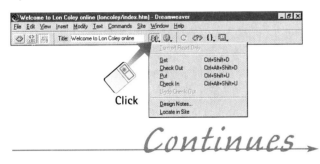

Click

Continues

How-To Hints

Using the Toolbar

If you have used previous versions of Dreamweaver, you won't be accustomed to having a toolbar at all. If you prefer not to use the toolbar, you can turn it off by choosing **View, Toolbar**.

View Options

After you become accustomed to using the toolbar, remember that you can use the view **Options** button in design view to turn the grid and ruler on and off without having to use the menus.

7 Preview in Browser

Check to make sure that your pages will appear in your visitors' browsers exactly as you intend the pages to look. Click the **Preview in Browser** button in the toolbar. The current page appears in your default browser. To see the current page in another browser you have installed on your computer, click and hold the **Preview in Browser** button and then select the desired browser.

Click

8 Add Other Browsers

It's a good idea to preview your pages in as many different browsers as you can to make sure that visitors to the page don't encounter any surprises. You can add additional browsers to the **Preview in Browser** list to make it easy for you to access these browsers. Click and hold the **Preview in Browser** button and choose **Edit Browser List** to open the **Preferences** dialog box to the **Preview in Browser** category. Click the + button to add a new browser to the list; the **Select Browser** dialog box opens.

Click

9 Locate the Browser to Add

Browse to find the **EXE** file for the browser you want to add and click **Open**. The selected browser is added to the **Preview in Browser** list

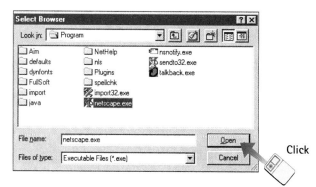

Click

10 Set a Default Browser

You can choose the browser you want to use as your default. Choose **Edit Browser List** to open the **Preferences** dialog box to the **Preview in Browser** category. From the **Browsers** list, select the browser you want to use as your default and enable the **Primary Browser** check box. After you have specified your default browser, you can display your page in it by clicking the **Preview in Browser** button in the toolbar or by pressing **F12**.

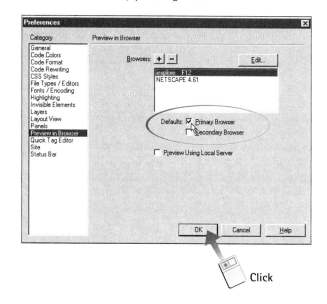

Click

11 Refresh the Design View

Another new feature in Dreamweaver 4 is the **Refresh Design View** button in the toolbar. Click this button to refresh the screen when you are in code view to ensure that the design view is always the most up-to-date screen possible.

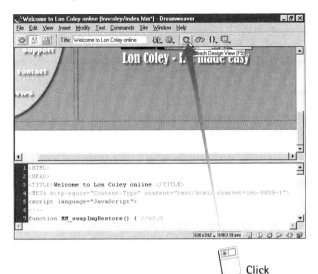

Click

12 Use the Reference Window

The **Reference** button in the toolbar is a new feature of Dreamweaver that allows you to see a definition of any HTML tag (whether that tag is used in your page or not). The screen that opens also shows a detailed example of the use of the tag. Click the **Reference** button on the toolbar to see this screen.

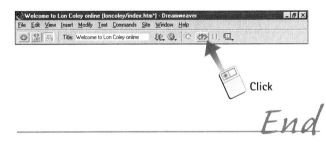

Click

End

How-To Hints

References

The new **Reference** feature allows you to learn the definitions of HTML codes and their attributes. The Reference feature also has a full definition of Cascading Style Sheets. If you want to read a list of the meanings of HTML tags, just click the **Reference** button on the toolbar and read. If you want to learn about a specific tag you have used in your page, select the tag you want to learn about from the **Tag Selector** area in the status bar and then click the **Reference** button. The screen opens to the definition of the tag you selected.

The **Reference** panel can be expanded to any size you want to make it easier to read the information. Simply drag a corner of the panel to expand its size.

How to Use the Menus

As with everything else in Dreamweaver, the menus are there to help you. Each menu has a list of options, grouped by the category of the menu title. Many menu items have subcategories, which are identified by the right-facing arrows on the right edge of the menu. Many menu options are addressed as we move through the book, but this task looks at the menu options in general terms.

Begin

1 View Context Menus

Perhaps the most forgotten type of menu is the *context menu*. This kind of menu gives you options based on the selected text or image. Right-click an object in the document window (**Ctrl**+click on a Macintosh) to open the context menu for that object. This example shows the context menu for the selected image.

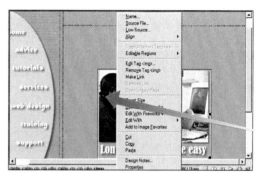

Right-click

2 The File and Edit Menus

The **File** menu contains commands relating to your files. Standard commands such as **Open** and **Save** are in the **File** menu. At the bottom of the File menu is a list of recently used files; click one to reopen that file quickly. The **Edit** menu contains commands that you'll find useful when editing a document: **Cut**, **Copy**, and **Paste** appear in this menu as well as some Dreamweaver-specific items such as **Select Parent Tag** and **Select Child**.

3 The View and Insert Menus

The **View** menu allows you to change the way you see the document window. You can use the options on this menu to display gridlines, borders, and rulers as well as the head content and metatags for your file. The **Insert** menu enables you to add images, tables, horizontal lines, and more to your page. In addition, this menu offers options such as **Layer** and **Server-Side Includes**, which are addressed later in the book.

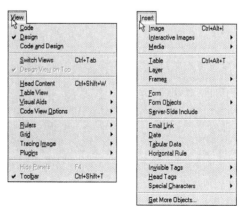

4 The Modify and Text Menus

The **Modify** menu lets you change the elements you have already inserted on the page. To change the appearance of tables, links, and so on, you use the **Modify** menu. The **Text** menu contains all the options you will ever need to make your text appear how you want it—including indents, fonts, styles, and sizes.

Modify	
Page Properties...	Ctrl+J
Selection Properties	Ctrl+Shift+J
Quick Tag Editor	Ctrl+T
Make Link	Ctrl+L
Remove Link	Ctrl+Shift+L
Open Linked Page...	
Link Target	▶
Table	▶
Frameset	▶
Navigation Bar	
Arrange	▶
Align	▶
Convert	▶
Library	▶
Templates	▶
Timeline	▶

Text	
Indent	Ctrl+Alt+]
Outdent	Ctrl+Alt+[
Paragraph Format	▶
Align	▶
List	▶
Font	▶
Style	▶
HTML Styles	▶
CSS Styles	▶
Size	▶
Size Change	▶
Color...	
Check Spelling	Shift+F7

5 The Commands and Site Menus

The **Commands** menu allows you to perform some advanced options such as cleaning up HTML imported from Microsoft Word and choosing preset color schemes. You use the **Site** menu to manage all the pages in your Web site. You can use this menu to check the links across an entire site and to define a new site.

Commands	
Start Recording	Ctrl+Shift+X
Play Recorded Command	Ctrl+P
Edit Command List...	
Get More Commands...	
Manage Extensions...	
Apply Source Formatting	
Clean Up HTML...	
Clean Up Word HTML...	
Add/Remove Netscape Resize Fix...	
Optimize Image in Fireworks...	
Create Web Photo Album...	
Set Color Scheme...	
Format Table...	
Sort Table...	
Window	▶
Lessons	

Site	
Site Files	F8
Site Map	Alt+F8
New Site...	
Open Site	▶
Define Sites...	
Get	Ctrl+Shift+D
Check Out	Ctrl+Alt+Shift+D
Put	Ctrl+Shift+U
Check In	Ctrl+Alt+Shift+U
Undo Check Out	
Reports...	
Check Links Sitewide	Ctrl+F8
Locate in Local Site	
Locate in Remote Site	

6 The Window and Help Menus

You will probably use the **Window** menu the most. You can display and hide all the Dreamweaver panels using this menu. Click to place a check mark next to a panel name to display that panel; click again to remove the check mark from the menu and the panel from the window. Use the **Help** menu to locate everything you need to know about Dreamweaver. Use this menu to access local and online help quickly and easily.

Window	
Objects	Ctrl+F2
Properties	Ctrl+F3
Launcher	
Site Files	F8
✓ Site Map	Alt+F8
Assets	F11
Behaviors	Shift+F3
Code Inspector	F10
CSS Styles	Shift+F11
Frames	Shift+F2
History	Shift+F10
HTML Styles	Ctrl+F11
Layers	F2
Library	
Reference	Ctrl+Shift+F1
Templates	
Timelines	Shift+F9
Arrange Panels	
Hide Panels	F4
Minimize All	Shift+F4
Restore All	Alt+Shift+F4
index.htm	

Help	
Welcome	
Using Dreamweaver	F1
Reference	Shift+F1
What's New	
Guided Tour	
Lessons	
Dreamweaver Exchange	
Dreamweaver Support Center	Ctrl+F1
Macromedia Online Forums	
Extending Dreamweaver	
Register Dreamweaver	
About Dreamweaver	

How-To Hints

Think About the Menu Names

When you first start using Dreamweaver, the mass of different views, options, and menus can be quite intimidating. One way to avoid the confusion is to use the menus. Each menu is named to help you find commands in that category: File commands are in the **File** menu, and so on. If you are struggling to locate the right option in the toolbars or panels, use the menus until you become more confident with the panels and inspectors.

End

How to Use the Objects Panel

The **Objects** panel contains many buttons for inserting, drawing, and creating objects on your pages. There are six different categories in the **Objects** panel that group the buttons logically. Each category in the **Objects** panel controls different objects and page elements. From inserting images to creating forms, the **Objects** panel contains a shortcut to do almost everything.

Begin

1 View the Common Category

The **Common** category of the **Objects** panel shows the most commonly used buttons for inserting tables, drawing layers, and so on. To insert an object, click the appropriate button on the **Objects** panel.

Click

2 Change to Layout View

Layout view is used to create the layout for your page without actually adding content to the page (see Part 7, "Considering Layout and Design"). To switch to Layout view, click the button at the bottom of the **Objects** panel.

Click

3 Switch Between Categories

To switch between categories in the **Objects** panel, click the down arrow at the top of the panel. A list of all the available categories appears. Select the category you want, and the **Objects** panel updates to display those option buttons.

Click

4 Insert an Object

To insert an object on your page using the **Objects** panel, just click the button for the object you want to insert. In most cases, a **Select** dialog box opens so that you can choose the file containing the item you want to insert. For example, to insert an image, click the **Insert Image** button in the **Common** category of the **Objects** panel.

Click

5 Browse to the Item to Insert

Use the dialog box that opens to locate the item you want to insert and click **Select**. The item is inserted into your page. Here you see the dialog box that opens when you click the **Insert Image** button.

Click

6 Complete the Properties Box

When you insert some types of objects, a properties dialog box might be displayed for you to complete. This example shows the dialog box that appears when you click the **Insert Table** button. Dreamweaver needs to know how many rows and columns you want in your table. Fill out the dialog box and click **OK** to insert the object.

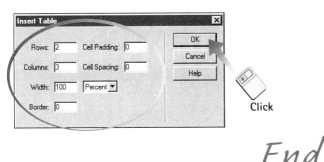

Click

End

How-To Hints

Remember the Categories

Throughout this book, we will look at many of the options available on the **Objects** panel. However, you should take the time now to familiarize yourself with the categories. For example, the **Character** category has buttons for inserting all those little symbols we use so often (such as © and ™), as well as a button that presents a table of less-common symbols you can choose from. The **Objects** panel contains many little gems, all designed to make your life easier. Make sure that you look at all the options.

How to Use the Properties Inspector

The **Properties Inspector** shows you information about the currently selected object or element on the page. Most of the properties displayed in the inspector can be edited as required. The **Properties Inspector** changes to show different properties for the different types of objects you select.

Begin

1 Show or Hide the Properties Inspector

Assuming that the **Properties Inspector** is onscreen (as it is by default when you open Dreamweaver), choose **Window, Properties** to remove the inspector from the screen. Choose **Window, Properties** again to bring the inspector back to the screen.

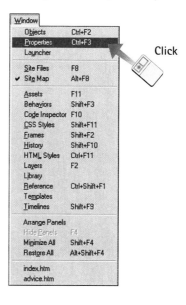

Click

2 Expand the Properties Inspector

Some objects have many properties, and you might not be able to see all of them in the **Properties Inspector** at once. Click the arrow in the bottom-right corner of the inspector to expand the panel so that it shows all the properties for the selected object.

Click

3 Get Help About Properties

To get help about any property you don't understand, click the **?** (question mark) in the **Properties Inspector**, and context specific help will be displayed where possible in your default browser. The help file displayed will tell you everything you need to know about the **Properties Inspector** and its options.

4 View Text Properties

The options in the **Properties Inspector** change depending on the type of object or element selected in the page. In this example, I've selected some text on the page; notice how the options in the **Properties Inspector** have changed from those shown in Step 3, when an image was selected.

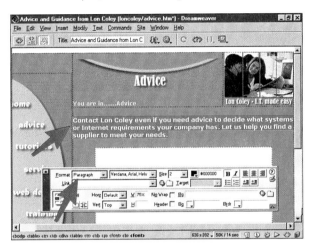

5 Change Some Values

You can use the **Properties Inspector** to change the properties of the element you have selected. In this example, I selected an image; notice that the **Properties Inspector** shows all the information about the image, including its width and height. If you change the value in only the height box, you can see how the image becomes distorted.

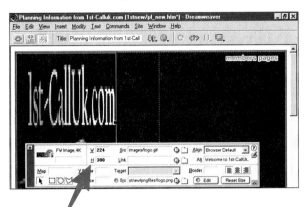

6 Reset the Size

If you mistakenly change the size of the selected image, you can use the **Reset Size** button in the **Properties Inspector** to restore the image to its original dimensions.

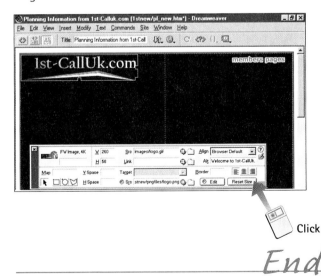

Click

End

How-To Hints

Properties of Other Objects

As you've seen, the options in the **Properties Inspector** change depending on what you have selected in the document window. In this task, we looked at the properties for text and images—two of the most common objects you'll work with in Dreamweaver. As you use Dreamweaver more, you will see how the **Properties Inspector** changes to display options for layers, frames, and hotspots as well. Use the **Properties Inspector** to make absolutely sure that you have selected the object you wanted to select. The object's name and properties will help ensure that you have the correct element selected.

How to Use the History Panel

The **History** panel keeps a running record of everything you do while you're using Dreamweaver. The **History** panel remembers information in steps as you work, and you can repeat, save, and use these steps again. If you save the steps as commands, you can then apply them to other objects at any time. All saved commands are available for use in any future document.

Begin

1 Open the History Panel

Choose **Window, History** or click the **History** button on the **Launcher** to open the **History** panel.

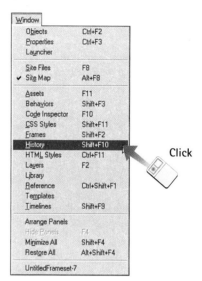

Click

2 Take Some Steps

Steps are all the actions you have performed on the current document since you opened it. The **History** panel shows all these steps in the order they were performed.

3 Use the Slider to Undo

You can use the slider to undo a single step or multiple steps that you have performed. Click and hold the mouse button on the slider as you drag it up through the steps in the **History** panel. Release the mouse button when you have undone the desired steps. Notice that, as you go backwards through your steps, you can see your actions unraveling in the document window. Drag the slider back down the list to redo the step. The **History** list is retained until you close the document.

Drag

4 Clear the History Panel

Although you can clear the **History** panel of all its steps, you will have no undo information for the current document if you do so. Make sure that you are satisfied with the steps you have taken on your page before you clear the **History** panel. Open the context menu by right-clicking anywhere in the **History** panel (Macintosh users press Ctrl+click) and choose **Clear History**.

Right-click

5 Set How Many Steps

By default, Dreamweaver retains 50 steps in the **History** panel—which should be more than enough for most people. If you want Dreamweaver to retain a different amount of steps, you can change this number. Choose **Edit, Preferences** to open the **Preferences** dialog box. From the **Category** list, select **General** to open the dialog box to that category of options.

Click

6 Enter a Number

In the **Maximum Number of History Steps** text box, type a new value for the number of steps to be remembered. Don't set this number too high, or you will consume a huge amount of system memory.

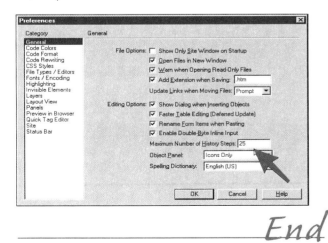

End

How-To Hints

Reusing the Steps

You can store information and steps from the **History** panel and use them again as a single command. This is handy if you want to apply the same formatting to elements on different pages or to additional elements later on the same page. We will look at reusing history steps in Part 13, "Reusing Information." Simply select the steps you want to reuse and click the save icon at the bottom of the panel. After you have named and saved it, the command is available from the **Commands** menu.

How to Customize the Way Panels Look

By now, you are familiar with how Dreamweaver looks. You have a lot of control over how the panels look in Dreamweaver, and you can move panels around and combine them easily. Dreamweaver uses the term *docking* to describe the process of combining panels into a single floating panel with lots of tabs. Some of the panels automatically display in combination with others, but even those can be changed and merged with different panels.

Begin

1 Decide What to Dock

Decide which panels you want to combine and make sure that all those panels are open onscreen. In this example, two panels are open, each with multiple tabs.

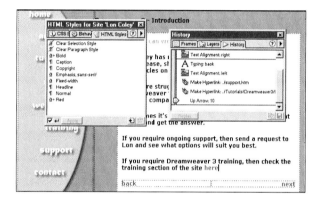

2 Drag and Drop the Panel

Drag the panel you want to move over to the desired location. As you drag, a highlighted border appears around the panel you are moving. Drop the panel when it is over its new location. In this example, I moved the **HTML Styles** panel out of the first group of panels and added it to the second group of panels. In Dreamweaver parlance, I "docked" the panel in a new location.

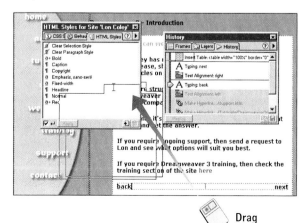

Drag

3 Make a Standalone Panel

To undock a panel after you have docked it, click the panel tab and drag it out of the combined panel. Drop the panel on a blank area of the screen. The panel reverts to being a standalone panel. In this example, I dragged the **History** panel out of the group and made it a standalone panel.

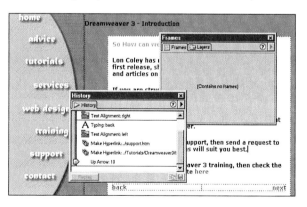

4 View Preferences

Choose **Edit, Preferences** to open the **Preferences** dialog box. Select **Panels** from the **Category** list to see the options available for panels. Note that the default is for all panels to appear in front of (or on top of) the document window—and on top of (that is, obstructing) your work.

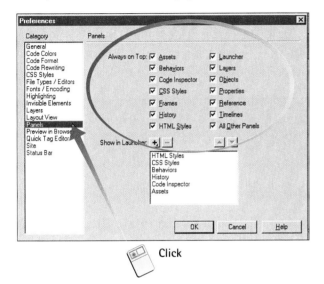

Click

5 Change the Preferences

In the **Always on Top** section, disable the check box for any of the options to make that panel stay behind the document window unless it is active. In simple terms, this means that when you open a new document, the disabled panel is not visible; those panels you have enabled (set to be on top) appear in all documents that you open.

Click

6 Snap Panels to the Edge

Dreamweaver 4 has an automatic snap to feature that brings panels back in line. Move a panel towards the edge of the screen, and it will snap to the edge automatically.

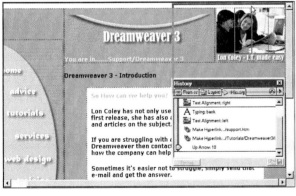

End

How-To Hints

Don't Get Carried Away

Although you can customize the appearance of panels to your heart's content, don't get too carried away. The panels that open together actually do so for a reason. As you use Dreamweaver more and more, you might develop a preference for a group of panels that you often use together. At that time, you can customize and group your panels.

Remember the Assets Panel

The **Assets** panel is a great innovation in this version of Dreamweaver so don't forget that it is there. As your site grows, the **Assets** panel will hold more and more information about objects and images you have used, giving you an at-a-glance reference to what is in your site.

Task

Working with Pages and Sites

Although you could just jump in and start creating pages in Dreamweaver, it is far better to plan your attack first. Many Web designers still use a pen and paper to draw a rough plan of how the finished site should look; other designers create a complete mock-up using graphics applications.

Regardless of how you plan your individual pages, working in a site is much better than simply creating pages. A site gives you somewhere to store all the information you want to use as well as a structure to work in.

You can check on the status of the site as a whole rather than checking every single page. Obviously, if you are planning a site that will only ever have one page, creating a site will probably be a touch of overkill. On the other hand, even sites that start small can grow and grow and grow! ●

How to Define a New Site

When you plan to create a Web site using Dream-weaver, you must first *define* the site before you can do any other work on the site. Dreamweaver allows you to create several Web sites, but you have to identify each one with a unique name. When you define a site, you create or specify a folder on your hard drive (called the *local folder*) in which all the files for this site are stored. You must define each Web site you create using Dreamweaver.

2 Name the Site

From the **Category** list on the left side of the dialog box, make sure that **Local Info** is selected. In the **Site Name** box, type a name for this Web site. Perhaps **MyFirstSite** would be a good idea. Choose a name that relates to the site content; the descriptive name will help you later on when you have several sites to choose from.

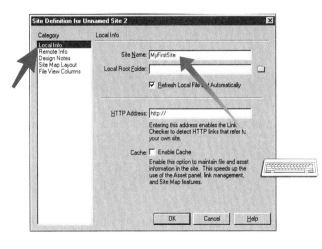

1 Open the Site Definition Dialog Box

Open Dreamweaver and choose **Site, New Site** to open the **Site Definition** dialog box.

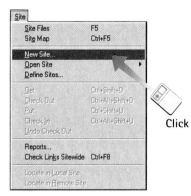

Click

3 Name the Location

Click the folder icon to the right of the **Local Root Folder** text box. The **Choose Local Folder** dialog box opens to enable you to navigate to the folder you want to use to store the files for this site. Select the folder you want to use and click **Select** (click **Choose** on the Mac). The path to the local root folder you have just chosen appears in the **Local Root Folder** text box.

Click

4 Create the Site

You don't have to fill in anything else in the **Site Definition** dialog box for now; click **OK** to register your site name and folder location. An alert box opens, asking whether you want to create a *cache* for your new site. A cache helps the management of the site and ensures that links are kept up to date. Click the **Create** button to create the cache.

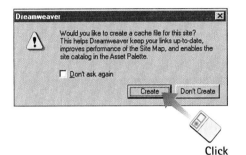

Click

6 Understand the Site Window

After you have some files for the site, the **Site** window will display information about each file (as this example shows). After you have uploaded your site to a remote server, you can display the remote server in the left pane and transfer files from your local hard drive to the remote server by simply dragging them from one location to the other. You can see how your Web pages are linked to one another by clicking the **Navigation** button. This example shows an existing site with the files showing on both the local hard drive and remote servers.

5 Open the Site Window

As soon as you click **Create** in Step 4, the screen changes to display the **Site** window. The right pane of the **Site** window shows the folder you have chosen to hold the files for your site. At the moment, there are no files for this new site, but when you do have files, they are displayed under the folder icon. Your site will soon grow and grow!

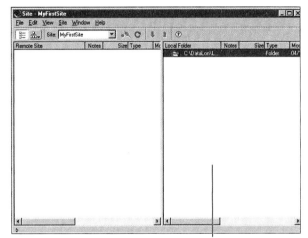

Files for the current site are displayed here

End

How to Create a New Page

Every Web site needs pages—and creating new pages in Dreamweaver is a nice, straightforward process. You can create all your pages before you start and add content later, or you can create the pages on the fly as you need them. As with most things in Web design, you will find the way that works for you. If you already have a clear idea of how the finished site will look, you might want to create the pages now.

2 Define a Home Page

Every Web site needs a *home page*, the first page that visitors to your site see. You establish the home page for your site by calling the file either **index.htm** or **default.htm**. You should never have one of each, and your hosting service will let you know which of the page names to use. The server knows to send that page first when a viewer accesses the address or URL for your site. Dreamweaver also recognizes a file with either of these names as your home page. From the **Site** menu, click **Site Files** to open the **Site** window. Click the **Navigation** button to see the **index.htm** file icon in the middle of the Navigation pane.

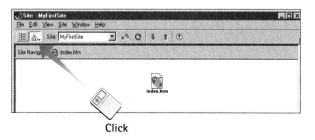

Click

1 Save Your First Page

As you know, simply opening Dreamweaver takes you to an empty document window. This is your first page—or at least it will be after you save it. Type a couple words at the top of the page and choose **File, Save**. Browse to the folder on your hard drive where the files for this site are going to be stored. In the **File name** box, type **Index** and click **Save**.

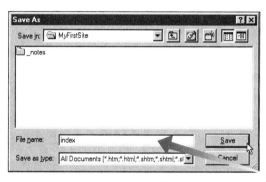

3 Create a New Blank Page

A Web site with only one page is a very small and probably incomplete site. As you develop content for your site, you will obviously need more and more pages. If the **Site** window is open, you can create a new page by choosing **File, New Window**. If you have closed the **Site** window and are back at your home page, choose **File, New Window** to create a new page.

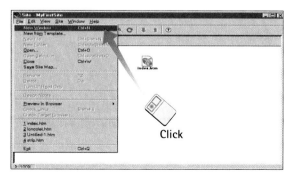

Click

4 Create a New Page from a Template

Note that the File menu contains a New from Template option. Unlike some other Web design software, Dreamweaver does not provide templates of predesigned Web pages. Dreamweaver expects you to make your own templates for your Web pages. You learn to create templates in Part 13, "Reusing Information." Although you can select File, New from Template, the Select Template dialog box that opens shows no templates.

You can't create a file from a template until you create some templates

5 Create a New Page from an Existing Page

If you have created pages using other software, you can edit those pages in Dreamweaver and make them a part of your new site. To use an existing HTML file, choose File, Open and browse to the file you want to open.

6 Save the Page to the Site

If the file you just opened is not already saved in the current site, choose File, Save As and browse to folder for the current site. Name the file and click Save.

Click

End

How-To Hints

Saving All the Elements of Existing Pages

If you are planning on using pages that have been created previously in other applications, remember that the image files contained in the existing pages must also be saved into the current site folder.

When you move image files to new folders, remember that the paths to these image files must be updated in your page files to reflect the new locations. Otherwise you will have broken image links when you upload your pages to the remote server.

How to Set Page Properties

Page properties control many things: color schemes, backgrounds, page titles, and even page margins. The **Page Properties** screen allows you to not only set page properties, but also to modify them at any time. Every Web page you create must have this information, so get into the habit of setting a title straight away and making sure that you are using matching colors.

Begin

1 Open the Page Properties Dialog Box

The main settings for your pages are kept in the **Page Properties** dialog box. To open this important dialog box, choose **Modify, Page Properties** from the main menu bar.

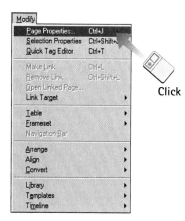

Click

2 Give the Page a Title

Each Web page needs a *title*—the text displayed in the title bar at the top of the Web browser. The title of the page is also the reference given to pages when a visitor creates a bookmark or favorite place in her browser. The title you give your page should specify the name of your site as well as the page within the site. In the **Title** field at the top of the **Page Properties** dialog box, type the title you want to assign this page and click **Apply**. The title immediately appears in the title bar of the document window.

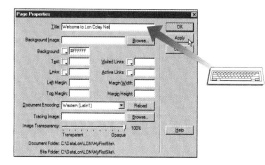

3 Set a Background Image

Background images in Dreamweaver tile to fill the screen exactly as they do in a Web browser. To select a background image for your page, click the **Browse** button next to the **Background Image** box in the **Page Properties** dialog box. Navigate to the image you want to use and click **Select** (click **Choose** on a Mac). You are prompted to save a copy of the image file into the site folder (you should do so). Click **Apply**; the image appears in the document window.

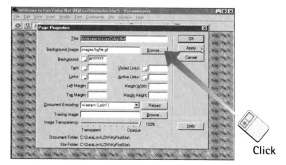

Click

4 Set a Background Color

Even if you use a background image, you should select a matching background color as well. The *background color* displays while the background image is loading and makes your text visible even if the image fails to load. To set a background color, click the button to the left of the **Background** box and choose a color from the palette that pops out. Click **Apply** to apply this color to your page.

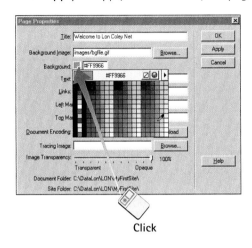

Click

5 Set Text and Link Colors

You can use the **Page Properties** dialog box to set default text and link colors for your page. Text automatically appears in this color when you type. There are three link colors to set on your page: **Links** (how links first appear to a visitor), **Visited Links** (how links appear after they have been clicked), and **Active Links** (the color a link changes to for the brief moment it is being clicked). Click the color palette button next to each option, make a selection, and click **Apply**.

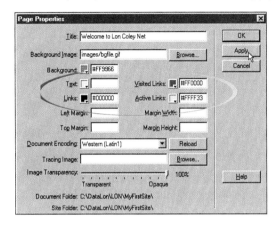

6 Set Margins

There are two sets of margin options available in the **Page Properties** dialog box, and these should be set to the same values. The **Left Margin** and **Top Margin** values are recognized by Internet Explorer; the **Margin Height** and **Margin Width** values are recognized by Netscape Navigator. The margins you set are visible only when you check your page in a browser window. When you finish setting page options, click **OK** to close the dialog box.

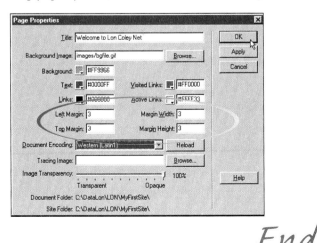

How-To Hints

Color Schemes

If you are not confident about getting your colors to coordinate properly, Dreamweaver allows you to choose from some predefined color schemes. Select **Commands, Set Color Scheme**. When you choose a background color, suggestions for coordinating text and link colors appear.

Background Logic

In this task, we set a background image *and* a background color. But only one of these will display in the final page. Almost everyone who sees your page will see the background image you set, and the page will display as you intended. However, you need the background color to display when the page is loading and also just in case some browsers don't have the capability to view images at all.

End

How to Set the Page View

Dreamweaver provides features that help you design and lay out your pages. One of the first page-design choices you should make is a pixel width for your pages. Most Web designers choose a width of either 640 pixels or 800 pixels to ensure that their pages can be viewed on monitors with a lower resolution. Dreamweaver lets you view your page at different resolutions as you work, letting you keep track of the page. Even more importantly, you can change the resolution to get an idea of what others will see when they view the page, regardless of your own screen size.

2 Show Rulers

Rulers in the document window show you exactly where each and every element has been placed. Rulers are particularly handy if you are not accustomed to using the pixel measurement system. Although rulers can be displayed in centimeters and inches, they appear in pixels by default. To show the rulers, select **View, Rulers, Show**. The rulers appear across the top and down the left edge of the document window.

Begin

1 Know Your Options

To help with your layout, you can show horizontal and vertical rulers and display gridlines. These options are available under the **View** menu. Other settings will resize your page to match a page displayed on a lower resolution monitor, as we will see in a few minutes.

3 Change and Remove Rulers

From the **View, Rulers** submenu, you can select a different unit of measurement for your rulers. If you want to turn off the rulers, you can. Just select **View, Rulers, Show** again.

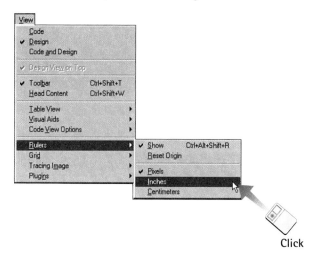

Click

4 Show and Remove Gridlines

Gridlines display on your page as squares set to a size of your choice. They can be used with or without the rulers to help you achieve exact placement of elements and layers on the page. Grids are commonly used for "snapping" layers, described in Part 7, "Considering Layout and Design." To show the grid, select **View**, **Grid**, **Show Grid**. Select this command again to turn off the grid.

5 Change Grid Settings

You can set the grid to look the way you want it to by using the **Grid Settings** dialog box (choose **View**, **Grid**, **Edit Grid**). You can change the appearance of the grid so that it displays as either lines or dots, and you can adjust the color and the measurement units.

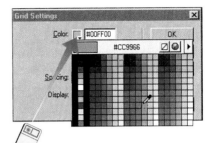

Click

6 Change the Window Size

You can change the size of the document window to check how your pages will look in different sized browser screens. The current window size in pixels is displayed in the status bar at the bottom of the screen. Click the arrow next to the current size to see a list of alternative options; click the one you want. The screen resizes immediately. Even when you work, the setting that Dreamweaver uses might not appear in the list. To create these screen shots, I am working on a large monitor set to low resolution, giving the rather strange size showing in my settings.

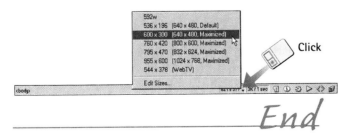

Click

End

How to Save and Name a Page

When you are creating a Web site, the way you name your files when you save them is important. If you don't follow certain rules, your server might not recognize your files. In this task, you learn some of the necessary tips for naming files in Dreamweaver.

Begin

1 Save for the First Time

It is a good idea to save your file as soon as you have created it. You should continue saving the file regularly as you add new content to the file. To save your work, simply choose **File, Save**. The **Save As** dialog box opens—but be careful. The **Save As** dialog box doesn't always go to the site folder you expect.

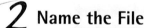

2 Name the File

By default, the page is saved with a **.htm** extension that is generally fine. However, some UNIX and Macintosh servers require the **.html** extension, so you must check with your server's administrator. In the **File name** box, type a meaningful name for the file. Don't put spaces in your filenames because browsers struggle to display these names correctly (spaces in filenames are what cause the **%20** characters that sometimes appear in Web addresses).

3 Save the File Again

When you have saved your work once, the filename is displayed in the title bar across the top of the page. To save the page again, simply select **File, Save**; the file is updated with the same name to the same location.

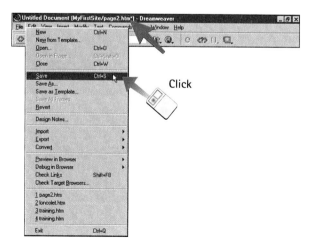

4 Use Save As

You can save a copy of the file by selecting **File, Save As** and choosing a different filename and location for the file you are copying. Your original file remains, and you have a copy with a new name.

6 Use the Keyboard

As you can with everything else in Dreamweaver, you can save files using the keyboard. Press **Ctrl+S** to save a file (press ⌘+S on a Macintosh); keyboard commands are displayed in the menus to the right of each command name.

5 Save Multiple Files

If you decide to create a frames-based Web site (as described in Part 9, "Using Frames and Framesets," you will always have more than one page open at a time. The page in this example contains three frames, each of which displays a separate page of information. Dreamweaver enables you to save all the pages in a frameset at once using the **File, Save All Frames** command.

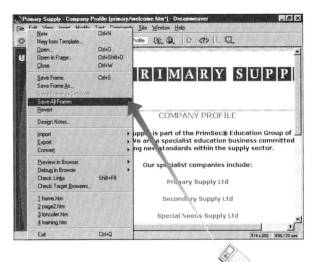

Click

End

How-To Hints

Naming Files

It is very tempting to call your early Web pages **Page1**, **Page2**, and so on. Although this naming convention works when you have only half a dozen pages to choose from, you might soon have 40 pages or more—will you know which page was about your family if you named it **Page3**?

Filenames and Cases

Although most Web servers can process filenames of any length and with capital letters, it is *always* best to stick to no more than eight lowercase characters in the filename. Following this naming convention prevents problems with any server.

How to Close and Retrieve Pages

Closing pages in Dreamweaver and being able to open them again quickly and easily is obviously a necessary part of using the software. This task explains how to do these necessary activities.

1 Close a Page

To close a page in Dreamweaver, make sure that the page is the current page and choose **File, Close**. If you haven't already saved a page when you try to close it, an alert box appears asking whether you want to save changes to the file. Click **Yes** to save an existing file or to display the **Save As** dialog box if it is a new page. Click **No** to close the file without saving it; click **Cancel** to return to the document window without saving or closing the page.

Click

2 Open a Page Using Shortcuts

Shortcuts to the most recent files you have had open are stored at the bottom of the **File** menu. Open the **File** menu to see a list of the documents you have recently used. Click the name of the file you want to open.

3 Open a Page Using the Site Window

You can open any page in the current site using the **Site** window. Choose **Site, Site Files** to open the **Site** window. In the list of files in the right pane, double-click the file you want to open.

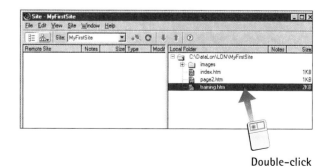

Double-click

4 Switch Between Open Pages

As you become more proficient with Dreamweaver, you will work with more than one file open at a time. You can switch between pages very simply by using the **Window** menu. Open the **Window** menu; a list of all your open files appears at the bottom of the menu. Click the one you want to make the current file.

Window		
	Objects	Ctrl+F2
	Properties	Ctrl+F3
	Launcher	F2
✓	Site Files	F5
	Site Map	Ctrl+F5
	Assets	F6
	Behaviors	F8
	Code Inspector	F10
	CSS Styles	F7
	Frames	Ctrl+F10
	History	F9
	HTML Styles	Ctrl+F7
	Layers	F11
	Library	Ctrl+F11
	Reference	Shift+F10
	Templates	
	Timelines	Ctrl+F9
	Arrange Panels	
	Hide Panels	F4
	Minimize All	Shift+F4
	Restore All	Alt+Shift+F4
	index.htm	
	page2.htm	
	home.htm	
	loncolet.htm	

5 Use the Open Command

You can also use the **File, Open** command to access any files on your computer. By default, the **Open** dialog box opens to the folder you last selected; you might have to browse to find the location of the file you want to open. Select the file and click **Open**.

End

How-To Hints

Opening Files Outside the Current Site

The **File, Open** command is the only way to access files that are stored outside the site folder you are currently working on. Use this command to edit or look at external files.

Open Files Created in Microsoft Word

Microsoft Word files saved in the HTML format include lots of unnecessary HTML tags. To use such a Word file in your site, bring the file into your Dreamweaver site and choose **Commands, Clean Up Word HTML**. This command removes all the extra tags quickly and easily.

How to Set a Browser to Preview Pages

Although the document window gives a reasonable interpretation of your finished pages, there is no substitute for checking how your pages will look in a real Web browser. In fact, you should open your pages in more than one browser to make sure that all your elements can be viewed in multiple browsers. Learning to recognize the differences in how browsers work is a vital part of designing any successful Web site.

Begin

1 Determine the Default Browser

When you installed Dreamweaver, the installation process identified your default browser; this browser appears in the **Preview in Browser** list by default. To see the current page in this browser, choose **File, Preview in Browser** and select the browser from the pop-out menu. The examples in this task show a page that already has some content so that there is something to display in the browser window.

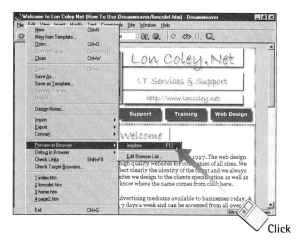

Click

2 See the Page

If it isn't already open, the selected browser opens, and the current page is displayed.

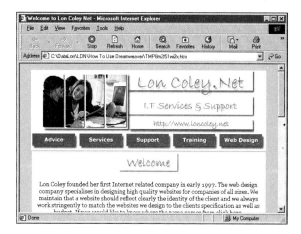

3 Set Another Browser

Assuming that you have at least one other browser installed on your computer, you can add it to the default **Preview in Browser** list. Choose **File, Preview in Browser, Edit Browser List** to open the **Preferences** dialog box.

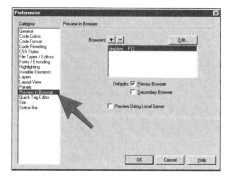

4 Complete the Information

Click the + button above the list of browsers to select a secondary browser. Type a name for this browser (for example, type **Netscape 4.61**) and click the **Browse** button to find the application file that relates to the browser you are trying to specify. In the **Select Browser** dialog box, navigate to the application file and click **Open**. Back in the **Add Browser** dialog box, click **OK**. The new browser now appears in the list in the **Preferences** dialog box.

Click

5 Remove a Browser from the List

Removing a browser from your list is simple. Repeat Step 3 to open the **Preferences** dialog box. Highlight the browser you want to delete and click the – button. The browser disappears from the list immediately, without any request for confirmation. (Note that the original application file still exists on your hard disk; it's just the name that's been deleted from this list.)

Click

6 Edit Browser Information

After you have added a browser to your **Preferences** list, you might want to change the name of it or change the path to where the application file is stored. Open the **Preferences** dialog box, select the browser whose information you want to edit, and click **Edit**. In the **Edit Browser** dialog box, change the information as required and click **OK**.

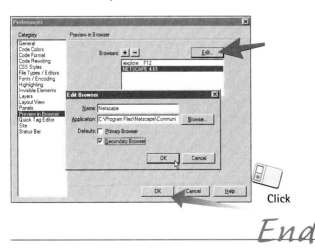

Click

End

How-To Hints

Using AOL

Even though you can now use other browsers when you are logged on to AOL, it is still a good idea to see how your pages look in the AOL browser. You can check your files in the AOL browser even when you're not connected to AOL or the Internet! Follow the information in Steps 2 and 3 to add a browser. Locate the AOL folder on your computer and select the **WAOL** application.

When you choose **File, Preview in Browser, AOL**, you will see the normal AOL signon screen. When this disappears, the AOL browser will open, and your pages will be displayed.

Task

Working with Text

Usually, the best way to learn about a new piece of software is step by step, and not by jumping into the deep end too quickly. Now that you have a solid understanding of the basics of Dreamweaver and know what is where and what some of the features do, the tasks in this part get you started with text—one of the most important features of any Web page.

Text might seem like an obvious element to a Web page—you type, it appears, and that's that. Well, actually there's more to it than that. You will soon discover that text can be formatted in only one of a limited number of fonts—those that are recognized by almost all computers—so forget all the "twirly," elaborate text you were planning.

When it's neatly aligned on a page, text can enhance the page, but be careful not to mix too many sizes and colors on the same page. Not only are too many sizes and colors hard on the eyes, but also all that fussiness will distract those trying to read your sales information or product details.

Text can be typed straight into a page or can be inserted into a layer or table cell. In fact, you can add text to your page just about anywhere you want it to be.

Formatting text can be done in different ways as well. In the manual approach, you select some text and apply a formatting command such as bold. You can also format text with HTML styles, which control only the text to which they are applied. Finally, you can use Cascading Style Sheets (CSS), which can be saved as external files and applied to an entire Web site. If you change the style sheet, you can update all the pages in your site in one fell swoop.

How to Enter and Format Normal Text

Normal text is just that: text that is typed in as plain text, not for use as a heading or a list. This task shows how to enter some text in a document and then perform some basic formatting on that text.

Begin

1 Enter Several Lines of Text

Start by typing something simple, such as **Welcome to my Web site**. To start a new line of text and to insert blank space between the lines, press **Enter**. Pressing **Enter** inserts an HTML **<p>** paragraph tag that provides extra space between lines. To start a new line without inserting extra space, press **Shift+Enter**. Pressing **Shift+Enter** inserts the HTML **
** break tag, which keeps the new line in the same paragraph as the previous one.

Press Enter to insert extra space

Press Shift+Enter to start a new line within the paragraph

2 Change the Color of Text

By default, the text you type appears black. To change the color and other formatting options, make sure that the **Properties Inspector** is displayed (choose it from the **Window** menu if it isn't). Select the text and use the color picker from the **Properties Inspector** to choose a color.

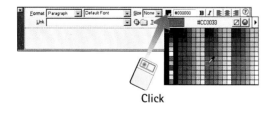

Click

3 Set a Specific Font Size

Text size in HTML can be specified in seven sizes, which more or less equate to standard point sizes: size 1 is 8 points, size 2 is 10 points, and so on. Remember that viewers of your site can change the size of the text that they see in their browser, so don't expect the text size to be fixed. To set a font size, select the text you want to affect, click the down arrow next to the **Size** field in the **Properties Inspector**, and pick a number from 1 to 7.

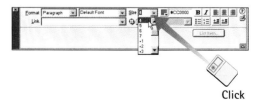

Click

4 Set a Relative Font Size

By default, the text you type is size 3. This is the **BASEFONT** size. You can set your text to be bigger or smaller than this by using the numbers preceded by a + or − in the **Size** list. Repeat Step 3, but this time choose a number with either a + or − in front of it. Given that there are only seven sizes of text in HTML, if your text is already size 5, you can make it only two sizes larger. Regardless of whether you select +2 or +4 for a size 5 text, the text still becomes size 7.

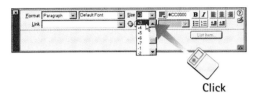

Click

6 Format Text with HTML Styles

You can apply a group of formatting options to text by using HTML styles; click **HTML Styles** in the **Launcher** to display the **HTML Styles** panel. Highlight some text and choose one of the styles in the panel to see how your text changes. To create your own HTML style, click the **New Style** button in the bottom-right corner of the **HTML Styles** panel to open the **Define HTML Style** dialog box. Choose a font, font size, color, and other attributes you want to apply and click **OK**. Your new style appears in the list in the **HTML Styles** panel.

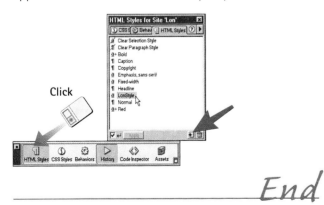

Click

End

5 Make Text Bold, Italic, or Underlined

You can make the text on your page bold or italic. Select the text you want to affect and click the **Bold** or **Italic** button in the **Properties Inspector**. To underline text, select the text and choose **Text, Underline** from the menu bar. Be careful when applying the underline attribute to text; most Web site visitors expect underlined text to be a hyperlink.

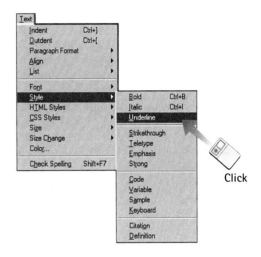

Click

How-To Hints

Remember, It's a Screen

When working with font sizes in Dreamweaver, remember that they are going to be seen and not printed. Don't assume that you have to set text to be the same size you would use in a printed letter or document. Let your eyes guide you to use the font size that looks right for the job. Text that is too big can spoil even the best-planned Web site.

Don't Go Crazy with Formatting

Use the bold, italic, and underline formatting options only when required. People read text onscreen differently than they read the printed word. Too many changes in formatting will make your site confusing to read and might deter people from staying around for long.

How to Align Text

Whether you can get your text to display correctly often makes the difference between a good Web site and a not-so-good one. Aligning text on a page is something you'll do all the time—placing it in the middle of the screen, moving it to the left or right, adding indents, and then removing them again—all these activities fall into the category of aligning text.

Begin

1 Center Some Text

When doing any kind of text formatting, you must first select the text you want to affect. For this step, select the text you want to center on the page and click the **Align Center** button in the **Properties Inspector**.

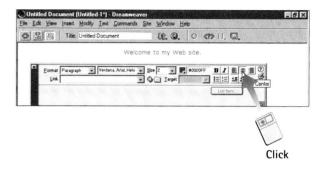

Click

2 Right-Align Text

To align text to the right side of the page, select the text and click the **Align Right** button in the **Properties Inspector**. The text moves to the right of the document window.

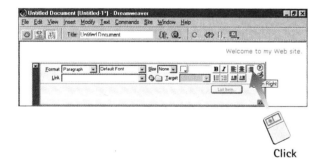

Click

3 Left-Align Text

By default, when you start typing, your text appears left aligned. Note that this default setting does not force your text to be left aligned, and some older browsers may display the text differently than you intend. To ensure that your text remains left aligned, select the text and click the **Align Left** button in the **Properties Inspector**.

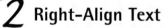

Click

4 Indent Text

You can indent text from the left margin. Select the text you want to indent and click the **Text Indent** button in the **Properties Inspector**. Click the button again to indent the text even more. We will look more at setting indents in Task 5, "How to Create Lists."

Click

5 Outdent Text

You can "outdent" text (that is, remove an indent) by selecting the previously indented text and clicking the **Text Outdent** button on the **Properties Inspector**. The text moves back to the normal alignment.

Click

End

How-To Hints

It Just Isn't Justified

Did you notice that there is no "justify" option in the **Text** menu or in the **Properties Inspector**? This is a deliberate omission because most browsers can't display justified text. The only way to add justified text is by using Cascading Style Sheets, which are discussed in Part 8, "Working with Layers and Cascading Style Sheets."

Note, however, that Cascading Style Sheets are interpreted consistently only by browsers of version 4.0 and later. Even browsers of version 4.0 and later may not display pages formatted with CSS as you might expect. Remember to check your pages in several versions of each browser.

How to Change the Font Face

In most browsers, the default text font is Times (unless the viewer has changed the settings). Although you can choose a different font for your page, remember that it must be one that almost all Macs and PCs have installed. Instead of selecting a single font, you select a group of similar fonts (such as Arial, Helvetica, and Sans Serif). This instructs the browser to display the text using Arial first. If that font isn't installed (which it won't be on most Macs), the browser looks for Helvetica, and so on. If none of these fonts are available, the browser uses the default font—Times.

Begin

1 See What's Available

You can see the font options that ship with Dreamweaver by choosing **Text, Font** or by clicking the **Font** menu in the **Properties Inspector**. The options appear in the submenu. To apply any of these font combinations to the currently selected text, choose the option from the menu. If you select the font before you begin typing, the new font is applied to the text you type.

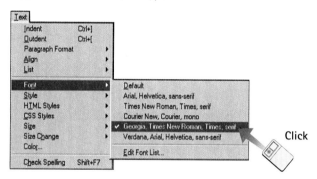

Click

2 Change the Font Combinations

If the font you want to use is not in the list, you can create your own font combination. Choose **Text, Font, Edit Font List**. The **Edit Font List** dialog box opens.

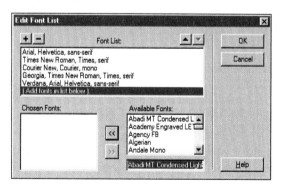

3 Create the Combination You Want

From the **Available Fonts** list, select the first font you want to include on your page by clicking the << button to move it to the **Chosen Fonts** list. Remember to choose fonts that are common to most computers; also remember that Macs have fonts that are different from PCs. Normally a group of fonts contains three or four fonts: a PC font or two, a similar Mac font, and a font family.

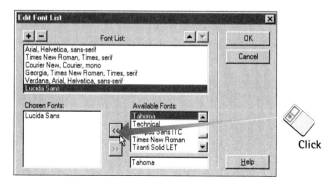

Click

4 Add a Font Family

After you have chosen the specific fonts you want, you should specify a *font family*. Any browser that can't display the specific fonts you have chosen will display a font from the family you specify last in your list. For example, if all the specific fonts you selected are sans serif, choose the **Sans Serif** family. (Font families appear at the bottom of the **Available Fonts** list.) When you are finished, click **OK**. The new font combination appears on the **Text, Font** submenu.

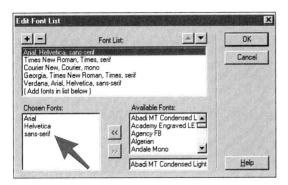

5 Edit a Font Combination

To edit the fonts included in a particular font combination, choose **Text, Font, Edit Font List** to display the **Edit Font List** dialog box. From the **Font List** at the top, choose the combination you want to edit. In the **Chosen Fonts** list, select the font you want to remove from this combination and click the >> button. (You can remove all the fonts from the **Chosen Fonts** list if you don't want this combination to appear in the **Font List** at all.) Alternatively, select from the **Available Fonts** list and click the << button to add a font to the combination.

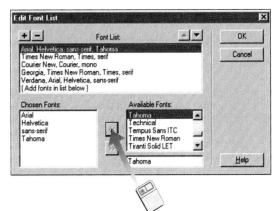

Click

6 Reorder the Font Combinations

You can make a particular combination appear at the top of the **Font List** in the **Edit Font List** dialog box and in the **Text, Font** submenu. In the **Font List** at the top of the dialog box, select the combination you want to move and use the up and down arrows to change the order of this entry in the list.

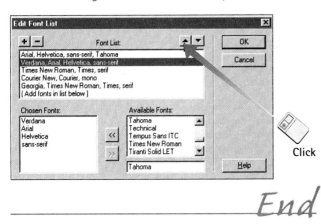

Click

End

How-To Hints

What Is a Font Family?

The term *font family* is a generic name for a group of similar fonts. Most computers and browsers acknowledge the following font families: cursive, fantasy, monospace, sans serif, and serif. If a browser cannot display any of the specific fonts you have chosen (as when the font is not installed on the user's computer), the browser displays the text using the default font associated with the font family. For example, on most computers, the default font for the monospace font family is Courier.

How to Import an HTML Document from Word

Being able to use previously created documents from Microsoft Word can save you a lot of time retyping information. However, if you don't import the Word file into Dreamweaver correctly, you can cause yourself a lot of trouble. Documents saved in Word in HTML format can have a lot of spurious and unnecessary tags. Dreamweaver can clean up the file for you. Make sure that you keep a copy of the original file in **.DOC** format; after Dreamweaver has cleaned up the HTML version, Word might not be able to open it.

Begin

1 Import the File

Choose **File, New** to open a blank document into which you will import the Word document. Then choose **File, Import, Word HTML** to open the **Select Word HTML File to Import** dialog box. Navigate to the Word file that was previously saved in HTML format (it won't have the **.DOC** extension but the **.HTM** extension) and click **Open**. The Word HTML file opens in the document window with the **Clean Up Word HTML** dialog box open in front.

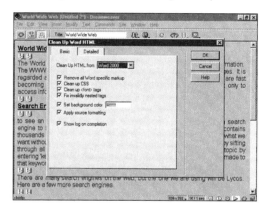

2 Clean Up the HTML

Dreamweaver is going to go through the document and remove a series of HTML tags that complicate the formatting of the document. All the kinds of potential trouble spots that Dreamweaver will look for and fix are marked with a check mark. Click the **Detailed** tab to open the second page of the dialog box.

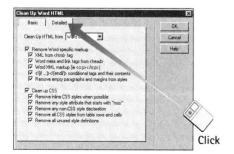

Click

3 Look at the Advanced Options

The **Detailed** tab lists all the specific tags that Dreamweaver intends to remove. These HTML tag descriptions are unlikely to mean much to you at this stage, so don't worry about them. In general, you want Dreamweaver to fix all potential problems with the HTML code Word has created, so leave all these options selected.

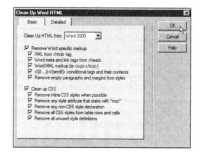

4 Start the Clean Up Process

You should not have to select the version of Word that created this HTML file; Dreamweaver detects and displays the appropriate version of Word in the list box at the top of the page. Click **OK** to accept the settings and start the clean up process.

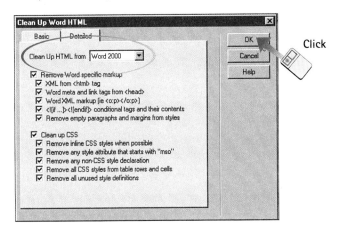

Click

5 Review the Changes

When it's done, Dreamweaver displays a screen showing you what tags have been removed from the Word HTML document. Click **OK** to continue.

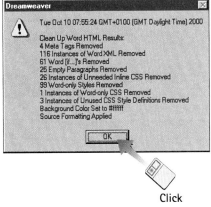

Click

6 Save the File

The document now has none of the unnecessary tags, but all the original formatting (such as italics and bold) is retained. Choose **File, Save As** to save the document as a Dreamweaver file into your site folder.

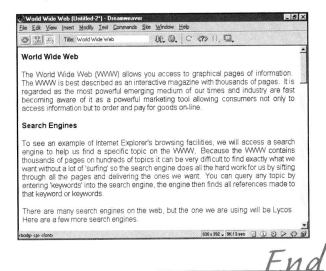

How-To Hints

Advanced Options

However good a word processor Microsoft Word is, it sure isn't great as an HTML editor. The **Clean Up Word HTML** utility is a lifesaver if you do a lot of your typing in Word and then want to use those documents in Dreamweaver. To make sure that the cleaned up file fits in with the rest of your site, you can set a background color as part of the clean up process by selecting the **Set background color** option on the **Basic** page of the dialog box. If you don't set one, the background color is automatically set to white.

End

How to Create Lists

In HTML documents, lists come in various shapes and sizes: bulleted lists, numbered lists, and definition lists. (In a *definition list,* you have a word on the left and its definition on the following line, slightly indented.) As you might guess, Dreamweaver makes it easy to format all these kinds of lists.

Begin

1 Create a New List

On the **Properties Inspector**, click either the **Bulleted List** (unordered list) button or the **Numbered List** button. A bullet or number appears in the document where the insertion point was. Type the first list item and press **Enter**. Pressing **Enter** adds a new bullet or number to the list. Continue until you have added all the items to appear in the list. To end the list, press **Enter** twice; the cursor returns to the normal alignment without a bullet or number.

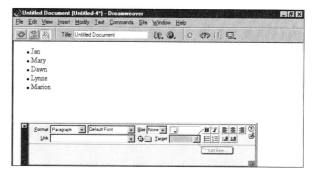

2 Create a List from Existing Text

You can turn text that already exists into a bulleted or numbered list. Each paragraph of text becomes a separate item in the list. Select the text you want to turn into a list and click the appropriate button in the **Properties Inspector**. The text is formatted into the list type you chose.

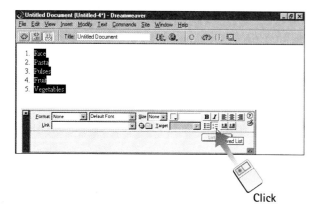

Click

3 Create a Definition List

To create a definition list, first type the items: Type the term to be defined, press **Enter**, and then type the definition or meaning on the next line. Choose **Text, List, Definition List** to format the text accordingly. In this example, the definition list format is used to list the titles of some company officers and the names of the people who hold those offices.

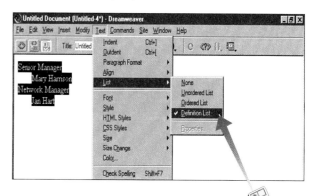

Click

4 Remove List Formatting

If you change your mind about the formatting you've applied to a list, you can "unformat" the text. Select the text that you've formatted as a list and click the button in the **Properties Inspector** that was used to apply the list formatting in the first place. If it's a definition list, choose **Text, List, Definition List**. The list formatting is removed from the text.

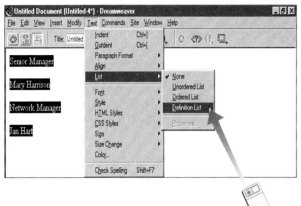

Click

5 Create a Nested List

A *nested list* is one in which certain items are "subpoints" under the main numbers or bullets. To create a nested list, select the items to be in the sublist and click the **Text Indent** button in the **Properties Inspector**.

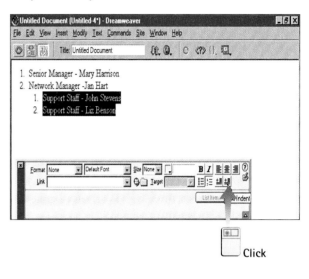

Click

6 Edit List Properties

You can change how your list appears, for example, whether you want round or square bullets and what number you want a numbered list to start on. Select a single item in the list and click the **List Items** button in the **Properties Inspector** to display the **List Properties** dialog box. From the **List Type** drop-down list, select the type of list item you want to work with. If you're working with a bulleted list, select the style of bullet you want from the **Style** list.

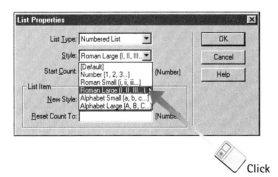

Click

7 Change the Numbers

If you want your numbered list to start at a number other than 1, open the **List Properties** dialog box and type the number you want the list to start at in the **Start Count** field. You can even change numbers within a numbered list. For example, items can be numbered 1, 2, 3, and can then start back at 1. Select the paragraph at which you want to reset the count and specify the number you want to reset the count to in the **Reset Count To** box.

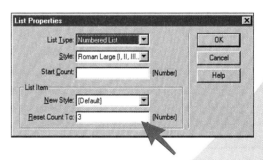

End

How to Define Cascading Styles for Text

Cascading Style Sheets (CSS) differ quite radically from the HTML styles we looked at earlier in this part. CSS can be used on multiple documents in a site; if you change the style sheet, all the pages to which it is applied are updated as well. We will look in greater detail at CSS in Part 8, "Working with Layers and Cascading Style Sheets."

Begin

1 Start with Some Text

Open a blank document window and type two or three lines of simple text that you can format with styles. Then click the **CSS Styles** button on the **Launcher** to open the **CSS Styles** panel. The panel list is empty because you have not yet defined any styles.

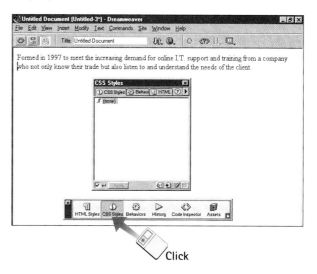

Click

2 Create a New Style Sheet

Before you can create a style, you must create a style sheet to contain the style. Click the **New Style** button at the bottom of the **CSS Styles** panel to open the **New Style** dialog box.

Click

3 Name the Style Sheet

Make sure that the **Make Custom Style** option is enabled. In the **Name** field, type a name for the style sheet you are creating. Click **OK** to save the file and open the **Style Definition** dialog box.

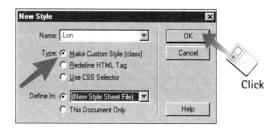

Click

4 Choose a Font Family

Use the **Font** drop-down list to choose a font family for the text that will be formatted with this style. You learned how to work with font families in Task 3, earlier in this part.

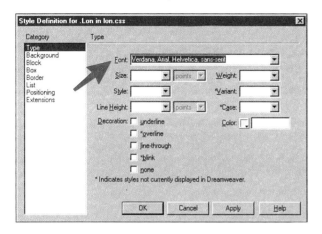

5 Choose a Color

Click the **Color** box and use the color picker to choose a color for the text. Note that you can select other options to further enhance the text. When you have made your selections, click **OK** to close the **Style Definition** dialog box and return to the **CSS Styles** panel.

6 Apply the Style

Select some existing text and choose the style you just created from the **CSS Styles** panel. With a single click, the text you selected now appears with the attributes you assigned to the style.

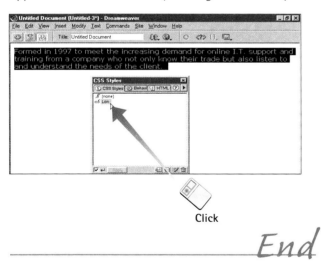

Click

End

How-To Hints

More About Style Sheets

Don't forget to check out Part 8 to learn more about defining styles. CSS is a very powerful tool that can aid you in formatting your entire site. In this task, we barely touched on one quick way of formatting text.

Styles Before You Type

After you have created a style or two, you can choose to apply a style *before* you start typing. If you do this, your text will take on the formats of the style as you create it, and you will have a better idea of how the text will appear on the page as you are creating the text.

How to Check Spelling

Making sure that you check the spelling of words in a Web page is just as important as it is in letters and other documents—probably more so. In a word processor, you can quickly make a change and reprint the information. To correct spelling on a Web page, you have to make the change locally and then upload the page to the server again. Get the page right the first time to avoid the tedium of uploading the page again later.

Begin

1 Start the Spell Check

The spell-check feature in Dreamweaver can check all or part of a page. To check a whole page, choose **Text, Check Spelling**. To check part of a page, select the text you want to check and then choose **Text, Check Spelling**. In both cases, the **Check Spelling** dialog box opens.

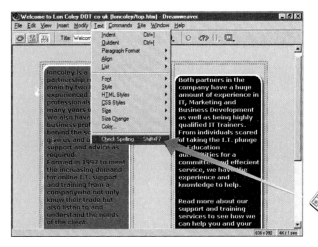

Click

2 Change a Word

When an unrecognized word is found, Dreamweaver highlights it on the page and offers you suggestions for replacements. If one of the words in the **Suggestions** list is the word you want to use to replace the highlighted word on the page, click the suggestion and then click **Change**. The text on the page is updated, and Dreamweaver continues through your page, looking for additional misspellings.

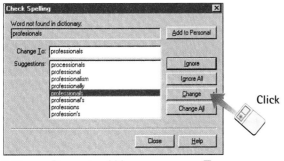

Click

3 Change All Instances

If you consistently misspell words when you type, you can change them one at a time as Dreamweaver locates them, or you can change them all at once. When Dreamweaver finds a word you misspell often, choose the correct spelling from the **Suggestions** list and click **Change All**. Dreamweaver will correct every instance of the misspelled word.

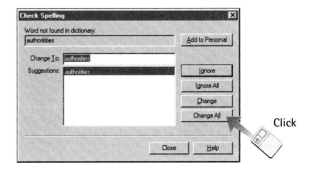

Click

4 Ignore a Word

If the word Dreamweaver has identified as an incorrectly spelled word is not incorrectly spelled (as is the case with many proper nouns), click **Ignore** button. The spell checker will continue to scan your document; it might find other instances of the same word and mark them as unknown. If you want to ignore all instances of the word, click **Ignore All**.

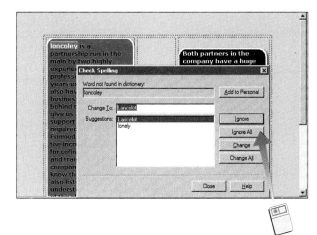

Click

5 Add to Personal Dictionary

You can add an unknown word to your personal dictionary if you want to prevent the spell checker from constantly stopping at it. When the spell checker stops at a word you use a lot, click **Add to Personal** to add this word to your personal dictionary. Now the spell checker won't stop when it encounters that word on this or any other page.

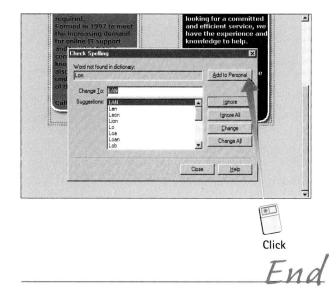

Click

End

How-To Hints

Which Language Do You Need?

By default, the Dreamweaver spell checker uses the U.S. English language dictionary. If, like me, you are British, you will want to change the language the spell checker uses so that it won't flag *criticise*, *colour*, and *favour* as wrong. To change the language, choose **Edit, Preferences** to open the **Preferences** dialog box. From the **Dictionary** drop-down list in the **General** category, select the language you want the spell checker to use. If you want neither U.S. nor UK English, go to the Macromedia Web site to locate other languages that are available for download.

How to Find and Replace Words on a Page

Even the most experienced Web designers and authors need to change things from time to time. Perhaps you have decided that a phrase you used several times in the document was wrong, or perhaps your company has changed part of its address. When this happens, you need to be able to find and change these instances of text quickly and easily. Dreamweaver lets you do just that.

Begin

1 Start the Search

The easiest way to find and replace words in your document is to use the **Replace** command. The **Find** command simply finds the word you specify; the **Replace** command allows you to easily change the words as well. To search for and replace a word or phrase, choose **Edit, Find and Replace**. The **Find and Replace** dialog box opens.

2 Type the Search Term

In the **Search For** text box, type the word or phrase for which you want to search and click **Find All**. Because you are going to be replacing this text with something new, put the new term in the **Replace With** box.

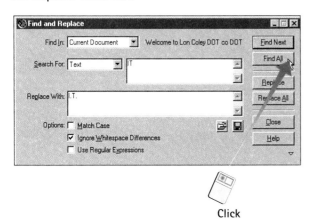

Click

3 Look at the Matches

Double-click any of the matching words in the bottom of the dialog box. Dreamweaver highlights the word in the document text.

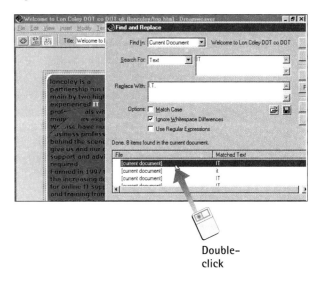

Double-click

4 Replace the Text

Click the **Replace** or **Replace All** button to change individual instances of the word or all of them at once. A dialog box appears to confirm the changes for you. Click **OK** to complete the process.

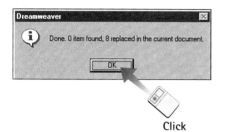

Click

5 Look in a Folder or the Site

If you want your search to look beyond the current document, use the **Find In** drop-down list in the **Find** or **Replace** dialog box to choose the **Current Site** or **Folder** option. If you select the **Folder** option, you'll be prompted to choose the folder you want to search. When the search is complete, double-click any item in the resulting list to open that document and view the text in context.

6 Try an Advanced Search

Use the **Search For** drop-down menu to specify that you want to search through the **HTML Source** code or for a specific **Tag**. If you select the **Text (Advanced)** option, you can specify a search for text inside HTML tags. For example, to find the text *Lon* that is not bold, you could search for the text **Lon**, specify the **Not Inside Tag** option, and then choose the **b** tag.

End

How-To Hints

Other Search Options

The **Find and Replace** dialog box offers three check boxes you can enable to further constrain your search. If you enable the **Match Case** option, Dreamweaver will search for text exactly as you type it in the text box. If you select the **Ignore Whitespace Differences** option, Dreamweaver will find all occurrences of the search term regardless of the number of spaces (or tab characters or paragraph returns) that appear. For example, a search for **Tom Jones** with this option enabled will return matches for **Tom<space><tab>Jones** and **Tom<paragraph return>Jones** but not **TomJones**. The **Use Regular Expressions** option is complicated enough to warrant your review of the Help files for explanation.

Task

5

Working with Hyperlinks

*H*yperlinks are what make the Internet the information superhighway. Being able move from page to page and site to site is possible only by the use of hyperlinks. *Hyperlinks* are the way visitors move between different Web pages. You know you are over a hyperlink on a Web page because the mouse pointer changes to a hand with one finger pointing upwards. When you click a hyperlink, a new page loads into your browser. The new page can be from the same site (an *internal hyperlink*) or from an entirely different site (an *external hyperlink*). There are many different ways of setting up the links on your Web page: You can use text, images, imagemaps, or even "jump menus" and navigation bars. The latter two are covered in later parts.

The tasks in this part of the book start you out by creating a simple hyperlink from one page of your site to another. As you work through these tasks, you will learn how to create links wherever and however you want—and not just links to other pages. You'll also learn to create email links, the easiest way to let site visitors contact you.

How to Create Hyperlinks

Hyperlinks come in many shapes and sizes, but there are only two real types of hyperlink: internal and external. Internal hyperlinks link from one page of your site to another page in your site; external hyperlinks link from one page of your site to another site entirely. Dreamweaver allows you to create hyperlinks by simply pointing to files within your site, by typing URLs straight into the **Properties Inspector**, and even by cutting and pasting from a browser window. After you know the options, you can decide which best suits you.

Begin

1 Select the Text

You can make a link out of any text on the page. First, select the text you want to turn into the link. Next, in the **Properties Inspector**, click the folder icon to the right of the **Link** field. The **Select File** dialog box opens.

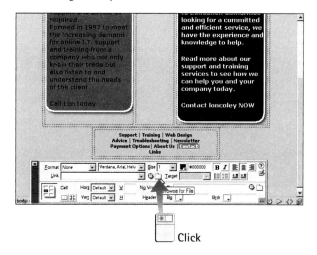

Click

2 Create the Link

Browse to the file you want the selected text to link to. The file should be in the same site folder as the current page. Select the file and click **Select**. The selected text changes to blue and is underlined, indicating that it is now a link. The **Link** box in the **Properties Inspector** now contains the filename of the linked page.

3 Use the Site Window to Create a Link

The **Site** window allows you create internal links without first selecting any text. Choose **Site, Site Map** to see the current files in the site. Your home page's icon appears in the middle of the **Site** window.

Home page icon

4 Drag to Create a Link

Single-click the home page icon; the mouse pointer changes to crosshairs. Drag the home page icon to any file in the **Local Folder** list on the right side of the screen. This action creates a link on the home page to the page you selected in the **Local Folder** list.

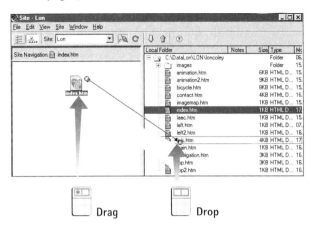

Drag   Drop

5 Find the Link on the Page

Open the home page in the document window. Note that Dreamweaver has automatically created a link to the selected page. This link appears as text at the bottom of your home page. The link is simply the filename (minus the **.htm** extension), which does not always make for a useful hyperlink. Here the link simply says *link*, but it, in fact, goes to a page full of useful hyperlinks.

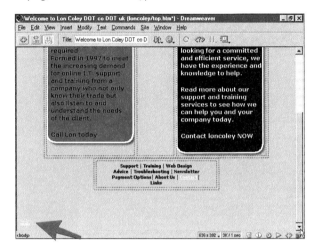

6 Use an Image as a Link

You can use an image as well as text as a hyperlink. Select the image that you want to use as a hyperlink. Use the folder icon to the right of the **Link** field in the **Properties Inspector** to browse to the file you want to link to; click **Select** to create the link.

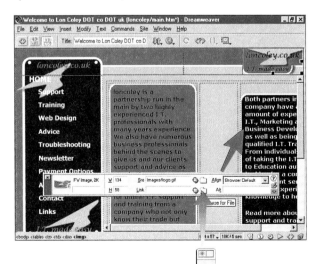

Click

7 Create an External Hyperlink

The process for creating an external link is very simple. Select the text or image that you want to use as the link and, in the **Link** field in the **Properties Inspector**, type the URL of the page to which you want to link.

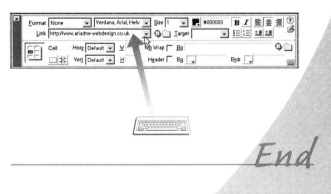

End

How to Edit or Delete a Hyperlink

At some point in your work creating and maintaining Web pages, you will have to change hyperlink information. For example, the URL to an external Web site might change, a link to an email address might change, or you might discover that the link you set up was wrong to start with! This task explains how you can change the information associated with the link—or even delete the link entirely.

Begin

1 Locate the Link to Change

Find the text or image that contains the link you want to change. Select the text or image and look for the **Link** box in the **Properties Inspector**. The current URL for the selected link appears there as soon as you select the link.

2 Change the Link Information

In the **Link** box, type the updated link information. If you want to delete the link (without deleting the text or image from the page), just clear the **Link** box of all address information. The link is now updated or removed.

3 Use Find and Replace

If a link appears several times in your page or throughout your site, you can use Find and Replace options to locate the link and change it. Choose **Edit, Find and Replace**; in the **Replace** dialog box, select **Source Code** from the **Search For** drop-down list, and type or paste the current (incorrect) link details into the text box.

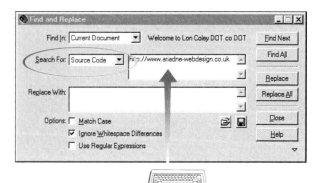

4 Enter the New Details

In the **Replace With** field, type the correct link details or leave the field empty if you want to remove the link altogether. From the **Find In** drop-down list, choose whether you want to search the current document or an entire site or folder. Click **Replace All**.

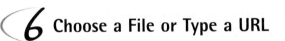

5 Use the Context Menu

If you don't want to make changes directly in the **Properties Inspector**, you can use the context menu. Select the text or image that contains the link you want to modify and right-click it (**Ctrl+click** for Mac users) to open the context menu. Choose **Remove Link** to eliminate the link completely or **Change Link** to make changes to the link. The **Select File** dialog box opens.

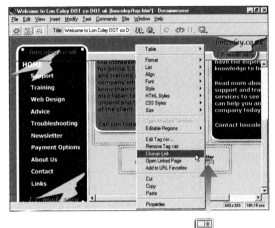

Right-click

6 Choose a File or Type a URL

In the **Select File** dialog box, either select the local file to which you want the link to refer or, in the **URL** box, change the URL as necessary to correct the link information. Click **Select** to make the change.

Click

End

How-To Hints

Look in the HTML Source Code

Remember that the text that appears on the Web page is not usually the same as the hyperlink itself (for example, the page might display a link which reads, *Lon's Great Web Site*, but the actual hyperlink is to **http://www.loncoley.co.uk**. The most important thing to remember is that changing the text on the page does not affect the actual hyperlink; you must remember to change both the text *and* the link information when necessary. The link information appears in the **Properties Inspector**, but many times you can't see the link onscreen. To look for the link information, you have to check the HTML source code, and the Find and Replace options are the best way to do that. If you can't remember how to use these features, refer to Part 4, "Working with Text."

How to Create an Email Hyperlink

Email hyperlinks are one of the mainstays of any successful Web site. When a visitor clicks the email link, their default email application opens to a new mail message, and the email address you've specified is already completed in the **To** field. Dreamweaver makes it easy to create email links, as shown in this task.

Begin

1 Select the Text or Choose a Location

Decide where on the page you want the email link to appear. Either select the text you want to use or click to position the insertion point on the page.

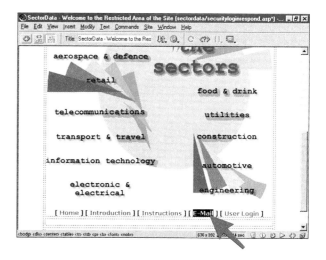

2 Use the Menus

Choose **Insert, Email Link** to open the **Insert Email Link** dialog box. In the **Text** box, type the text that will contain the email link (if you selected text in Step 1, the **Text** field is already filled in); in the **E-Mail** box, type the email address to link to. Click **OK**.

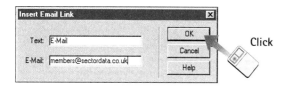

Click

3 Use the Properties Inspector

Instead of the menus, you can enter the email link information in the **Properties Inspector**. Select the text or image to be used as the link. In the **Link** field, type **mailto:** and then the email address you want to link to (make sure that there is no space between the colon and the email address you type).

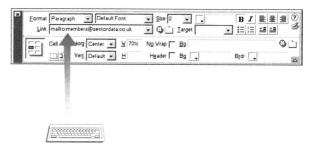

4 Use the Objects Panel

Another alternative to creating an email link is to click the **Insert Email Link** button on the **Objects** panel. The **Insert Email Link** dialog box opens, as shown in Step 2; type the text and email address to link to and click **OK**.

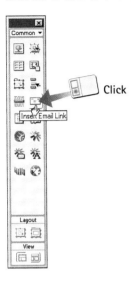

Click

Insert Email Link

5 Test the Link

Choose **File, Preview in Browser** to open the page in the default browser. Click the email link; your default email application should open to a blank document; check the email address that appears in the **To** field.

Click

End

How-To Hints

Mail Call!

Provide email links on your pages so that site visitors have a direct route back to you. Although you shouldn't fill your pages with unnecessary links, giving people a line of communication that is simple to find and use will hopefully prompt them to contact you frequently.

How to Create Anchors and Thumbnails

You can set up an *anchor* on a page so that you can hyperlink directly to that point on the page. Normally when you hyperlink to a page, the page opens at the top. Anchors are often used to allow people to jump back to the top of a page from somewhere further down the page. Because you must set up the anchor on the page before you can link to it, you cannot jump to anchors on other sites. A *thumbnail* image is a smaller version of a graphic that, when clicked, opens to a larger version of the same image (see Task 4 in Part 15, "Working with Images in Fireworks," for details about resizing images).

Begin

1 Insert the Small Image

If you want to show a thumbnail image on your page that links to a larger image, choose **Insert, Image**. Browse to the file containing the small image you want to insert and click **Select**. The image appears on your page. Save the page.

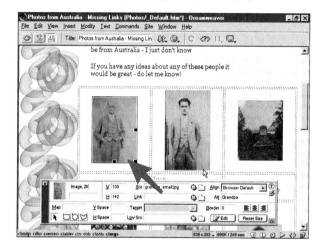

2 Create the Link

Select the image you just inserted. In the **Properties Inspector**, click the folder icon next to the **Link** field to open the **Select File** dialog box. Browse to the full-sized image file and click **Select**.

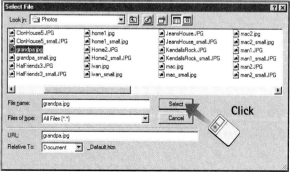

3 Test the Link

Save the page and prepare to preview the page: Choose **File, Preview In Browser**. When the page opens in the browser, click the thumbnail image; the full-sized version of the image should appear.

4 Create an Anchor

Before you can link to a specific point in a document, you must create the anchor. Open the page to which you want to add an anchor point and click in the document where you want the anchor. On the **Invisibles** page of the **Objects** panel, click the **Insert Named Anchor** button to open the **Insert Named Anchor** dialog box.

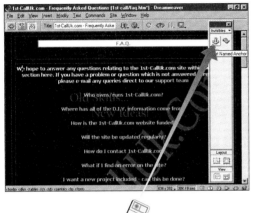

Click

5 Name the Anchor

Type a name for the anchor you're creating and click **OK**. If you are creating a link back to the top of the page, a good anchor name is **Top**; if you're creating an anchor to a particular section in a long, text-filled page, make the anchor name similar to the title of the section. The anchor icon appears in the document window. If you don't see the icon, open the **View** menu and make sure that the **Invisible Elements** option is enabled.

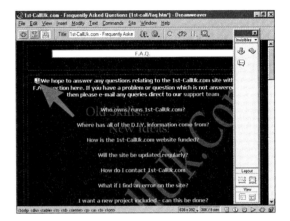

6 Link to the Anchor

To link to the anchor you just created, select the text you want to use as a link to your anchor. (If you just created an anchor at the top of the page, for example, you can insert the text *Back to the top* somewhere else on the page as the link to the top of the page.) In the **Link** field in the **Properties Inspector**, type **#anchorname** (for example, type **#Top**). You can also create a link to an anchor in a different file: In the **Properties Inspector**, click the folder icon next to the **Link** field, browse to the file, and click **Select**. Following the filename in the **Link** field, type **#** and the name of the anchor on that page to which you want to link.

End

How-To Hints

Use Point to File

The **Point to File** icon on the **Properties Inspector** is a handy tool that helps with creating links. When you drag the **Point To File** icon over the named anchor you just created, the name of the anchor automatically fills in the **Link** box in the **Properties Inspector**. Simply let go of the mouse when the icon is over the anchor, and the link will be complete.

Use the Menus or Keyboard to Create Anchors

You can also create anchors by choosing **Insert, Named Anchor** or by pressing **Ctrl+Alt+A** (Windows users) or ⌘+**Option+A** (Mac users).

How to Change the Way Links Look

Links must be highly visible to site visitors. By default, Dreamweaver formats links as underlined, blue text so that the links stand out from the rest of the page. You can make changes to the default settings for links, as explained in this task.

Begin

1 See the Defaults

Open a new page in Dreamweaver and create a simple link to another page in your site. Notice the link on the page: The text is blue and underlined. This is the default setting for links; you didn't format the link like that, the HTML standards did. Furthermore, the standards automatically change the color of the link to red as you click it and to purple after you've visited the linked page.

2 Choose Your Colors

To change the colors of the links on your page, choose **Modify, Page Properties** to open the **Page Properties** dialog box. Use the color picker to select new colors for the **Links, Visited Links,** and **Active Links** options.

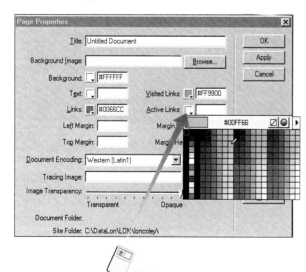

Click

3 Check That the Colors Work

Remember that you have three link colors to consider; make sure that none of these colors disappears against the background color of the page or image. Preview the page in a browser to make sure that you can see all three link colors. If you use an image as a link, any border you place around the image takes on the link colors you've specified. (To add a border to an image, type the number of pixels thick that you want the border to be in the **Border** box in the **Properties Inspector.**)

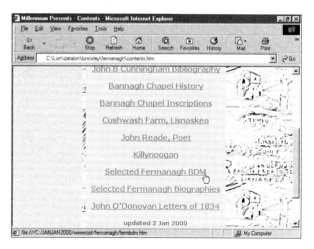

4 Use a Color Scheme

Dreamweaver color schemes allow you use a preset combination of text and link colors designed to work well together. To see the color scheme options, choose **Commands, Set Color Scheme** to open the **Set Color Scheme Command** dialog box. Select from the **Background** and **Text and Links** lists and preview these combinations. Click **OK** when you've found a color combination you like.

Click

5 Make Links Stand Out

If your links still don't look obvious enough on the page, try making the link text bold. Select the link text and click the **Bold** button in the **Properties Inspector**.

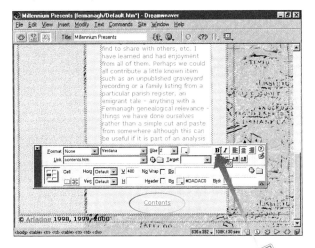

Click

End

How-To Hints

Links with Style

Make sure that your link colors are significantly different from the color of text on the page. You don't want visitors to miss vital information because they didn't notice that a link was there. You can create links using *styles*, which remove the underline formatting in certain browsers. Part 8, "Working with Layers and Cascading Style Sheets," describes styles in detail.

Think Background Colors—and Not Just Page Backgrounds

When you change link colors, make sure that you check the page in a browser. Don't forget that the link color changes after you've visited the link—there are far too many Web sites on which links disappear after they've been clicked because the creator forgot to check the colors. You will have to think about link colors when you change background colors on different parts of the same page. (Tables and layers make it possible to separate the page into areas that can have separate background colors.)

How to Follow and Check Hyperlinks

Checking your hyperlinks before uploading the site is not only a good idea, but also it's vital if you are going to have a successful Web site. Internal links can be checked (followed) from within Dreamweaver; you check external links from a separate browser. You learn to do both in this task.

Begin

1 Follow an Internal Hyperlink

Open the page in Dreamweaver and select a link that has already been created. Open the context menu by right-clicking the link (**Ctrl+click** for Mac users).

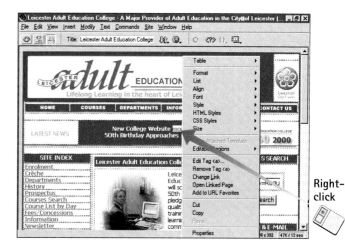

Right-click

2 Open the Linked Page

Choose **Open Linked Page** from the context menu. The page you linked to opens for editing into the document window. This result tells you that the link is correct and that it works.

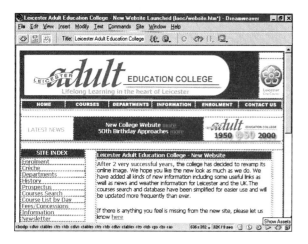

3 Check an Email Link

To check whether an email link works, open the page in the default browser by choosing **File, Preview In Browser**. Click the link to make sure that the default email application opens and that the correct email address is inserted into the **To** field.

Click

4 Check an External Hyperlink

To check an external hyperlink, you must first open the page in the default browser. Make sure that you are connected to the Internet and click the external link. You should see the correct page in the browser window.

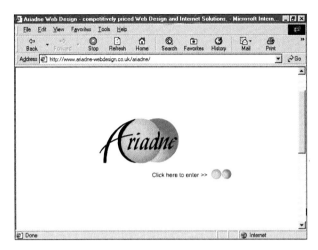

5 Check All Local Links

Dreamweaver can check the internal links in a document, folder, or site for you. Choose **File, Check Links** to open the **Link Checker** dialog box. Use the **Show** drop-down list to select which links you want to show and check. When you select **Broken Links** from the list, Dreamweaver runs a complete check on links in your local site. Here, the dialog box tells you about broken links. Double-click any files displayed to edit them and repair the link information.

Double-click

6 Check Links in Part of a Site

Open the **Site** window and open the context menu by right-clicking anywhere inside the right pane (**Ctrl+click** for Mac users). Choose **Check Links** and then choose whether you want to check the entire site or just selected folders. If you choose **Selected Files/Folders**, a dialog box opens from which you can select the folders in the local site you want to check for broken links.

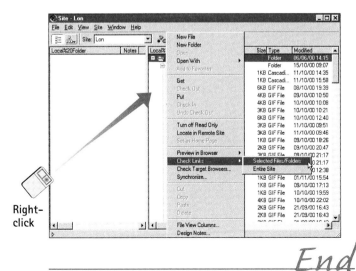

Right-click

How-To Hints

Checking Links

Dreamweaver can open links to local files only through the context menu. External hyperlinks and **mailto:** email links can be checked only using the **File, Preview In Browser** menu option. If you use the **File, Check Links** command, Dreamweaver creates a list of external links but cannot check whether they are still in working order.

End

Task

Working with Graphics

*M*ore and more, graphics are being used in Web sites for many reasons: Effect, fun, and advertising are all valid reasons for enhancing your pages with a picture file or two. In Part 15 of this book, "Working with Images in Fireworks," we will look at creating and editing images in Fireworks; in the tasks in this part, we focus on how to use existing images.

If by chance you don't already have a supply of image files on your computer, use a general search engine on the Internet to search for either clipart or Web graphics. You should be able to find many sites that offer images that can be used royalty free. Starting off with some professional-quality images will certainly help you feel confident enough to tackle the creation of your own images. Alternatively, you can jump to Part 15, to learn how to make your own images in Fireworks. Then come back here and see how to use them.

The file formats of your images are important. For most purposes, stick with the GIF and JPG or JPEG formats, which are supported in all but the oldest browsers.

The Graphic Interchange Format (GIF) format uses a maximum of 256 colors; combinations of these colors simulate all other colors. The GIF format is best for displaying images such as logos, icons, and buttons. You should also use GIF when you need transparency, interlacing (when an image appears to load into the browser bit by bit), or the ability to create animations. The Joint Photographic Expert Group (JPG or JPEG) format is the file format used with photographs or other images that require the support of large numbers of colors. The JPEG format supports millions of colors. Although you can't have transparency or interlacing with a JPEG image, the JPEG format does allow you to specify the degree of file compression so that you can create a balance between image quality and file size.

How to Organize and Import Images

You should always make sure that the image files you intend to use on your pages are stored within your site's subfolders on the hard disk. Proper organization of your graphics files ensures that the images will appear correctly on your local machine and (more importantly) on the remote server as well. When you *import* an image, you bring the file into your site folder; when you *insert* an image, you place it on a page for people to see.

2 Create a Folder

To begin tidying up the unorganized files shown in the preceding figure, you'll need to create some subfolders to hold the image files for this site. In the right pane of the **Site** window, click the root folder for the site (for example, **C:\datalon\LON\loncoley**) Then right-click (**Ctrl+click** on a Macintosh) to open the context menu and choose New Folder.

Right-click

Begin

1 Open the Site Window

Open the **Site** window for the site you want to work with. As you already know, it is good practice to keep the image files you plan to use for a site in subfolders under the main site folder. If you keep your image files organized in this fashion, you'll know where they are, and the **Site** window won't be filled with unrelated files. In the example shown here, image files are strewn among HTML files, making it difficult to determine what's what.

3 Name the Folder

Dreamweaver creates a new subfolder in the root folder of the current site. The folder is already selected and ready for you to rename from the meaningless default; type a meaningful name (such as **images**) and press Enter.

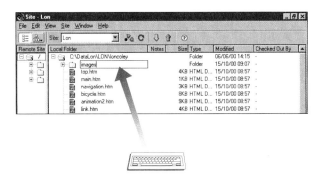

4 Move Image Files to the **images** Folder

If you already have image files in the site folder, you can move these files into the **images** folder simply and quickly. Click the **Type** heading at the top of the **Site** window to organize the files in the window by file extension (all GIF files are grouped together, all HTML files are grouped together, and so on). Select the file or files you want to move and drag them to the **images** folder. You can select multiple files using the **Shift+click** technique.

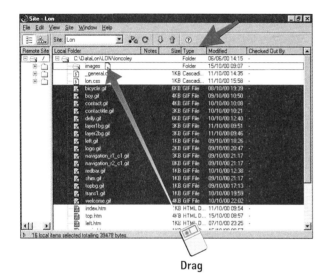

Drag

5 Update Links

Dreamweaver knows when you move files and prompts you to update links to the files you are moving. In this example, Dreamweaver asks whether you want to update the links to the dozen or so image files in the eight HTML files listed. Click **Update** to complete the move and update the HTML files. If you don't click the **Update** button, all the existing image references in the HTML pages for the site will be broken, and your pages will not be able to find the images.

Click

6 Use File Management Software

Now that you have an **images** folder for your Web site, you can copy images from other locations on your hard drive to this folder to use in your pages. To copy files from other folders, you'll have to use your file management program (such as Windows Explorer); the **Site** window lets you access only the folders in the current site.

7 Locate the Images to Copy

Navigate to the location for the images you want to use in your current site, select the files, and click the **Copy** button in the toolbar.

Click

Continues

8 Paste Images into Site Folder

Still in your file management software, browse to the **images** subfolder you created in the current site folder. Click the folder to select it and click the **Paste** button in the toolbar. The selected image files are copied to the **images** folder, ready for you to use in the site.

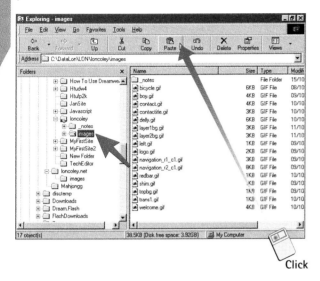

Click

9 Check That the Files Are There

Close the file management software window and switch back to the **Site** window in Dreamweaver. Make sure that the files you just copied to the **Images** folder are there and ready for you to use.

10 Save New Images into the Folder

When you create or import new images for use in the site, use the new **Images** folder as the save or export location from your imaging application. Part 15, "Working with Images in Fireworks," addresses the creation and storage of images you create in Fireworks.

11 Download Images to the Folder

If you are downloading image files from the Internet for use in your site, you should specify the **images** folder as the save location. Right-click the image you want to save to your hard disk and select **Save Picture As** from the context menu (Mac users press and hold **Ctrl**, click the image, and select **Download Image to Disk**). Then browse to the **images** folder to complete the download.

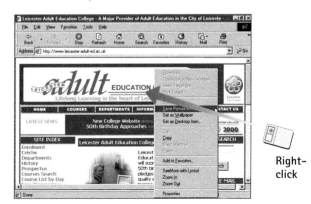

Right-click

12 Save an Inserted Image to the Site

If you insert an image into an existing page from another location, Dreamweaver will prompt you to copy the image into your site folder. Click **Yes** to continue; the **Copy File As** dialog box opens.

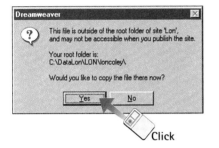

Click

13 Insert an Image into an Unsaved Page

When you insert an image from an external location into a new unsaved page, Dreamweaver notifies you that the file path will be updated when the file is saved. Click **OK** to continue; the **Copy File As** dialog box opens.

Click

14 Select the Images Folder

The **Copy File As** dialog box opens as soon as you agree to copy a file into your local site. You'll see the same dialog box whether you are working with an unsaved page or an existing page. To complete the copy, in the **Copy File As** dialog box, select the **images** folder and click **Save**. The image file is saved with the correct reference in the correct folder.

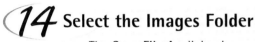

Click

End

How-To Hints

Organization Skills

In this task, we have created a single **images** folder in which you can keep the graphics for your site. As your site grows, it is a good idea to divide your graphics files into subdirectories for buttons, backgrounds, logos, and so on. Keep your files organized from the start, and you won't have to constantly tidy up later.

Fireworks Files

Even though this task is concerned about organizing existing image files, you can use your local site directory to store other image files that don't actually appear in the Web pages. For example, you can use the local site to store your original PNG files from Fireworks so that the files are close at hand when you need to edit them.

How to Insert Images

So far, we have simply "plonked" a picture into a page so that we can do things with it or learn about palettes. This task looks at all the different ways you can insert images into a page. The information in this task is expanded on in Part 8, "Working with Layers and Cascading Style Sheets," which includes discussions of how to put images in layers. For now, this task examines all the options Dreamweaver provides for inserting images directly into a page.

Begin

1 Use the Menu to Insert an Image

Before you add an image to a Web page, make sure that you save the page file. Click in the page where you want your image to appear first and then choose **Insert, Image** to open the **Select Image Source** dialog box. Go to Step 4.

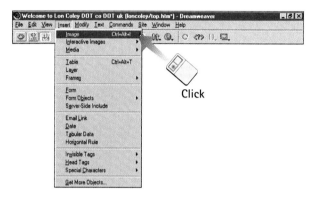

Click

2 Use the Objects Panel

Alternatively, you can open the **Select Image Source** dialog box by clicking on the Web page where you want the image to appear and then, in the **Objects** panel, clicking **Insert Image.** Go to Step 4.

Click

3 Drag the Icon

If you don't want to first click on the page where you want the image, you can drag the **Insert Image** icon from the **Objects** panel to the location you want on the page. This action opens the **Select Image Source** dialog box. (The image will be inserted where you dropped the icon.)

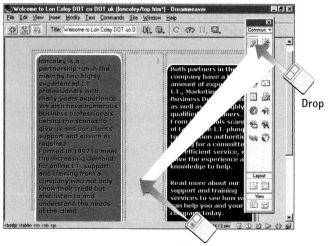

Drop

Drag

4 Select the Image

In the **Select Image Source** dialog box that opens as a result of Step 1, 2, or 3, browse to the image file you want to insert. (Ideally, the image file is located in the **images** folder you created for your site as described in Task 1 of this part.) Click **Select** to insert the selected image into the page at the location specified in Step 1, 2, or 3.

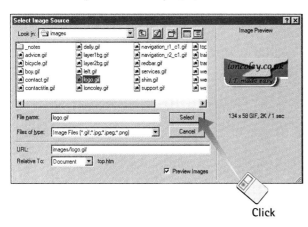

Click

5 Insert an Image from Your Desktop

Dreamweaver also allows you to drag an image from your desktop directly into your page. Dreamweaver then prompts you to save the file into your site folder.

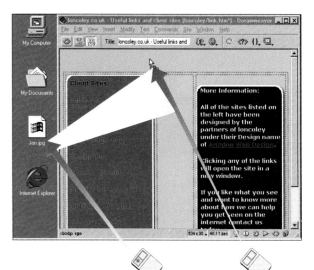

Drag   Drop

6 Use a Placeholder

If you don't know which image you are going to use or haven't created the image yet, you can insert an image placeholder where you want the picture to appear. Click on the page to identify the location for the image and then press and hold the **Ctrl** key (Mac users press **Option**) and click the **Insert Image** button in the **Objects** panel.

Ctrl + Click

How-To Hints

Don't Copy and Paste

Depending on the software you are used to, you might think that simply copying an image from your imaging application and pasting it into a Dreamweaver page is a good plan. Not only is this *not* a good idea (you can't set transparencies or background colors), Dreamweaver simply doesn't allow it.

Check the File Path

You should get into good habits with images early on to avoid missing files and bad file paths. There's nothing worse than surfing to a page that looks good but has the awful little red cross where an image should be. This situation is usually caused by a file path pointing incorrectly to a local file system—so be careful!

End

How to Set Image Properties

Image *properties* cover many things—size and position on the page being the most obvious. The **Properties Inspector** is your key to identifying and changing properties for the images on your pages. In addition to explaining how to set the size and position properties for an image, this task shows you how to set other properties (such as alternative text and borders) as well.

Begin

1 Look at the Properties Inspector

Launch the **Properties Inspector** (choose **Window, Properties**). Click an image on your page (refer to Task 2 for instructions on inserting an image, if necessary). Look at the **Properties Inspector** to see what it shows you.

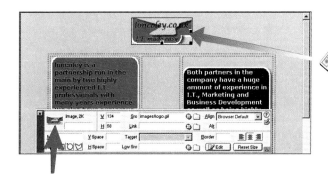

Click

2 Check Width and Height

The Width and Height fields in the **Properties Inspector** contain the dimensions for the selected image. To change the dimensions for the image on the page, simply edit these values in the **Properties Inspector**. A note of caution: Changing the height and width values can change the proportion of the image; making the image too large can cause it to become pixilated because you're not editing the image, only the size it displays on the screen. Although these weird effects might be exactly what you want to accomplish by editing the image properties, they usually are not!

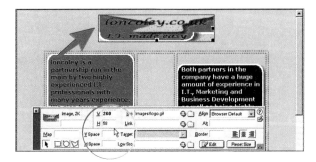

3 Identify the Image Source

The **Src** field shows the path of the source file for the selected image. There's no need to change this value because it is generated when the image is inserted on the page. If you want to change the image and know the exact path and filename of the file you want to use instead, type directly into the **Src** field.

4 Set the Alignment

Use the alignment buttons (**Align Left**, **Align Right**, and **Align Center**) to position the image onscreen. The **Align** drop-down menu allows you to control how the image is aligned when positioned with text (refer to Task 7, "How to Wrap Text Around Images").

5 Check the Link

The **Link** field shows the file, image, or URL that the selected image links to. By default, the **Link** field is empty and is filled in only when (or if) you link an object to this image.

6 Specify Alternative Text

The text you type in the **Alt** field displays as the image itself is downloaded. This text also appears instead of the image in browsers that don't support the display of images or as a tooltip when a visitor holds the mouse over the image in a browser. Type the descriptive text you want to appear in these situations into the field.

Continues

How-To Hints

Image Sizes

In the preceding steps, we looked at how easy it is to change the display dimensions of image files. It is important to realize that changing the dimensions of the image changes *only* the display size, not the underlying image. If you want to change an image drastically, it is always better to use a graphics application and edit the original image file. For example, if you have a large image that takes a long time to download, changing the dimensions in Dreamweaver does not affect the file size or download time—only the space the image takes up in the browser window.

7 Set V and H Spaces

The Vertical and Horizontal fields set a whitespace area (specified in pixels) around the image. These fields are a nice way to create a buffer between an image and the text that surrounds it; note that the H value you specify is used on both sides of the image, and that the V value is used both above and below the image. Notice here that a vertical space of 15 pixels creates a gap at the top of the page, above the image, and pushes the other page content down away from the image.

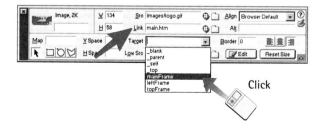

8 Specify a Low-Resolution Source Image

The **Low Src** field specifies a low-resolution image that will load quickly into the browser before the high-res image. This field is really used only with images with a large filesize and long download time (quick-loading images with short download times don't need this option). Click the folder icon to browse to a low-resolution version of the image, which will display quickly when the page is loaded.

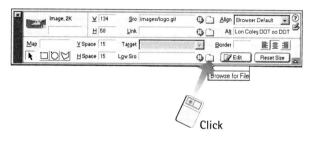

Click

9 Specify Target and Map

Targets are used only when working with hyperlinks on pages that use frames and framesets You were introduced to targets in Part 5, "Working with Hyperlinks," and will meet up with them again when we address frames in Part 9, "Using Frames and Framesets." In this example, you can see that the image is linked and is being assigned a target frame of **mainFrame**.

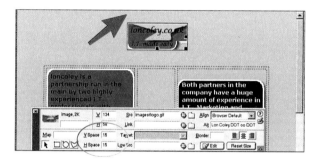

Click

10 Specify a Border Thickness

You can have Dreamweaver draw a border around your image. Type a number in the **Border** box to specify the pixel thickness of the border to be drawn. Be warned that your viewers might perceive that a bordered image contains a hyperlink.

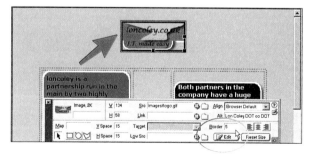

11 Edit the Image

To edit the graphics file, click the **Edit** button in the **Properties Inspector**. The image opens into your default imaging application. Make any changes to the image and save it to make the changed image appear in your page. Here you see the logo image opened in Fireworks, which you learn more about in Part 15, "Working with Images in Fireworks."

12 Return to the Original Proportions

Click the **Reset Size** button in the **Properties Inspector** to return the Width and Height properties to their original values. This button is handy if you have been fiddling with these values and the image no longer looks correct.

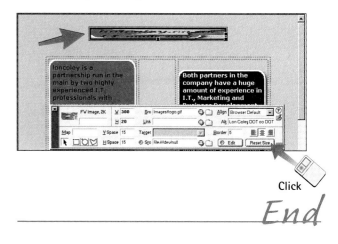

Click

End

How-To Hints

Editing Images

Remember that this book covers Fireworks as well as Dreamweaver. If you are new to image editing and creation, take a look at Parts 15 onward to learn how it is done. The Fireworks section of the book teaches you not only how to make images, but also how to optimize them for use in your pages.

How to Link Images

In Part 5, "Working with Hyperlinks," you learned how to create a hyperlink using text. A Web site filled with nothing but text can become boring. Using images for hyperlinks can not only serve a useful purpose, it can brighten up your page as well. Images can be used for internal, external, and email links in the same way as text can be used. This task shows you how.

Begin

1 Insert an Image

Decide on the image you want to use as a link on the page you are working on. If you don't already have images in place, insert one now. Choose **Insert, Image** from the menu, navigate to the image you want to insert, and click **OK** to insert that image on your page.

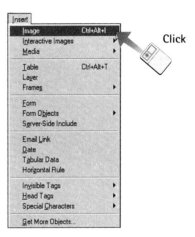

Click

2 Link to a Local File

Click to select the image you want to link. In the **Properties Inspector**, click the folder icon next to the **Link** field to open the **Select File** dialog box. Browse to the page or file in the local folder that you want this graphic to link to. Click **Select** to close the dialog box and return to the page. The link is created.

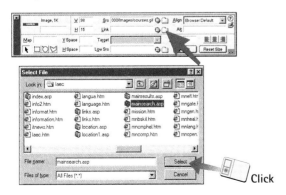

Click

3 Link to an External Site

Click to select the image you want to link. In the **Link** field in the **Properties Inspector**, type the full URL of the remote site to which you want to link. (Note that the full URL of many sites begins with **http://**.)

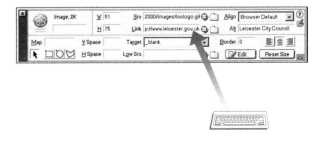

4 Link to a Different File Type

You can link the graphic image directly to another type of file (for example, you can link a graphic of a question mark to a help TXT file). Click to select the image you want to link. Right-click the image and select **Make Link** from the context menu. The **Select File** dialog box opens.

5 Select the File

In the **Select File** dialog box, make sure that all files are being displayed. Choose the image file or non-Web-page file to which you want to link the selected graphic. Click **Select**.

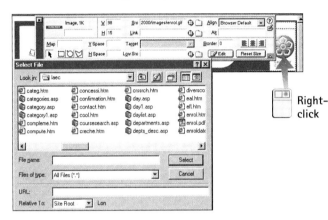

Right-click

Click

End

How-To Hints

Make It Obvious!

When using images as hyperlinks, make sure that the site visitor knows that the image is a link! There's no point in using images as links if the people visiting your pages don't know that the images are navigation tools.

To make it more obvious that the image is a link, add a border to the image—the color of the border will change to agree with the link colors you've set up when you make the image into a link. Another option is to fill in the **Alt** field in the **Properties Inspector** with some text such as **click here to see full-size image**. This text will display as a tooltip in the visitor's browser window when the mouse passes over the image.

How to Create Imagemaps

In simple terms, an *imagemap* is a single image with areas that are links to multiple places. Imagemaps allow you to use a nice large image as a starting point for your site. For example, you can create a graphic of a geographic map with town labels that act as the *hotspot* links; when viewers click a town label, they are linked to pages about that town.

Begin

1 Insert the File to Be Mapped

Decide which file you want to use as the basis for your imagemap. Select **Insert, Image** to open the **Select Image Source** dialog box and navigate to the image you want to insert. Insert the image into the page you want and make sure that the image you choose is pretty large.

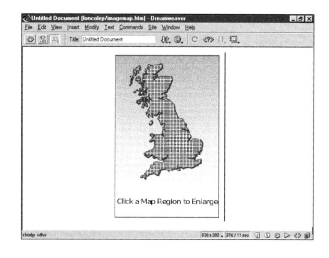

2 Expand the Property Inspector

Click to select the image file. Open the **Properties Inspector** by choosing **Window, Properties**, and then click the **Expand** button in the bottom-right corner of the **Properties Inspector** to see all the properties for the image.

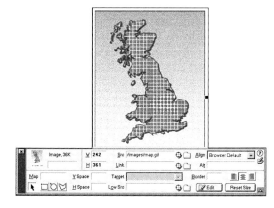

3 Name the Imagemap

In the **Map** box in the **Properties Inspector**, type a unique name for the imagemap you are going to create from the selected image.

4 Choose the Hotspot Shape

Circles and rectangles are the easiest hotspot shapes to create. Click the circle or rectangle icon on the **Properties Inspector** to select the desired shape of the hotspot. The mouse pointer changes to a crosshair that you can position over the image.

Click

5 Draw the Hotspot

Move the mouse over the image and drag to draw a hotspot where you want the link to appear. In this example, we are creating a hotspot that covers the northwest coast of Scotland. We will create the link for this hotspot in Step 9.

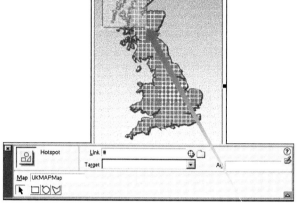

Drag

Continues

How-To Hints

Mix and Match

Don't think that just because the first hotspot you drew was a rectangle that they must all be—you can use as many of the three options as necessary to cover your image or the part of it to be mapped. Your options for hotspot shapes are circle, square, and polygon.

Don't Get Too Complicated

Remember that visitors to your site will click on the hotspots you are creating. For this reason, make sure that all the hotspots you create are big enough for a mouse to go over. Too many small, complex hotspots will cause confusion for your visitors.

Not Just Maps

The term *imagemap* is used to identify any image that has multiple hotspots placed on it. We are using an actual map of the United Kingdom in these examples, but imagemaps can be any graphic that you want to use to point to different pages. Just remember to make it obvious to your site visitors that there are links on the image.

6 Select a Polygonal Hotspot Shape

Polygonal hotspots are used for irregularly shaped areas. You create them by clicking the corners of the shape you want to create. In the **Properties Inspector**, click the polygon icon. In the image, click once to mark the first corner of the area you want to outline.

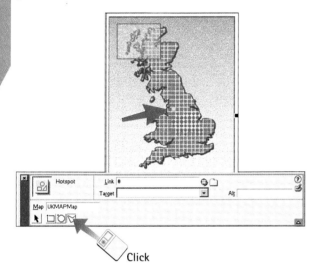

Click

7 Add the Points

Continue creating the polygon shape on the image by clicking the corners of the shape. Here you see an irregular shape outlined in the midlands area of England on the map.

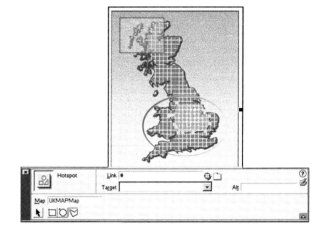

8 Turn Off the Polygon Tool

Click the arrow in the **Properties Inspector** to turn off the polygon drawing tool. This action returns the mouse pointer to a normal pointer.

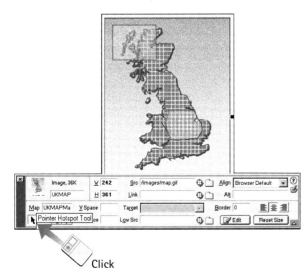

Click

9 Display the Hotspot Properties

No matter what shape your hotspot is, the link to that area is created in the same way. Click one of the hotspots you drew earlier to select that hotspot. Notice that the **Properties Inspector** changes to show only those fields associated with hotspots.

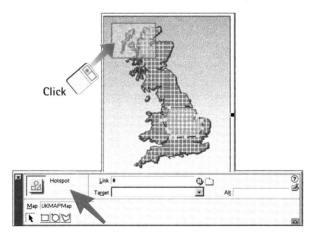

Click

10 Create the Link

In the **Properties Inspector**, create the link by either typing the URL to link to in the **Link** field or clicking the folder icon next to the **Link** field and navigating to the file in the local folder.

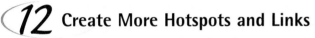

11 Set Alternate Text

Use the **Alt** box to add alternative text for each hotspot on the imagemap. You can also set alternative text for the complete image by selecting it and typing in the **Alt** box in the **Properties Inspector**.

12 Create More Hotspots and Links

Repeat the steps in this task to create additional hotspots on the image and to link those hotspots to other pages in the local site or to remote sites.

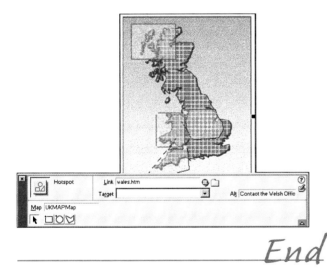

End

How-To Hints

Alternative Text

The text you type in the **Alt** field for each hotspot can inform the viewer about what each spot links to. Note that in addition to providing Alt text for each hotspot, you should also provide some Alt text for the imagemap as a whole; that text appears as the imagemap downloads and is visible if you hover the mouse over any non-mapped parts of the image.

How to Edit Imagemaps

In the preceding task, you learned how to create an imagemap as a navigational tool for your site. In an ideal world, your imagemap would be perfect and never need changing. However, in reality, you will have occasion to edit the imagemap at somepoint. In this task, you will learn how to change, move, and even delete hotspots.

Begin

1 Delete a Hotspot

To remove a hotspot completely from an imagemap, click the **Hotspot Pointer** tool in the **Properties Inspector,** click the hotspot in the image, and press the **Delete** key on the keyboard.

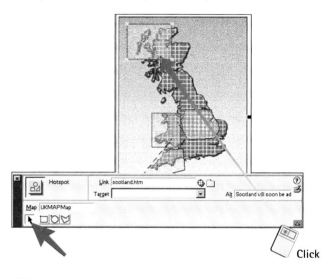

Click

2 Change the Size of a Hotspot

Click the **Hotspot Pointer** tool in the **Properties Inspector** and then click any hotspot you have already created. Notice that the selected hotspot has handles around its edges. Drag a handle to resize the hotspot to whatever size you want.

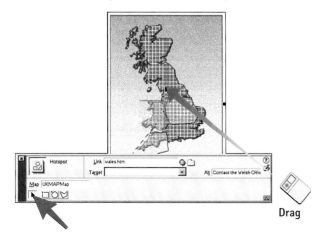

Drag

3 Change the Link

Select the hotspot whose link you want to change. In the **Properties Inspector,** click the folder icon next to the **Link** field and navigate to a different file; alternatively, type a new URL in the **Link** field.

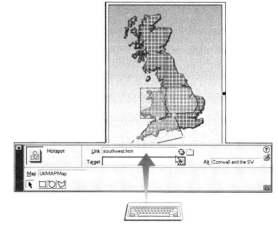

4 Move a Hotspot

If you want to move a hotspot to a different part of the image, click the **Hotspot Pointer** tool in the **Properties Inspector** and drag and drop the hotspot shape where you want it to appear. The existing link information for that hotspot is retained, and might need to be changed to reflect the new location.

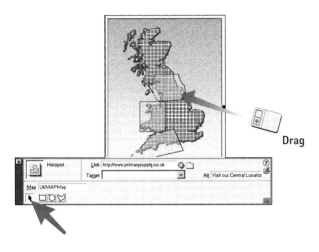

Drag

5 Remove Overlapping

Hotspots should not overlap on an imagemap. Web browsers can interpret only one link at a time, so it's best not confuse them by giving them a choice of links to respond to! If you have overlapping hotspots, resize or move them to solve the problem.

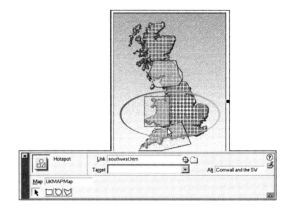

6 Select Multiple Hotspots

If you want all your hotspots to appear in a line either vertically or horizontally, press and hold the **Shift** key as you click the hotspots you want to select. Here we have an example of multiple hotspots on an image.

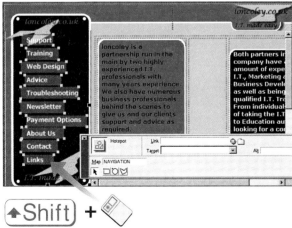

↑Shift + Click

7 Align the Hotspots

Choose **Modify, Align** and then select the alignment or sizing option you want to apply to the selected hotspots.

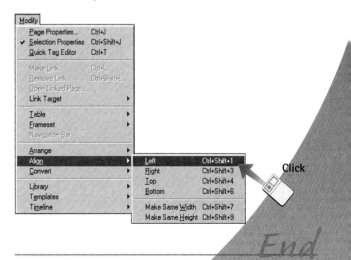

Click

End

How to Wrap Text Around Images

The image-alignment options on the **Properties Inspector** allow you to set the alignment for the image in relation to other page content. You can vertically align images to any other content on the same line as the image, including other images or text. When vertically aligning images with text, only the text on the same line as the image is affected. If you choose one of the horizontal alignment options (such as left), the text is pushed to the right of the image.

Begin

1 View the Browser Default

In the example shown here, no wrapping effect is in place—the image is simply "plonked" onto the page. In the **Align** field in the **Properties Inspector**, notice that **Browser Default** is the selected option.

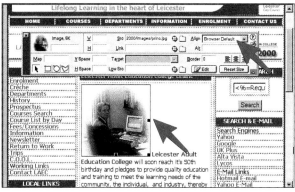

2 Choose Baseline or Bottom Alignment

When you change the **Align** field to the **Baseline** or **Bottom** option, the baseline of only one line of text is aligned with the bottom of the image. The rest of the text falls underneath the image.

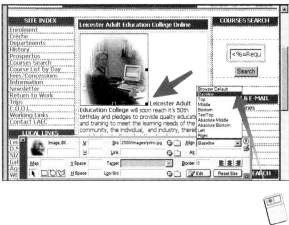

Click

3 Choose Absolute Bottom Alignment

When you change the **Align** field to the **Absolute Bottom** option, the very bottom of the text is aligned to the bottom of the image. The "absolute bottom" of the text refers to the bottom of descenders in letters such as *g* and *j*. In this example, notice that the text *Leicester Adult* has moved up slightly.

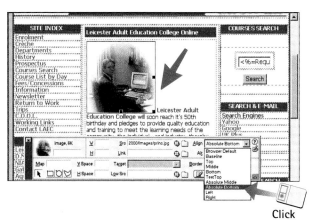

Click

4 Choose Top or Text Top Alignment

When you change the **Align** field to the **Top** or **Text Top** option, the top of the ascenders in letters such as *t* and *h* align with the top of the image. If you are aligning the image to another image, the **Top** alignment option sets the top of both images to be level.

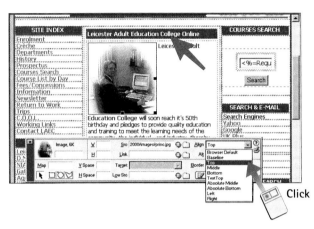

Click

5 Choose Middle or Absolute Middle Alignment

When you change the **Align** field to the **Middle** option, the baseline of the text aligns with the middle of the image. If you select **Absolute Middle**, the midline of the text is aligned with the middle of the image.

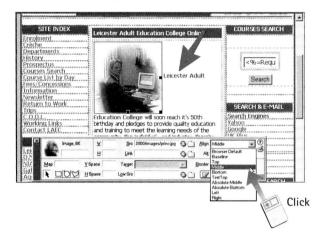

Click

6 Choose Left or Right Alignment

When you change the **Align** field to the **Left** or **Right** option, the image is pushed to the left or right edge of the cell or page and the text wraps around the image. Note that the left and right alignment setting relates to the *image* and not to the text.

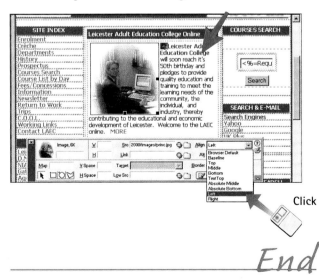

Click

End

Task

Considering Layout and Design

*B*y now you should know your way around the software and certainly know how to insert and delete most of the things you are going to need. Now it's time to make it look nice—and more importantly, make it look the way you want onscreen. HTML is not the same as desktop publishing, but here we will look at ways of getting your pages to look the way you imagine them to be.

Tables are the mainstay of Web designers; they allow you control over the design and layout of your pages. Dreamweaver has built-in facilities to help you design your pages successfully. Tables can be created with individual cell and background colors to create the effect of color. Spacing and padding options allow you to place information inside a cell with gaps around the text or image, and you can change the number of rows and columns in the table whenever you want.

Even the width of tables and other design elements can be used to give you control over the look of the page. Tables and lines can have either percentage widths (they fill the specified percentage of the screen, regardless of how the screen is displayed) or fixed-pixel widths (they always display at the specified number of pixels).

Tables give you control over the general layout of your site. With that in mind, Macromedia has introduced a new Dreamweaver feature that enhances your ability to create flexible layouts that work properly in all browsers. The Layout view allows you to draw table cells straight into the work area and to create nested tables. You add table cells to your page by working in Layout view, which can be accessed using the new buttons at the bottom of the **Objects** panel.

After you become familiar with tables, don't forget to check out Part 8, "Working with Layers and Cascading Style Sheets," which explains how you can take even more control over the exact placement of elements on the pages. ●

How to Use Layout View

You can create layout cells on your page only when you're working in **Layout** view. In this task, you add layout cells to your page, but Dreamweaver automatically adds a layout table around the cells. This table acts as a container for your cells (you cannot have cells without a table to hold them). The layout you create can be as simple or as complicated as you want. In this task, we will create a layout to hold page content as follows: a cell to hold a logo and links at the top of the page, a cell for a navigation bar on the left, a cell to hold the main contents, and a cell to hold copyright information and the date the page was modified.

Begin

1 Switch to Layout View

Open a blank document. In the **Objects** panel, click the **Layout View** button. Alternatively, choose **View, Table View, Layout View**.

Click

2 Read the Information

The first time you use **Layout** view, an information screen appears, telling you about Layout view and how to use it. Click **OK** to continue. You can prevent this screen from displaying again by enabling the **Don't show me this message again** check box.

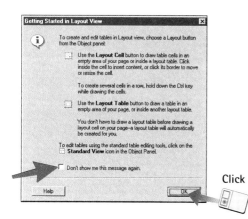

Click

3 Get Ready to Draw a Cell

To draw a layout cell on the page, click the **Draw Layout Cell** button at the bottom of the **Objects** panel. The mouse pointer changes to crosshairs when you do this.

Click

4 Draw a Layout Cell

Draw the first layout cell where you want it to appear on the page: Click the mouse where you want the layout cell to start and drag the cell to the size you want it to be.

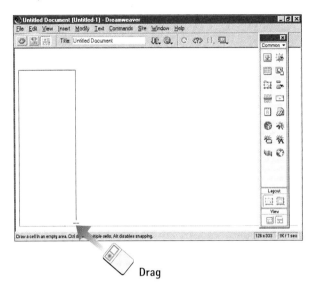

Drag

5 Look at the Layout Table

As soon as you let go of the mouse, Dreamweaver adds not only the cell that you drew but also a layout table. This first layout table is sized to completely fill the document window. The layout table is outlined in green and has a green label at the top.

6 Insert More Layout Tables

Click the **Draw Layout Table** button on the **Objects** panel to draw more layout tables within the existing table. Working this way gives you more control over the way the content will fit into the cells. Notice that when you draw tables close to one another, they automatically snap together.

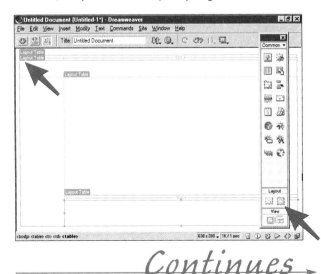

Continues

How-To Hints

Layout Cells and Table Cells

It is a good idea to use multiple layout cells (and thus multiple layout tables) because they act as individual elements on the page. If you use a normal table to design your page layout and then add content to one cell, that content affects the width of the cells adjacent to the first cell. If you use individual layout cells, changing the content of one cell does not affect any other cell.

7 Insert More Cells

Inside each of the layout tables, add a layout cell by repeating Step 4. Create a layout similar to the one shown here (refer to the introduction to this task for details about the page we're designing here). When you are comfortable using the layout cells and tables, you can be as creative as you like. If you want to draw multiple cells, hold down the **Ctrl** key (⌘ on a Macintosh) to avoid the need to click the **Draw Layout Cell** button between cells. You can stop tables from snapping to each other by holding down the **Alt** key (**Option** on a Macintosh) while dragging.

8 Resize Cells or Tables

All the cells and tables you create in **Layout** view can be resized at any time. Select a cell by holding down the **Ctrl** key (⌘ on a Mac) and clicking anywhere inside the cell; select a table by clicking its edge. In either case, selection handles appear, and you can resize the cell or table by dragging it to the dimensions you want.

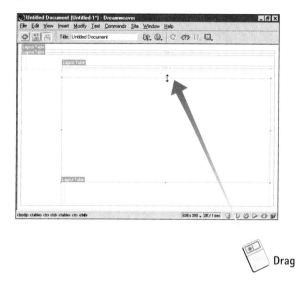

Drag

9 Move Layout Cells

You can move layout cells within your design to any location you choose. Note that you cannot have overlapping layout cells, and the cells must always remain inside the table container. Click the edge of the cell you want to move and drag it to the desired location or use the arrow keys to nudge it one pixel at a time in any direction.

Drag

10 Format Layout Cells

You can format your layout cells using the **Properties Inspector**. To each cell, you can apply a background color; you can set the alignment for the cell's contents using the **Horiz** and **Vert** drop-down menus. You can also set the word wrapping option for each cell: Enable the **No Wrap** option if you want the contents of the cell to force the cell to widen without a line break.

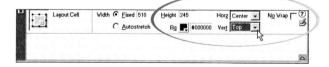

11 Format the Layout Width

The width of the layout can be formatted in one of two ways: **Fixed** or **Autostretch**. Typically, you would set the cell containing a navigation bar to a fixed width (because you know the size of the buttons in the bar); you set the main content area to the **Autostretch** width option. Use the **Properties Inspector** to turn on the **Autostretch** option. You are prompted to let Dreamweaver create a *spacer GIF* for you (an invisible GIF image used to control the size of your cells). Click **OK** to continue.

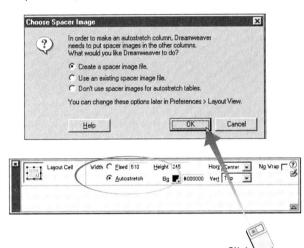

Click

12 Switch Back to Standard View

Click the **Standard View** button on the **Objects** panel to switch back to Standard view and start inserting your page content. The table and cell lines are not visible in the Web browser when the page is displayed there.

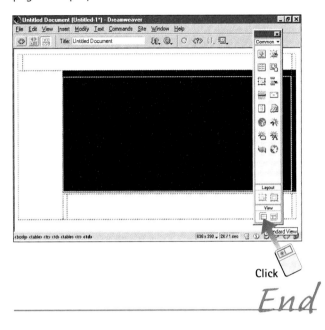

Click

End

How-To Hints

Cell and Table Background Colors

If you select the entire table and use the **Bg** button to select a background color, the color affects the entire table. If you select a single cell and then use this option, the color affects only the selected cell, overriding the color set for the rest of the table. Think of it as different layers: The page background sits on the bottom of the stack, a table background is on top of that, and then a cell background tops off the stack.

For Experienced Users

Those of you who have used previous versions of Dreamweaver or other Web design applications will be used to using tables within a design environment. The neat thing about Dreamweaver 4 is that you can still create your pages on the fly without using the layout view if you choose to do so.

How to Insert Text and Images into Tables

Tables are generally used to create a layout grid into which you can place objects and text on your page. With tables, you have more layout possibilities than what is possible by simply having text and images one after the other in a single column down the page.

Begin

1 Insert a Table

Open a new document window and click **Insert Table** from the **Objects** panel. The **Insert Table** dialog box opens for you to specify the number of rows and columns you want for your table. In the **Rows** and **Columns** fields, type the number of rows and columns you initially want the table to have and click **OK**. In this example, we are creating a table with two rows and three columns.

Click

2 Select and Align the Table

Click anywhere inside the table and then click the **<table>** tag in the bottom-left corner of the screen to select the entire table. In the **Properties Inspector**, use the **Align** drop-down list to select how you want the table to be positioned on the page. By default, tables are left-aligned in the browser window. For this example, select **Center** to center the table in the page. If necessary, expand the **Properties Inspector** by clicking the down arrow in the lower-right corner so that you can see all the properties of the table.

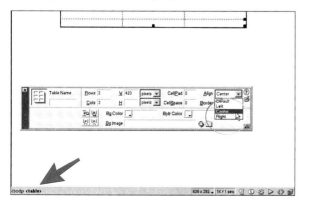

3 Insert Some Text

Click in any cell to select that cell and start typing. The text appears in the cell and wraps within the cell you selected. Notice that the depth of the cell changes to accommodate the text you insert. If you already have the text in another location, you can cut and paste the text from there.

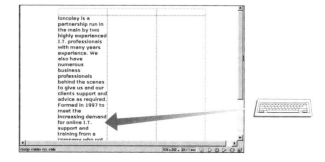

4 Insert an Image

Click to select a different cell. In the **Objects** panel, click **Insert Image**. Navigate to the image file you want to insert and click **OK**. The image appears in the selected cell, which expands to accommodate the image; notice that other cells in the table are resized.

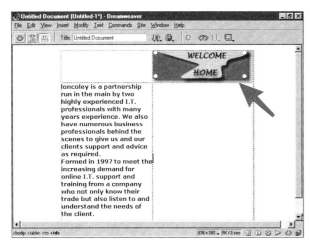

6 Set the Table Width and Height

Use the **W** field to set the width of the table either in pixels or as a percentage of the width of the page. Define the width in pixels to ensure that the table is always the same size regardless of the width of the browser window. Define the width in percentages if you want the table to resize itself to fit the browser window, even if the viewer resizes the window. Use the **H** field to set the height of the page in the same way.

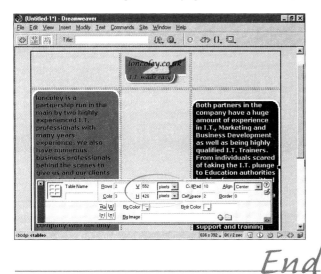

5 Set Cell Padding and Spacing

Cell padding inserts space between the edge of a cell and the cell content; *cell spacing* inserts space between the cells in the table. Select the table and then use the **Properties Inspector** to add a value of **10** in the **CellPad** field. Notice that there is now a noticeable gap around the contents of each cell. Now type a value of **10** in the **CellSpace** field and see the difference that change makes on the page. There should be a definite gap between each of the cells as well.

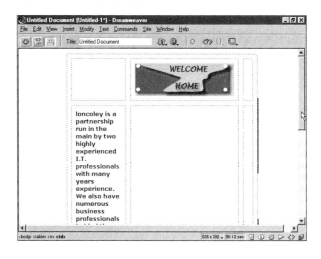

How-To Hints

Align the Contents of a Cell

Select a cell and use the **Horz** and **Vert** drop-down lists in the **Properties Inspector** to specify whether the contents of the selected cell are centered, left aligned, or right aligned. You can also use the alignment buttons in the top-right corner of the **Properties Inspector** to align text in a cell.

Make It a Header Cell

It's easy to make text in a cell look like a header: Type the text and enable the **Header** check box in the **Properties Inspector**. By default, text in header cells is bold and centered.

End

How to Change Cell Properties

You can have a lot of control over the finished look of your site simply by setting and changing the properties of the cells in the table you use to lay out your pages. Merging and splitting cells can make life a lot easier as you change your mind about how to lay out your page. Adding or changing table borders can also add to effects that you create as you go. Just be careful not to do too much changing at once, or you can get confused!

Begin

1 Split Cells

A cell can be split into more than one, giving you more options and greater control over the finished product. Click in the cell you want to split. Right-click in the cell to open the context menu and choose **Table, Split Cell**.

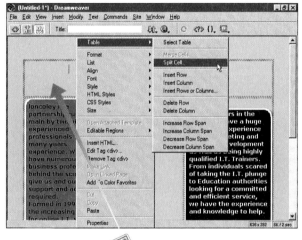

Right-click

2 Split into Rows or Columns

In the **Split Cell** dialog box, choose whether you want to split the cell into **Rows** or **Columns** and enter the number of rows or columns you want to split the single cell into. Click **OK**, and the cell splits based on your choices.

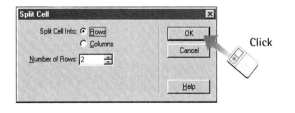

Click

3 Select the Cells to Merge

By combining several cells, you can have more control over your layout. To merge cells together, you must first select the cells you want to merge. Click in one cell, hold down the mouse button, and drag across the cells you want to select. The cells are highlighted.

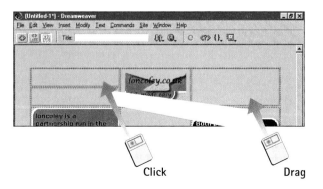

Click   Drag

4 Merge the Cells

Choose **Modify, Table, Merge Cells**. The selected cells are combined into a single cell. When merging cells that have both text and images, the results might not always be what you expected, so be prepared for a few surprises. Merging multiple cells containing text puts all the text into one cell, starting with the text in the left (or top) cell of those cells merged.

5 Set the Cell Width

You can specify a particular width for a cell. Click inside a cell to select it; in the **W** box in the **Properties Inspector**, type a value, in pixels, for the cell width. The cell expands or contracts to that width. Remember that the width of an individual cell must fit in with the other cells and the overall width of the table. Notice here that expanding the cell with the red background has caused the background image in that cell to tile and the black cell to shrink noticeably.

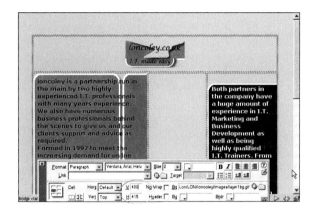

6 Set the Table Height

Select the entire table. In the **H** box in the **Properties Inspector**, type a value, in pixels, for the height of the entire table. The table expands or contracts to the specified height. (Note that it normally isn't necessary to specify a height for individual cells because they expand and contract based on the content. Notice how expanding the overall table height has expanded the top cell to be much bigger than it was originally.

7 Add a Row

You can add rows and columns to your table at any time. Select a cell in the row under which you want to insert a new row. Choose **Modify, Table, Insert Row**. A new row is inserted underneath the current cell. Notice that this new row takes on the same properties and background as the row above it—which can look a little strange! (In this example, I will remove the cell background images immediately.)

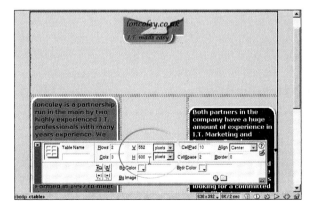

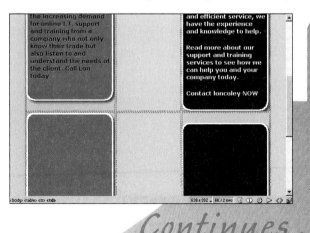

Continues

8 Add a Column

You can add columns to your table in almost the same way as rows. Select a cell and choose **Modify, Table, Insert Column**. A new column is added to the left of the cell you selected. This new column of cells takes on the properties of the column it was added from and causes the existing columns in the table to adjust to accommodate the new column.

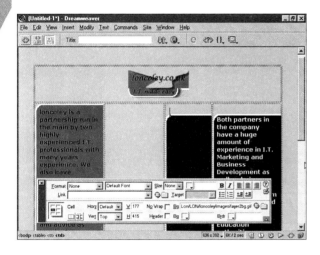

9 Select Rows or Columns

To select an entire row of cells, click the right edge of the table. To select an entire column of cells, click the top edge of the table above the desired column. The mouse pointer changes to a black arrow pointing to the row or column you've selected.

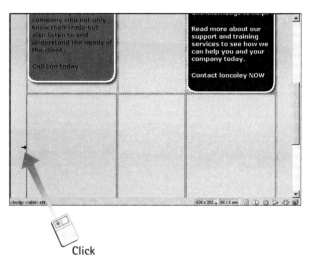

Click

10 Delete Rows or Columns

You can delete an entire row or column of cells—and all the cell contents—easily. Click to select a single cell in the row or column you want to delete and choose **Modify, Table, Delete Row** or **Delete Column**.

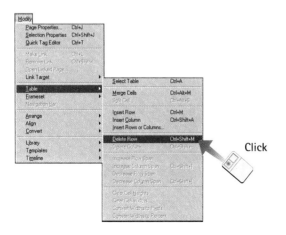

Click

11 Resize Cells by Dragging

In addition to specifying pixel values for the height and width of a cell, you can drag a cell to the size you want. Move the mouse pointer over the intersection of any two cells; the pointer changes to an "adjust" cursor. Click and drag the mouse to resize the cells.

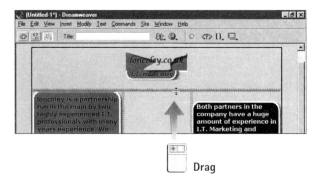

Drag

12 Remove Height Settings

Select the entire table and click the **Clear Row Heights** button in the **Properties Inspector**. The Height setting (the **H** field) value disappears and the table will shrink to the minimum possible height, allowing for content and specific cell settings.

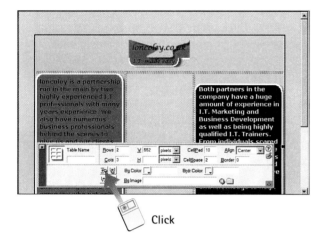

Click

13 Remove Width Settings

Select the entire table and click the **Clear Column Widths** button in the **Properties Inspector**. The table removes any widths attached to the cells so that the cells are spaced proportionately over the width of the table or based on any images in the cells.

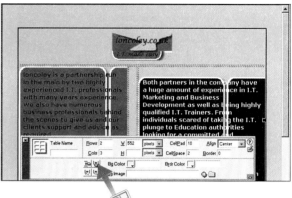

Click

14 Change the Cell Borders

Use the **Border** field in the **Properties Inspector** to change or add a table border. Any number greater than 0 adds a border around the entire table and individual cells. Use the **Bdr Color** picker to specify or change the border color. In the color picker window, click the square with a line through it to reset the borders to their default color.

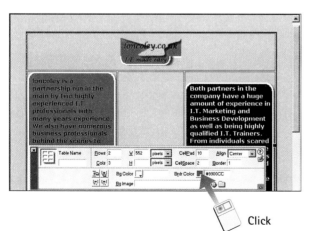

Click

How-To Hints

A Table Is a Group of Cells

Although it might seem obvious, notice that adjusting the size or shape of a single table element affects the rest of the table as well. Adding a new cell into a fixed-width table causes the other cells to shrink to fit. Your entire amount of rows and columns must fit within the width and height settings you specified for the table.

End

How to Nest Tables

A *nested table* is simply a table inside another table. For example, you might be using one table as the design grid for the page, but you want to display on that page a chart of information. The chart can be presented as a table of information nested within the design-grid table. The more complicated your designs get, the more you will want to use the nested tables feature.

1 Select the Cell to Hold the Table

Click inside the cell in which you want the new table to appear. Click the **Insert Table** button on the **Objects** panel to display the **Insert Table** dialog box.

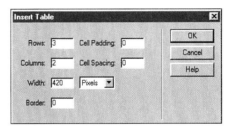

2 Set the Shape

Even though you are defining a table that will appear inside another cell, you can still specify the numbers of rows and columns you want this new table to have. Type the appropriate values in the **Rows** and **Columns** fields and click **OK** to insert the new table in the selected cell.

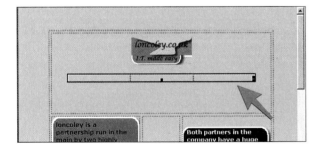

3 Set the Width

Remember that the size of the original cell constrains the size of the new table. You can't specify a width of 400 pixels for the new table if the original cell is only 150 pixels wide. To maximize the width of the nested table, select the new table and set the **W** field in the **Properties Inspector** to 100%—which means that the new table will fill the original cell.

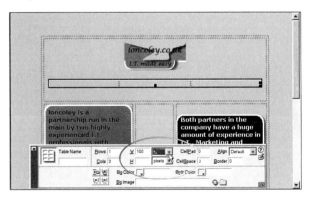

4 Set a Background

By default, the color of the underlying cell will be seen through the nested table. You can change the background color of the nested table. Select the nested table by clicking inside it and then clicking the second **<table>** tag in the bottom-left corner of the screen. In the **Properties Inspector**, click the **Bg Color** button and select a background color for the nested table.

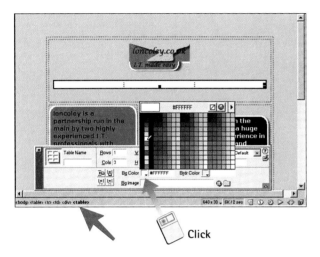

Click

5 Set a Border and Spacing

The nested table can have its own borders and cell spacing and padding. Use the **Properties Inspector** to give the nested table the look you want it to have.

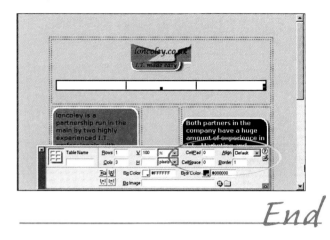

End

How-To Hints

Tables, Tables, and More Tables

By now you know that tables are a flexible way to manage your text and other objects on a page. You should use tables to create complex layouts, but note that too many tables add to the download time of your page. Think about the page layout before you start and try not to use more tables than necessary.

Cut, Copy, and Paste

Not only can you paste information into a cell from another document, but you can also cut and paste cells from one table to another. The only rule to remember is that if you are going to copy more than one cell, you must copy cells that form a complete rectangle (that is, you cannot copy random cells in the same copy operation).

How to Import Tabular Data

Tabular data is information created in another application (such as Microsoft Excel) and saved in a delimited format (comma or tab separated). This kind of data is easy to import into Dreamweaver, as this task explains.

Begin

1 Open the Dialog Box

In the **Objects** panel, click **Insert Tabular Data**. The **Insert Tabular Data** dialog box opens.

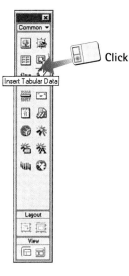

Click

Insert Tabular Data

2 Find the File

Click the **Browse** button to open the **Open** dialog box so that you can navigate to the file containing the data you want to import. Select the file and click **Open**.

Click

3 Choose the File Type

In the **Delimiter** field, select the separator used in the data file. Spreadsheet and databases normally use a comma or tab to separate fields. Refer to your spreadsheet or database application's documentation to determine which separator it uses.

4 Set the Table Width

Use the **Table Width** options to specify a width for the data table. You can specify a particular width for the table, or you can let Dreamweaver fit the width based on the data.

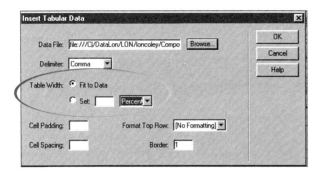

5 Format the Table

Set **Cell Padding** and **Cell Spacing** values to suit your tastes. Use the **Format Top Row** drop-down list to select a formatting option for the column headings. Click **OK** to insert the data.

Click

6 Tweak the Table

Use the **Properties Inspector** to fine-tune the settings for the new table. Refer to Task 3, "How to Change Cell Properties," for more information about adjusting the properties for any table.

End

How-To Hints

Get It Right

Make sure that you choose the correct **Delimiter** option when importing the tabular data. If you choose the wrong delimiter, the data will be imported incorrectly. Note that Dreamweaver will not notify you that an error has occurred.

Sort Your Data

Dreamweaver can even sort your data for you. As long as you are not using any merged cells in your table, choose **Commands, Sort Table** to let Dreamweaver organize your data either alphabetically or numerically.

TASK **6**

How to Use Horizontal Rules

Horizontal rules (lines) are used a lot in Web pages—sometimes to split content, sometimes just for an optical effect. For something so easy to insert, they have a lot of different uses.

Begin

1 Insert a Horizontal Line

Click to position the cursor on the page where you want to insert a horizontal rule. Choose **Insert, Horizontal Rule**.

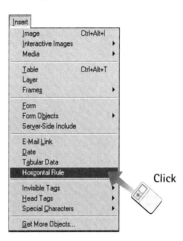

Click

2 Set the Width and Height

The **Properties Inspector** shows you the options you can set for your horizontal rule. Click the rule on the page to select it. In the **Properties Inspector**, type a width for the rule; you can specify the width as a particular number of pixels or as a percentage of the width of the page. Specify a height for the rule as well; this value is always given in pixels.

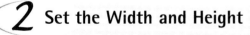
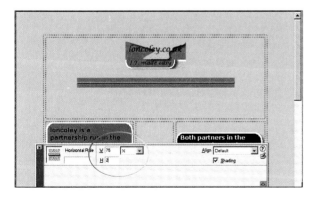

3 Choose the Alignment

Horizontal rules can be aligned to the right or left of the page, or they can be centered on the page. Use the **Align** drop-down list to choose the alignment you want for the rule.

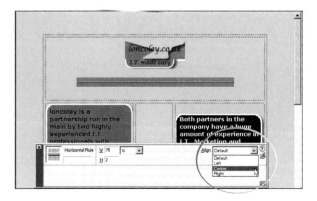

4 Remove Shading

By default, all horizontal rules are shaded. To remove the shading and be left with a solid line, disable the **Shading** check box.

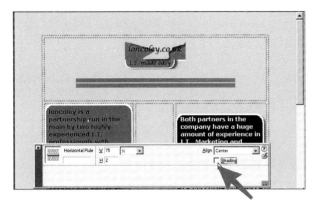

5 Change the Color

Notice that the **Properties Inspector** for the horizontal rule does not have a color picker. To change the color of a horizontal rule, you have to work directly in the HTML source code for the page. Select the horizontal rule and click the **Code Inspector** button on the **Launcher** to open the **Code Inspector** window.

6 Add the Color to the Code

Locate the **<HR>** tag in the code. Immediately after the **<HR** characters, type a space and then type **color="#000000"** (or the hex code for whatever color you want). The horizontal rule will change, but the color will be visible only when you preview the page in a browser. We will look more at code in Part 14, "Dreamweaver and Beyond."

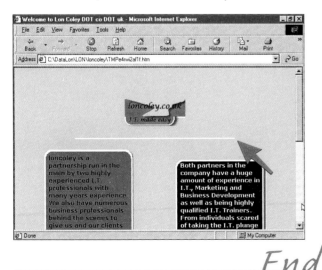

End

How-To Hints

Make Your Own Rules!

If you can't get a horizontal rule to look the way you want, don't give up the idea—try to create your own rule! Fireworks is a great graphics editor that you can use right away to create and edit simple graphics such as rules. Refer to Part 15, "Working with Images in Fireworks," for details.

Download Rules

As there are for many types of images, there are literally thousands of Web sites that have all kinds of patterned, shaded, and textured lines available for free download and use. Simply go to any search engine and type **Web Graphics** to see lists of sites you can visit for cool rules and other simple graphics you can use on your pages.

Task

8

Working with Layers and Cascading Style Sheets

n Part 7, "Considering Layout and Design," we looked at using tables to control page layout. In the tasks in this part, we look at layers, Cascading Style Sheets (CSS), and a little DHTML.

Layers are best described as containers or holders for your page content. Layers can hold any page element, have their own properties and settings, and also have the advantage of being positioned exactly on the page (this is where the Dynamic HTML comes in). In Web design terms, layers are still an innovation, implemented quite recently into the vocabulary of Web designers and developers. The idea behind layers was to give Web designers complete control over the appearance of their content at all times.

So if layers are so wonderful, why did we spend Part 7 talking about tables? It's simple really: Layers are new, and if you use them, anyone with a browser before version 4 will simply see a garbled mess (or nothing at all) instead of your page. Even some of the newer browsers are a little buggy in their support of layers. Unless you are designing your site for only those people who have new browsers, you should remember that your site visitors might have display problems with layers.

The good thing is that Dreamweaver has a built-in command that allows you to convert your layers to tables. This command gives you the flexibility to design with layers, but ensures a greater audience by also posting the page converted to tables.

Cascading Style Sheets (CSS) is a styling language that allows you to attach a style to an HTML tag or tags. The actual style sheets are templates that contain rules. These rules are then applied to your file or files in a way that is similar to how a desktop publishing application uses styles.

How to Create Layers

Dreamweaver gives you options on how to create layers—all are easy to use and straightforward. Layers do not have to be created on blank pages; you can use an existing page and move content into the layer. However, for this task, we'll start from scratch. You can have as many layers as you need to hold your page content. Layers can be as large or small as you want, and each layer can contain text, images, plug-ins, or any combination of these elements. You can place layers inside other layers to create nested layers or stack them on top of other layers, and you can use the **Layers** panel to control and manage your layers.

Begin

1 Use the Objects Panel

Open a blank document in Dreamweaver and click the **Draw Layer** button in the **Objects** panel. The mouse pointer changes to crosshairs.

Click

2 Draw the Layer

Draw the layer on the page where you want it by dragging the crosshairs to define a rectangle of the size you want. Normally, you will know what content you are planning to place in the layer, so draw the layer to an appropriate size. Remember that you can draw a layer anywhere in the document window.

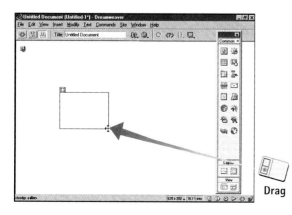

Drag

3 Draw Multiple Layers

Click the **Draw Layer** button on the **Objects** panel again and hold down the **Ctrl** key as you drag another rectangular layer. You can draw as many layers as you want for the layout of the page as long as you hold the **Ctrl** key as you drag. As you draw each layer, a marker appears at the top of the screen. (If you don't see these markers, check the How-To Hints box at the end of this task.)

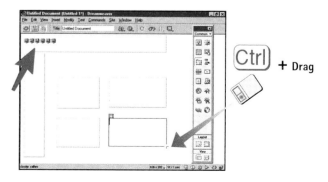

Ctrl + Drag

④ Insert Layers Using the Menu

Instead of dragging a rectangular layer on the page, you can let Dreamweaver insert layers for you. Choose **Insert, Layer**. A rectangular layer appears automatically at the top of your screen.

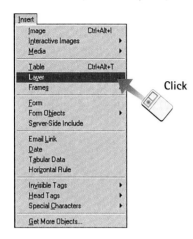

Click

⑤ Move the Layer

You can move and resize the default layer that Dreamweaver inserts at the top of the screen. Click the square at the top left of the layer to select it. Now drag the layer to reposition it, or resize it by dragging the handles.

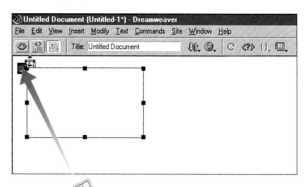

Click

⑥ Drag from the Objects Panel

You can drag the **Draw Layer** icon from the **Objects** panel onto the page to insert a layer. On a blank page, this layer appears at the top of the screen and can be resized or repositioned as described in Step 5.

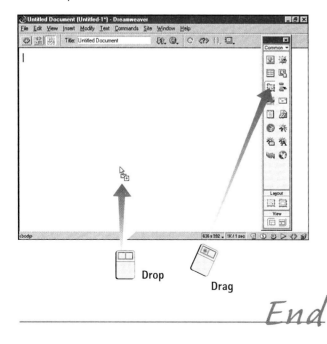

Drop

Drag

End

How-To Hints

Can't See the Layer Icon?

For each layer you insert on the page, a layer icon appears in the top-left corner of the page. If you can't see the layer icon, open the **View** menu and make sure that the **Invisible Elements** option is enabled. When you insert layers into a blank page, the layer icons appear at the top of the document window. The icons appear further down the page after you add contents or insert paragraph breaks in the page. These layer icons are a quick and easy way to select layers and view their properties in the **Layers** panel (described in Task 2).

How to Work with Layers

Layers give you control and flexibility over the exact layout of your pages. You can insert content into your layers in the same way you can with tables except that layers are more flexible and easier to manipulate than tables. When you work with layers, you'll make extensive use of the **Layers** panel.

Begin

1 Understand the Layers Panel

Choose **Window, Layers** to display the **Layers** panel. The **Layers** panel shows all the layers you have created for the page, with the most recent layer at the top of the list. Click any layer in the panel to select it. When selected, the layer has handles around it, and its icon at the top of the screen is highlighted.

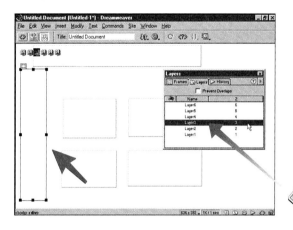

Click

2 Look at the Layer's Properties

When a layer is selected, its properties are visible in the **Properties Inspector**. The **Properties Inspector** shows you the name of the layer, the width and height of the layer in pixels, as well as the layer's location on the screen. (The **T** entry means the distance from the top of the page, and the **L** entry refers to the distance from the left edge of the page.)

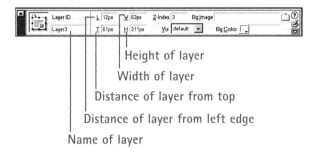

Height of layer
Width of layer
Distance of layer from top
Distance of layer from left edge
Name of layer

3 Create a Nested Layer

A *nested layer* is a layer inside another layer. By default, the nested layer has the same properties and visibility (which we will look at in the next task) as its parent. To create a nested layer, click inside an existing layer and choose **Insert, Layer**. You can immediately resize this layer to fit neatly inside the existing layer. Notice that the layer icon for the nested layer appears inside the parent, not at the top of the screen.

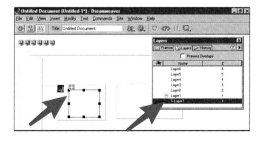

4 Ensure That It Is Nested

Choose **Edit, Preferences, Layers** to open the **Preferences** dialog box. Select **Layers** from the **Category** list and enable the **Nest When Created Within a Layer** option to ensure that the new layer will appear as a nested layer. This option also ensures that any new layers you draw inside existing layers in the future will automatically be nested.

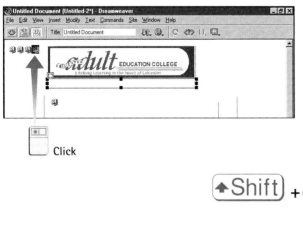

5 Activate a Layer

Before you can insert content into a layer, you must first activate the layer by clicking anywhere inside the layer box. The active layer has a border around the edge. Note that activating a layer is not the same as selecting a layer. Activating a layer simply means that the insertion point is within the layer, ready for you to insert content.

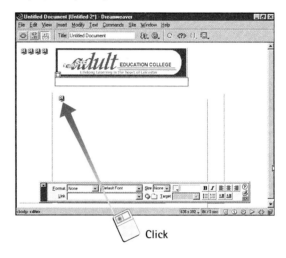

Click

6 Select a Layer

To select a layer, click the layer icon for the layer you want. The icon is highlighted, handles appear around the selected layer on the page, and the layer's properties are displayed in the **Properties Inspector**. Selecting a layer allows you to move it, resize it, and (if you want) even delete it.

Click

7 Select More Than One Layer

You can select multiple layers on the page by holding **Shift** as you click the border of the layers you want to select. Each selected layer has handles around it. With multiple layers selected, you can move them all at once—a great thing to do if you find that you need to move all your layers to the left, right, up, or down.

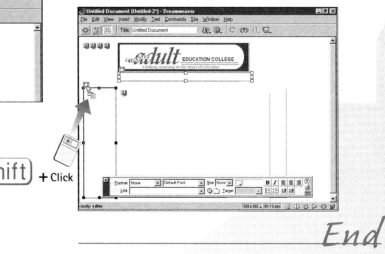

▲Shift + Click

End

How to Set Layer Properties

Each layer you create has individual properties you can view and edit through the **Properties Inspector**. Most of the properties are set automatically when you draw or insert a layer, but you can change them in the **Properties Inspector** at any time. You can rename the layers from the **Layer1**, **Layer2** defaults Dreamweaver generates, and control the background image or color of the layer. You also can control the visibility of the layer (whether the layer is seen onscreen at all times) and whether visitors can scroll through the layer if the content outsizes the layer's dimensions.

Begin

1 View the Properties

Select a single layer in Dreamweaver and view the **Properties Inspector**. To see all the properties for the layer, click the down arrow in the bottom-right corner of the **Properties Inspector** to expand it.

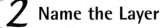

Click

2 Name the Layer

By default, Dreamweaver assigns the layers you create sequential numbers: **Layer1**, **Layer2**, and so on. In the **Layer ID** box in the **Properties Inspector**, type a unique name for the layer (note that you can use only letters or numbers for the name, no spaces or punctuation). It is best to give the layer an appropriate name; in this example, the layer contains the navigation links at the top of the page, so I have named the layer **NavTop**.

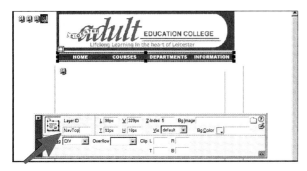

3 Set the Position

The **T** and **L** boxes in the **Properties Inspector** show the position on the page of the layer, in pixels from the top and left corners of the screen. If the layer is not exactly where you want it, change these values. These fields are especially handy when you want layers to line up with one another exactly.

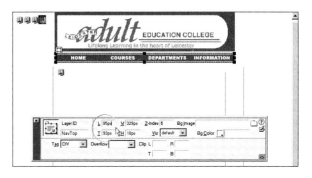

4 Set the Size

The **W** and **H** boxes determine the width and height of the layer in pixels. Note that you can specify a different unit of measure by typing the measurement unit in the field. For example, type **80mm** if you want to use millimeters or **7in** if you want to use inches. When working with nested layers, you can even specify that a nested layer is a percentage of its parent by typing **60%**.

5 Set a Background

You can set a background image or color for the layer. Click the box next to the **BgColor** field and use the color picker to select a color (or type the hex value of the color if you know it). Click the folder icon next to the **BgImage** field and browse to the image file you want to use. Note that the background image and color you set for the current layer affect any layers nested within the current layer.

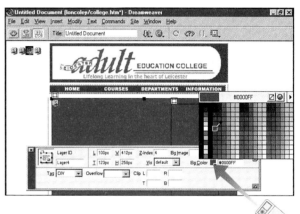

Click

6 Understand the Z Index

Each layer has a number within the *Z index* that indicates its stacking order. The higher the number in the **Z index** field, the higher up the layer appears in the stacking order. In this example, the current layer has a Z index value of 5; this layer appears on top of the other layers, which have lower Z index values. Change the number in the **Z Index** field to change the stacking order of the layer. In this example, I deliberately moved the layers around and set the backgrounds to make the stacking order more obvious. See how the layers sit on top of one another.

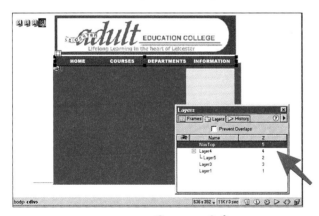

Continues

How-To Hints

Background Image Files

Background images are used all over the Internet and come in many different guises. The best file type to use for backgrounds tends to be a GIF file because these files are small and quick to download. With any background—for a page, a table, or a layer—you must use a file that appears very quickly. If you don't, your text might be invisible to the visitor until the background loads (imagine a nice black background image with white text; no background equals no text). Although you can use JPEG files for backgrounds, this is less common because they tend to be larger files and take longer to download.

7 Set the Visibility

Layers are normally visible unless you tell them not to be. Nested layers inherit properties from their parent unless you choose to change the visibility for the child. We will look more at visibility in Part 10, "Using Scripts and Behaviors in Dreamweaver." Having invisible layers might seem an odd concept, but when you are creating timelines and animations, they are a great way to control what is seen and when. When a layer is set to **hidden**, the layer icon remains visible onscreen.

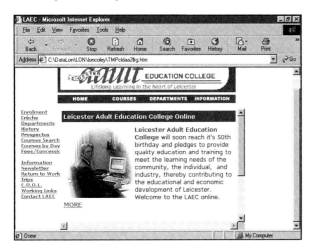

Click

8 Choose the Tag

There are two types of layers: CSS layers (which use **SPAN** and **DIV** tags) and Netscape layers (which use **LAYER** and **ILAYER** tags. Netscape tags are supported only by the Netscape Navigator browser. To stick with the default CSS layers, leave the default **DIV** setting in the **Tag** field. These HTML tags are created whenever a layer is created in Dreamweaver. CSS layers will give you the greatest audience for your layered site.

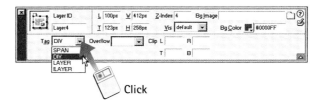

Click

9 Set Overflow Settings

The **Overflow** option is relevant only to CSS tags; it determines what will happen if you insert content that is too big for the layer to hold. If you choose the **visible** option, the layer expands to hold the content; the **hidden** option cuts the content to fit the layer; the **scroll** option adds scrollbars to the layer whether they are needed or not (as you can see in this example); and the **auto** option adds scrollbars only when they are needed.

10 Specify Clip Settings

You can use the **Clip** options to set a visible area within the layer. These options can be useful if you are placing an image in the layer and want to crop part of it without editing the image. The values you enter in this field are in pixels. The top, left, right, and bottom values you enter here relate to the current layer, not to the page.

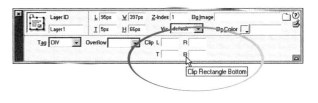

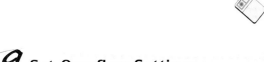

11 Set Properties for Multiple Layers

After you use **Shift+click** to select multiple layers, you can then set properties for all the selected layers simultaneously. The **Property Inspector** tells you that you have multiple layers selected. You can add a background color or image to all selected layers, set text attributes across the layers, and even set the visibility for multiple layers at the same time. The **Properties Inspector** shows only those options that can be changed across layers.

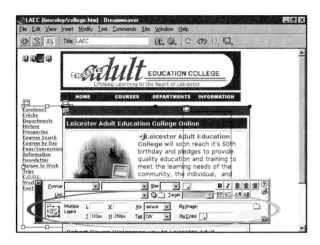

12 Snap Layers to the Grid

Dreamweaver has a design grid that you can display to help you position and resize layers and other elements on the page. Choose **View, Grid, Show Grid** to turn on the grid, and then choose **View, Grid, Snap To Grid** so that the layers will snap to the lines of the grid.

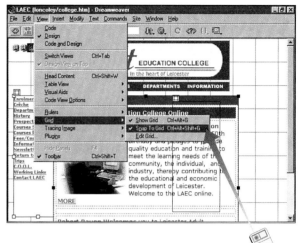

Click

13 Snap a Layer

With the grid displayed and the **Snap To** feature enabled, drag a layer to reposition it on the page. Note that the layer snaps to the nearest grid line as you drag. Choose **View, Grid, Edit Grid** to change the spacing of the grid lines and to specify how close the object has to be to a grid line before it snaps to the line.

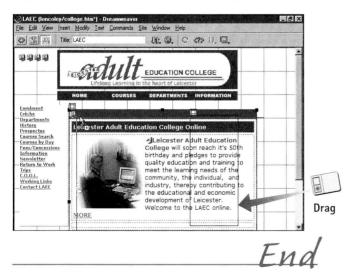

Drag

How-To Hints

Layer Tags

As with everything in Dreamweaver, when you insert layers on a page, the HTML code is created for you. Four tags are actually used for layers: **DIV**, **SPAN**, **LAYER**, and **ILAYER**. Dreamweaver automatically uses the **DIV** tag for layers because it is the most widely supported tag. The **LAYER** and **ILAYER** tags are supported only in Netscape 4.0 (even Netscape no longer supports those tags). If you use **LAYER** tags in older browsers, the content of the layer should be visible, but it will not appear in the correct position.

End

How to Format Using Cascading Style Sheets

Cascading Style Sheets (CSS) allow you complete control over formatting options. You can use CSS to format all your text as well as the complete page or site. You can create style sheets externally and link them into Dreamweaver. The "cascading" part of the name comes from the fact that the styles you create can cascade through your entire site. Still, most people simply say "style sheet" or "CSS."

Begin

1 Create a Style Sheet

Click the **CSS Styles** button on the **Launcher** to open the **CSS Styles** panel. Click the **New Style** button at the bottom of the panel to open the **New Style** dialog box.

Click

2 Select the Type of Style

We are going to redefine some HTML tags so that the styles we create will update the properties for the HTML tags in any pages to which we link the style sheet. In the **New Style** dialog box, enable the **Redefine HTML Tag** option. Use the **Tag** drop-down menu to select a tag to redefine. In this example, we will define the **H5** tag (a fifth-level heading tag). Click **OK** to continue.

Click

3 Name and Save the File

The **Save Style Sheet File As** dialog box opens. Name the file (**style1** or **mystyle** is appropriate) and navigate to select your site folder as the **Save in** location. Click **Save** to continue.

Click

4 Redefine the HTML Tag

In the **Style Definition** dialog box that opens, select the font, size, color, and any other attributes you want to apply to all the text formatted with the **H5** tag in your file. Click **OK** to continue.

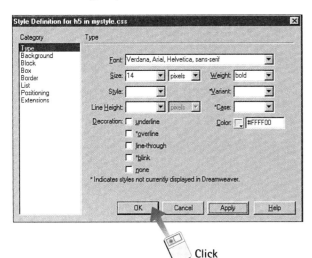

Click

5 See the Effect

In the document window, you should be able to see immediately that all the **H5** tags in the file have been updated to reflect the properties we defined in Step 4. In this example, there is now one very yellow line of text.

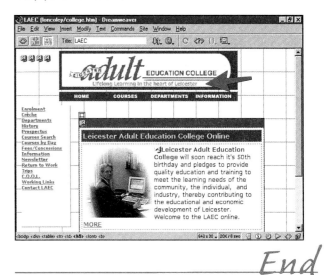

End

How-To Hints

Don't Apply HTML Formatting to CSS

When you use a CSS style sheet, you just type the text and then apply the appropriate style; the style sheet does the rest. Don't apply HTML formatting tags to text that's been formatted with CSS, or you will override the style sheet. Any text formatted without using the style sheet won't be updated if you amend the style sheet.

Why Use a Linked Sheet?

Linking a style sheet to your page gives you more flexibility than setting up a separate style sheet for each page. If you link the same style sheet to several pages, you can update the style sheet and watch the changes affect all the pages linked to that style sheet.

Import a Style Sheet

If someone else has developed a style sheet for use with Dreamweaver that you want to use, it's easy to import that external style sheet to your site. CSS files are simply text files that hold the formatting options for your pages. If you want to use someone else's CSS, start by putting the file from them on your hard drive (the CSS file must be located in your site folder). Now you can link your page to that file from the **CSS Styles** panel: Click the **Edit Style** button, select the **Link** radio button, and browse to the location of the CSS file you want to link to. Click **Done** to link the file.

How to Edit Cascading Style Sheets

In the last task, you created a very basic style sheet (it has only one style: Heading5). In this task, you learn to edit the style sheet so that it contains more styles and to modify the existing style. When you're done modifying the style sheet, make sure that you save the sheet. Now all the updated styles will be applied to all the pages linked to this style sheet.

Begin

1 Open the Style Sheet

Click the **CSS Styles** button on the **Launcher** to open the **CSS Styles** panel. Click the **Edit Style Sheet** button at the bottom of the palette. The **Edit Style Sheet** dialog box opens, listing all the style sheets that are linked to this page.

2 Choose Edit

Select the style sheet you created in the last task. At the bottom of the dialog box is a list of all the styles contained in the selected style sheet. Select the style you want to edit (for the current style sheet, the only style available is the **H5** tag) and click the **Edit** button. The **Style Definition** dialog box opens.

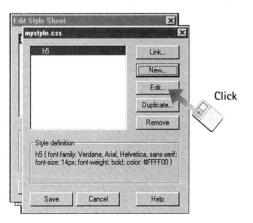

Click

3 Make Some Changes

Change the font color or size you selected for the **H5** style and click Apply; then click **Save**; then click **Done** to close all the dialog boxes. The H5 text in your document is immediately updated to reflect the change.

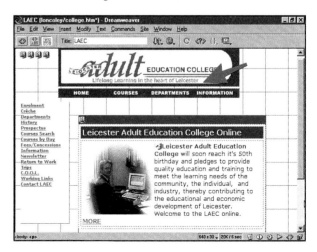

4 Add More Styles

In the **Edit Style Sheet** dialog box, select the style sheet to which you want to add some new styles and click **Edit**. Then click **New** to open the **New Style** dialog box where you can select the next tag to define. Make sure that the **Redefine HTML Tag** option is selected and choose another HTML tag from the **Tag** drop-down list; click **OK** to open the **Style Definition** dialog box.

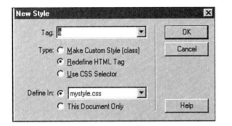

5 Select an HTML Tag to Format

Choose the desired formatting options for this tag and click **OK**. The new style appears in the list of styles for the selected style sheet. Click **Apply** and repeat this step to continue adding styles to the style sheet. When you're done adding styles, click **OK** to go back to the style sheet dialog box. Click **Save** to save the style sheet and all its additions. In this example, I amended the **body** tag to change the background color for the page to blue.

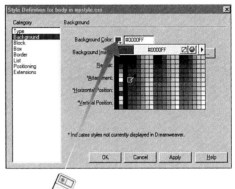

Click

6 Apply the Style Sheet to Another Document

Open the page to which you want to apply the style sheet. Click the **CSS Styles** button on the **Launcher** to open the **CSS Styles** panel. Click the **Open Style Sheet** button at the bottom-right corner of the panel to open the **Edit Style Sheet** dialog box. Click **Link** and browse to the style sheet you want to attach to this document. All the styles in the selected style sheet are applied to the current page.

Blue background

End

How-To Hints

Other Types of Styles

This task looked only at the **Redefine HTML Tag** option in the **New Style** dialog box because, until your confidence with HTML and CSS grows, it is the easiest and safest way to create style sheets. You can choose the **Make Custom Style (class)** option to create a style that you can then apply to a block or section of text rather than to a whole page or site. These styles are applied using a class attribute (for a paragraph style, the attribute is **p class ="nameofstyle"**). The **Use CSS Selector** option is used for combinations of tags such as **td H5**, which would then be applied to any **H5** tags inside a table. These styles are applied using an id attribute (for example, **#nameofstyle** is applied to any tags that have the value pair **ID="nameofstyle"**). CSS could take a whole book to define, so start by redefining HTML tags and move on when you are confident with those skills.

How to Convert Layers to Tables

Because some older browsers do not support layers, Dreamweaver allows you to convert layers to tables in a simple manner. However, you cannot convert layers that overlap; if your page design contains overlapping layers, you will have to redesign the page before you can convert the layout to tables. Note that "overlapping" includes nested layers, so you must move or delete any nested layers before converting the file.

Begin

1 Convert Layers to a Table

To convert all the layers on your page to tables, choose **Modify, Convert, Layers to Table**. The **Convert Layers to Table** dialog box opens.

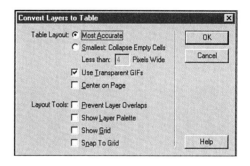

2 Select Conversion Options

I recommend that you select the **Most Accurate** and **Use Transparent GIFs** options to achieve the most accurate conversion possible. The **Most Accurate** option creates a table cell for each of your layers (plus additional cells for the areas in between); the **Use Transparent GIFs** option creates a table that views the same in all browsers. Click **OK** when you are done.

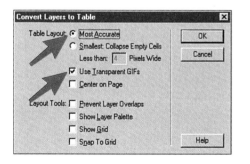

3 View the Result

Look at the result of the page conversion in your default browser. Make sure that the page still looks the way you want it to look. If the conversion went awry, go back to the Dreamweaver document window and choose **Edit, Undo** to return the page to the layer layout.

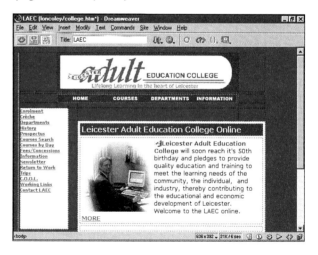

4 Convert for Version 3 Browsers

Choose **File, Convert, 3.0 Browser Compatible** to create a version of your page that is compatible with older browsers. The **Convert to 3.0 Browser Compatible** dialog box opens. Choose whether you want to convert **Layers to Table, CSS Styles to HTML Markup,** or **Both.** (I suggest **Both.**) Click **OK** to close the dialog box and begin the conversion.

5 View the Results

Dreamweaver creates a new, unsaved, untitled version of your document, leaving the original intact. In this example, you can see how different this page is from the original shown in Step 3.

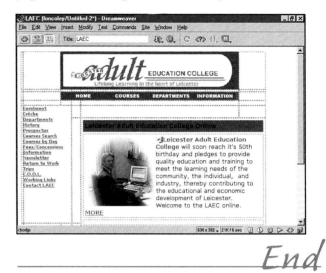

End

How-To Hints

Save Some Time

If you convert your page to a page that version 3.0 browsers can view, make sure that you have completed development of the page before you convert it. Because Dreamweaver creates a new page when it does the conversion, you will have to keep converting the original to a version 3.0-compatible page whenever you change the original. It makes more sense to complete the page and convert it once.

Task

Using Frames and Framesets

*I*n simple terms, *frames* are individual Web pages held together in a set; when the browser sees them, it draws the frames together to give the impression of a single page. To use frames, you must create a *frameset*—an HTML page that holds all the information for all the frames you want to appear together. You must also create the individual pages to be displayed as frames. It isn't as complicated as it sounds—honestly!

You have undoubtedly seen frame-based sites on the Internet. The "standard" page layout has a title frame at the top of the page, a narrow navigation frame on the left that contains the links for the page, and a contents frame where the main body of information appears. Although this is a standard use of frames, you can use many alternatives instead.

In the standard frame-based page just described, the frameset contains the three frames—three individual Web pages that are viewed together inside the frameset. The frameset is never actually displayed in the browser—it is there to contain the information about the structure and properties of the individual frames.

Each individual frame within the frameset is an HTML page with its own content, properties, and settings. You can be as creative as you like with frames as long as you remember to check that the frames work together both visually and functionally when they appear together on the page. Each frame can have its own scrollbars if needed or can be "scroll free" and give the effect of a single page. ●

How to Create a New Frameset

Dreamweaver makes creating a frameset a painless task, not to mention a quick one. Making the frameset, or container, for a frame-based site is the starting point for any framed site. After the frameset is created, you can either make new pages to use within the frameset or use pages you already have.

Begin

1 Show Frame Borders

The first thing to do is to make sure that you can see the borders for the frameset. The borders give you a view of how your frameset will look. Choose **View, Visual Aids, Frame Borders**. A visible line appears all around your document window.

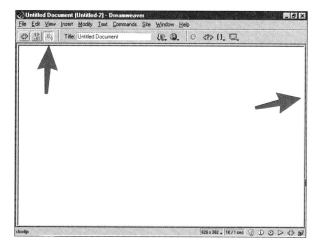

2 Create a Frameset with a Vertical Split

You have to split the original frame (if you don't, you simple have a page and not a frameset). Choose **Modify, Frameset, Split Frame Right** or **Split Frame Left**. This command places a vertical division in the document window so that you have two frames inside the frameset. A frameset split into left and right frames lets you have a navigation panel on the left and a content screen on the right.

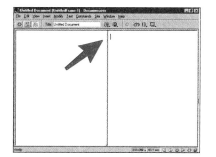

3 Add a Horizontal Split

Click in the right frame you created in the preceding step and choose **Modify, Frameset, Split Frame Up**, or **Split Frame Down**. The **Split Frame** commands give you the general layout for the frameset and the page; we'll worry about dimensions in a minute. Use both the vertical and horizontal split options to create the exact layout you want.

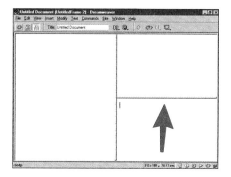

4 Create a Four-Framed Set

Press and hold the **Alt** key (Mac users press **Option**) and drag from any corner of the border to create a frameset with four frames. Although four frames on a single page isn't common, this is where the term *frameset* comes from. Note that this technique can be employed only from a new blank page.

Alt + Drag
Option +

5 Delete a Frame

To delete a frame, drag the frame border all the way out of the document window.

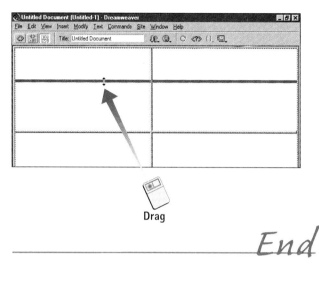

Drag

End

How-To Hints

Play Before Work

Before you start trying to input content into frames, make sure that you understand how the frames and the frameset work. In many ways, the most important thing to understand about frames is the structure. Get the structure of your frameset right to start with, and everything else will be fine.

How to Use a Predefined Frameset

Dreamweaver comes with a number of predefined framesets from which you can choose. Predefined framesets come in the most commonly used arrangements. They save you the time and effort of having to drag and split frames into the shapes you want.

Begin

1 Look at the Options

From the drop-down menu at the top of the **Objects** panel, choose **Frames**. When the **Frames** panel displays, note that there are eight predefined layouts for you to choose from.

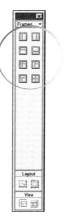

2 Decide Which Suits Your Needs

Each of the eight frameset options is represented by a thumbnail icon that shows how the frameset will look on your page. Hover the mouse pointer over each option to see a text description as well.

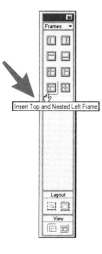

3 Understand How the Framesets Work

When you select one of the predefined framesets, you create extra blank HTML pages in each of the frames. One of the frames will contain the document you have open. The frame in a predefined frameset that will hold the current document is designated by the blue shading on the thumbnail icon in the **Objects** panel. This example shows an open page; look at the icons in the **Objects** panel to determine where that document will appear in the different framesets.

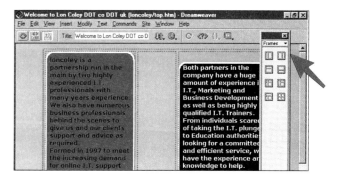

4 Insert a Frameset

Click the icon for the frameset you want to use. This example uses the **Insert Top and Nested Left Frame** frameset. Look at how the existing page appears in the document window. The new frames have been inserted around the existing document, which is now in a separate frame.

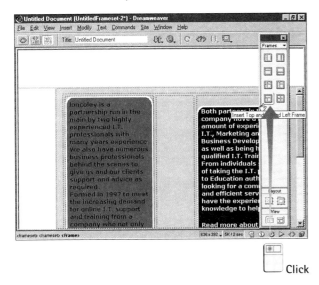

Click

5 Name the Frames

When you start working with frames, keeping them straight can be confusing. Let's type some identifying text into the two new frames. In the top frame, type the word **Top**; in the left frame, type the word **Left**. We will get rid of these labels in the following tasks, but first we'll use them to understand how the frameset works.

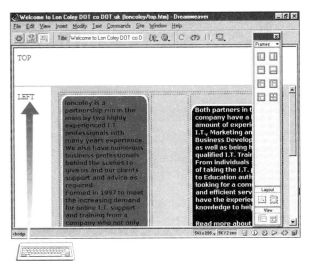

6 Save All Frames

Select **File, Save All Frames** to open the **Save As** dialog box. The first thing you have to save is the frameset, so type the name you want to give to this frameset (I suggest **Frameset1** as a good name for this first attempt at frames). Click **Save** to continue on to saving the individual frames.

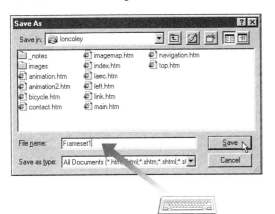

7 Save the Frame Pages

After you have named and saved the frameset, Dreamweaver highlights each frame in turn and prompts you to save the frames individually. I suggest that you name the two new HTML documents **Top** and **Left**, respectively.

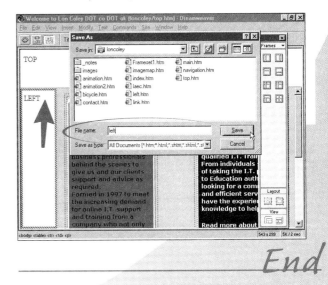

End

How to Set Frameset Properties

When you're working with frames and framesets, you'll want to use the **Frames** panel, which makes it easy to choose the frame or frameset you want to work with. After you select a frame or frameset, the properties for that item become visible in the **Property Inspector**. Among other things, the properties of a frame or frameset control the size of the frame, whether a scrollbar is visible, and whether the visitor can resize the frame.

Begin

1 View the Frameset Properties

Choose **Window, Frames** to display the **Frames** panel. A visual representation of the frameset currently applied to your page is displayed in the panel.

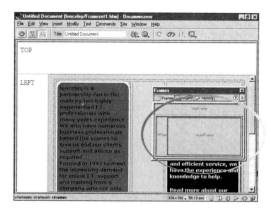

2 Select the Frameset

To see the properties for the whole frameset, show the **Properties Inspector** by choosing **Window, Properties.** In the **Frames** panel, click the frameset border; the **Properties Inspector** now shows the properties of the frameset for the page.

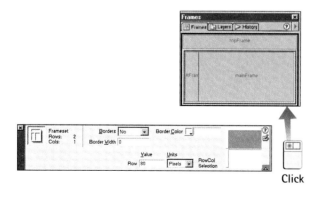

Click

3 Set Borders for a Frameset

From the **Borders** drop-down menu in the **Properties Inspector**, choose whether or not you want to have a visible border between frames. In this example, visible borders have been turned on. Compare the results on the page in the background in this example with the frames in the background in Step 1. Although the difference might be subtle, the border line that displayed as a visual aid in Step 1 now appears raised up slightly—and will appear in the browser.

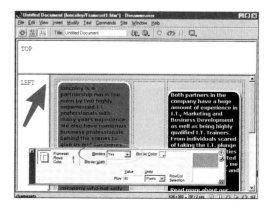

4 Set Border Properties for a Frameset

If you turned on the visible borders in Step 3, you can set the size and color of the borders. In the **Border Width** field in the **Properties Inspector**, type the width, in pixels, for the border. Click the **Border Color** box and use the color picker to choose a color for the borders (if you know the color you want, you can simply type the hex code for that color).

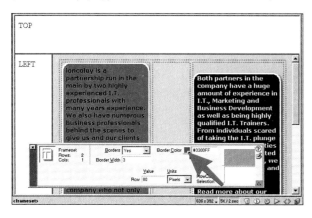

5 Set the Column Width

Use the **Frames** panel to set the column width or row height for your frames. You can set these values to be a relative percentage of the total frameset or a set number of pixels. This image shows the left frameset with a width of 200 pixels—notice how much wider that frame is now.

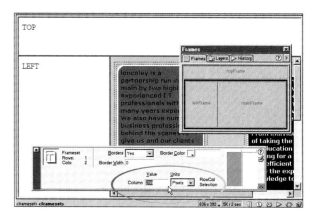

6 Give the Frameset a Title

In the **Frames** panel, make sure that the frameset is selected (click the outside border of the frameset and check the **Properties Inspector** to make sure that the frameset is selected and not an HTML page within another frame), and then choose **Modify, Page Properties**. In the **Page Properties** dialog box that opens, type a title for the frameset page in the same way you do for any other page and click **OK**. This text will appear in the title bar of the browser when the page is displayed. When you use frames, remember that the individual page titles are no longer visible in the title bar; only the title of the frameset appears there.

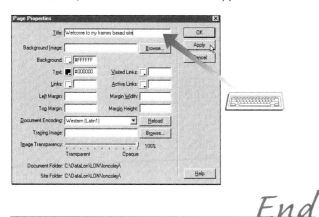

How-To Hints

Understanding the Frames Panel

The great thing about using the **Frames** panel is that it gives you the best possible view of your frameset. Moving between frames in the panel is easy: just click inside the frame you are interested in. The selected frame always appears highlighted for you. Experiment to note that the frameset is highlighted by a large, thick border, and the individual frames are highlighted by a thinner line.

End

How to Set Frame Properties

Each frame within the frameset contains an HTML document. You can specify properties for each frame within the frameset. You can select individual frames using the **Frames** panel and use the **Properties Inspector** to change the settings. Note that any frame properties you set will override the frameset properties.

Begin

1 View Frame Properties

In the **Frames** panel, click the frame whose properties you want to see. The **Properties Inspector** displays the property information for the frame you have selected.

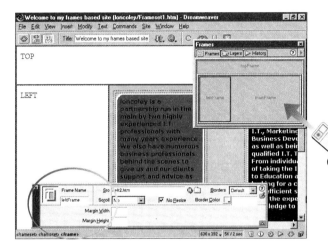

Click

2 Name the Frame

In the **Frame Name** field in the **Properties Inspector**, type a name for the frame. This name is used for targeting hyperlinks. Make sure that the name you supply is relevant. If you are planning to use any scripting in your site, avoid using scripting words such as **top** or **navigator**. This example names the selected frame **Content**; you can also use the default name that Dreamweaver creates for you.

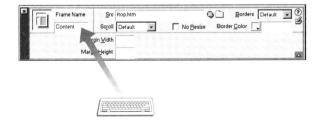

3 Set Scroll Properties

From the **Scroll** drop-down menu, choose whether scrollbars will appear at the edge of the frame. Most browsers show scrollbars only when browser size requires them. Select **Yes** to force scrollbars; select **No** to never show them. Selecting **No** means that you must ensure that your content never outsizes the frame because your viewers won't be able to scroll to see the content. In most browsers, the default setting is **Auto**, but you should set your own properties to be certain that the end result is what you want.

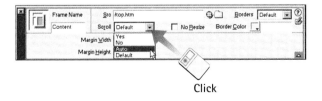

Click

4 Set Border Properties

Setting a border color for a frame overrides any border colors you set in the frameset **Properties Inspector**. Use the color picker to set a new color. You can turn off borders in the **Properties Inspector** for the frame only if the **Borders** option for every adjacent frame in the frameset is set to **No**. In this example, notice that changing the border color for this frame affects the adjacent frames as well.

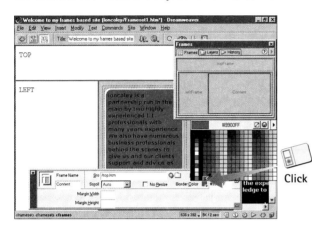

Click

5 Set Resize Options

Although you can allow visitors to your site to resize frames in the browser window, this flexibility is usually not provided. Frames should be sized by you at the design stage rather than allowing visitors to resize the frames. Enable the **No Resize** box to ensure that visitors cannot affect the size of the frames.

6 Set Margins

If you can't see the margin options, expand the **Properties Inspector** window by clicking the arrow in the bottom-right corner. The margin controls set the distance between the edge of the frame and the frame contents. In the **Margin Width** and **Margin Height** fields, type the number of pixels you want for a margin. Notice the difference in the margins between this example and the example in Step 4.

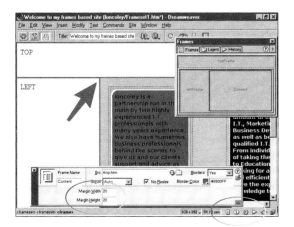

7 Set Background Color

Frames don't specifically have a background color; the background color for the frame is set in the underlying HTML document. (Therefore, the frame's background color is not specified in the **Properties Inspector**; it is set in the **Page Properties** dialog box.) Select and then right-click the frame for which you want to change the background and choose **Page Properties** from the context menu. Click the arrow in the **Background** field and use the color picker to select a color.

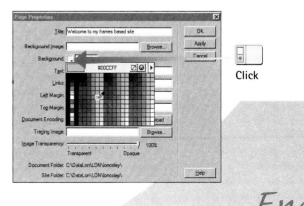

Click

End

How to Use NoFrames and Nested Frames

Even in these days of advanced browsers, there are still some browsers that cannot display frames. The **NoFrames** option allows you to control what the visitor sees if he is using a browser that cannot display frames. Frames are also flexible enough that you can have frames within frames (just as you can with tables). The **Nested Frameset** option refers, as the name implies, to frames within frames and simplifies your work with these more complex arrangements.

Begin

1 See the NoFrames Content

You can modify the default message that appears to a visitor using a browser that doesn't support frames. If your page uses frames, you should take the time to modify the default message so that the visitor isn't frustrated at being unable to access the content of your page. To view the default message, choose **Modify, Frameset, Edit NoFrames Content.**

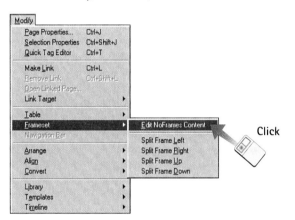

Click

2 Enter the Content

The screen refreshes to a screen that simply says **NoFrames content.** You can type whatever content or instructions you want onto this page to tell visitors why they can't see your page and what they can do instead.

3 Return to Frames View

After you have entered the information you want to display, choose **Modify, Frameset, Edit NoFrames Content** again to return to the normal view of your frames. Note that you don't have to actually save the **NoFrames** message information separately because it is stored with the frameset.

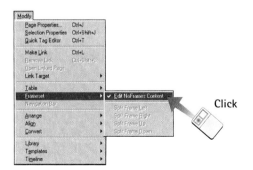

Click

4 Insert a Nested Frameset

Nested framesets are framesets within framesets. They are used to further divide existing frames; when used carefully, they can create interesting effects. Click inside the frame you want to hold the new frameset and use the **Frames** page of the **Objects** panel to insert a new predefined frameset. In this example, wc insert a new top frame in the existing top frame on the page.

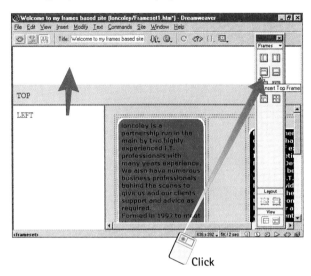

Click

6 Save the New Layout

Choose **File, Save All Frames** to save the newly created top frame. Make sure that you give this new frame a unique name within the frameset.

Click

5 Format the Nested Frameset

Nested frames and framesets can be formatted in the same way as first-level frames. Open the **Frames** panel and click inside the new frame; use the **Properties Inspector** to set the properties for it.

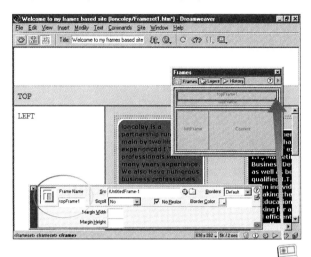

Click

End

How-To Hints

Use a Framed Page as Your Home Page

If you want to use a page formatted with a frameset as the home page for your site, you must name the frameset accordingly. To make a page the home page, the frameset must be named either **index.htm** or **default.htm**. (Your ISP will tell you which name to use.)

Saving Frames

Did you notice that when we saved the new frames page, the option we selected on the File menu was **Save All Frames**? Continue to use this option to save all the frames in your frameset at once. If you want to save the frameset with a different name, select the entire frameset in the **Frames** panel and choose **File, Save Frameset As**. This option is available only after you have selected the frameset.

How to Edit Frames

You can change the layout of your frameset even after you have started working on its content. Frames can be deleted or split at any time to create new frames. If you want, you can add existing HTML pages to a frame instead of using the new blank HTML pages that Dreamweaver automatically adds when you insert a frame. This task explains some of the editorial jobs you can accomplish with frames.

Begin

1 Delete a Frame

Deleting a frame is simple even if you have started working with the content of the frame. Select the frameset using the **Frames** panel. In the document window, simply drag the frame border off the page.

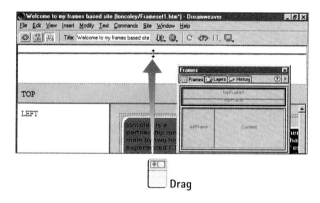

Drag

2 See the Effect

The frame you dragged disappears, and the contents of the rest of the frames adjust to fill the screen. In this example, we deleted the top frame; the contents of the bottom frame adjust to fill in the gap.

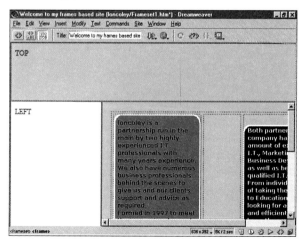

3 Split a Frame

You can split an existing frame into more than one frame. Select the frame you want to split by clicking in the **Frames** panel. Then hold down the **Alt** key. (Mac users press **Option**.) In the document window, drag the frame border to split the frame.

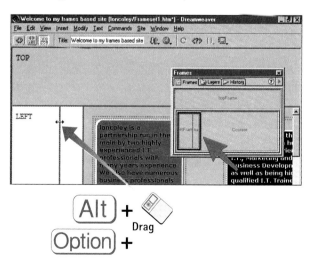

Alt + Drag

Option +

4 Change the Page to Be Displayed

You can fill a frame with a previously created document. In the **Frames** panel, select the frame you want to change. In the **Properties Inspector**, click the folder icon next to the **Src** field and browse to choose the HTML page you want displayed in that frame.

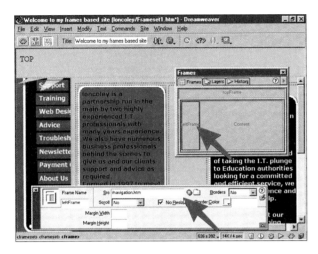

5 Adjust the Frame Width

If the frame is not wide enough to display the contents of the page you choose, drag the frame border to widen the frame. Alternatively, change the value in the **Column** box in the **Properties Inspector**.

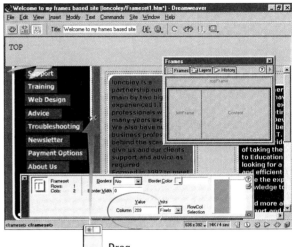

Drag

6 Preview the Page

Choose **File, Preview in Browser** to check that the page looks how you expect. Verify that the frames contain the chosen pages in the correct places, that the scrollbars work as expected, and so on.

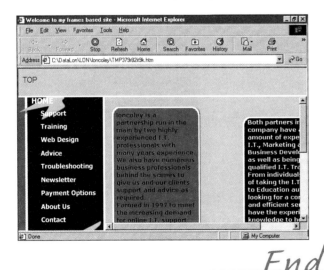

How-To Hints

Don't Forget

The pages that display in the frames are complete HTML pages in their own right and can be edited either as part of the frameset or as an individual page. To open the page away from the frameset, just open the page from the **Site** window.

End

How to Set Links in a Frameset

The way links in framesets work is unique. Get the links right, and your site will look wonderful. Get the links wrong, and it will look like your worst Web design nightmare with pages opening in the wrong places. When we looked at hyperlinks in Part 5, "Working with Hyperlinks," we mentioned the target options; now is the time to use those options.

Begin

1 Get Familiar with Frame Names

Open the **Frames** panel for your frameset. Note the names for each frame on the page. Recall that you can change the names of the frames in the **Frame Name** field in the **Properties Inspector.** You'll refer to these frame names when you create your links.

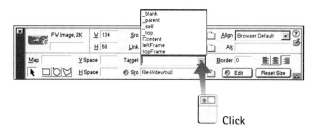

2 Create a Hyperlink

In any frame in the document window, type a line of text or a word to use as a hyperlink. If you are using an existing page, simply select the text or image you want to use as a link. Then use the **Link** field in the **Properties Inspector** to specify the file or URL to be linked to.

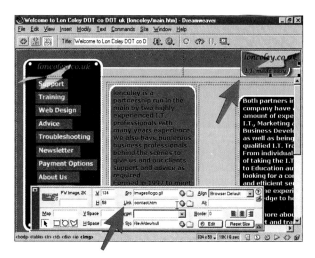

3 Look at the Targets

Often, you will want the page to which the hyperlink points to display in a different frame on your page. You can choose the frame in which you want the linked page to open from the **Target** drop-down menu in the **Properties Inspector.** Click the arrow next to the **Target** field to display the list of frames in the page.

Click

4 Choose the Target Frame

In this example, we want the page referenced by the selected link to display in the **Content** frame rather than in the **topFrame** frame. Select the desired frame from the list.

Click

5 Open a Link Outside the Frameset

It is considered very bad manners to open other peoples' Web sites inside your own frameset. If the link you want to display is to an external site, you can specify that the contents open either in a new window (use the **blank** option) or into a complete page in the same browser window without frames (use the **top** option).

Click

6 Open a Link in the Same Frame

To open a linked page in the same frame as the link itself, choose **_self** from the **Target** menu. In this example, we want the link on the page in the **Content** frame to open its referenced page in the **Content** frame. To make this happen, select the link text and choose **Content** or **_self** from the **Target** drop-down menu.

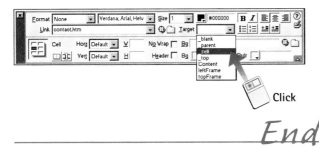

Click

End

How-To Hints

What Does _parent Do?

If you create a nested frameset, the outer frameset become the parent frame. When targeting your links, use the **_parent** option to point a link to the parent frameset and out of the nested frame.

How to Fix Links in a Frameset

When you use frames on your page, it is essential that you check the links between the frames. Your site will simply not work if you have full pages opening in navigation-sized frames and other peoples' sites trying to open into your layout. In this task, you learn how to check the links in your frameset—and how to fix any errors you find.

Begin

1 Preview the Page in a Browser

When you are done with your preliminary page design—including frames and links—open the frameset into the default browser for testing. To do this, choose File, Preview in Browser.

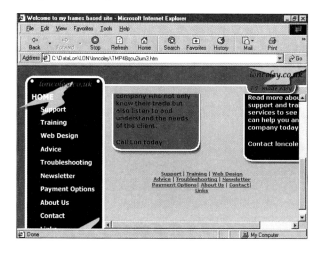

2 Check Internal Links

Click each of the internal links to make certain that they open where they should. Make a note of any links that don't act as expected.

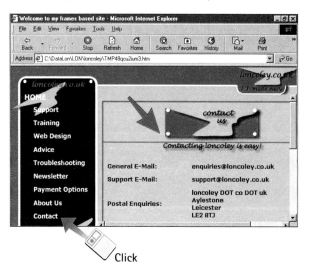

Click

3 Fix Any Problems

Switch back to Dreamweaver and open the Site window. Choose the frameset you want to work with (opening the frameset file opens all the associated HTML pages as well). Use the Link and Target fields in the Properties Inspector to retarget any links that went wrong during testing.

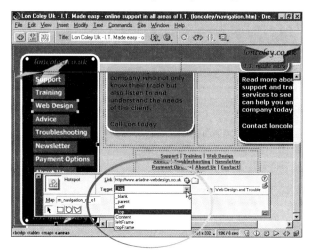

4 Check Links from Other Pages

It makes sense to manually work through all the links in a logical fashion because Dreamweaver has no feature that checks the target of links for you. Work through the links on each page in succession and then move to the next page. This logical approach is the only way to guarantee success with targeted links. In this example, you can see what happens when a page that should open outside the frameset is targeted incorrectly.

5 Set a Base Target Command

If you know that all the links on your HTML page have to open in a particular frame or window, you can edit the HTML code to set a base target that will operate for all the links on the page. Open the HTML source for the page by clicking the **Code Inspector** icon and add the following line into the **<Head>** tag: **<base target="_self">**. Setting the base target to **_self** tells all links to open into the same frame as the link appears; setting the base frame to **_blank** opens all links in a new browser window.

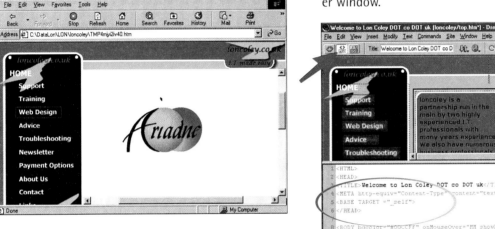

End

Task

10

Using Scripts and Behaviors in Dreamweaver

*S*cripts allow you a huge amount of flexibility and power in Dreamweaver. *Behaviors* are Dreamweaver-specific scripts. You can use them in many different ways to show and hide elements such as layers, to create messages in the status bar, and to create navigation bars. Scripts are perhaps the single most powerful element of the software.

To create this type of interaction with almost any other piece of software, you would need to learn how to code in HTML and JavaScript. The great thing about Dreamweaver behaviors is that the JavaScript is all inserted for you, giving you the power to have things happen (actions) when the site visitors perform actions such as clicking a particular area or when the page loads into the browser (events).

The only drawback to using behaviors is that some older browsers offer little or no support for JavaScript. For this reason, Dreamweaver lets you choose the type of browser you anticipate that your visitors will have. The newer the browser version you choose, the more behaviors you have access to. Even better is that the behaviors that ship with Dreamweaver are written to work with both Internet Explorer and Netscape.

How to Attach a Behavior to a Page Element

Attaching a behavior involves defining an action that will take place when the visitor to the page causes an event to occur. The easiest way of remembering this is *an event plus an action equals a behavior*. It's a simple process in Dreamweaver as long as you are careful. In this task, we will attach a behavior that shows text in the status bar when the user moves the mouse pointer over a hyperlink.

Begin

1 Open the Behaviors Panel

All behaviors are inserted and controlled from the **Behaviors** panel. To open the **Behaviors** panel, choose **Window, Behaviors**.

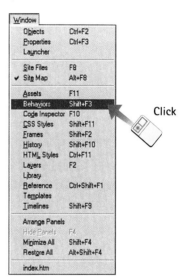

Click

2 Select the Element to Be Affected

Select a hyperlink or image you have inserted on any page or create a new page element for this exercise. Behaviors cannot be attached to plain text, only to hyperlinks or images.

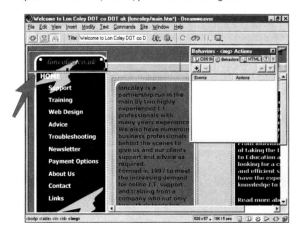
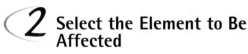

3 Choose the Action

In the **Behaviors** Panel, click the + button to display the list of actions available for the currently selected page element. Choose **Set Text, Set Text of Status Bar**.

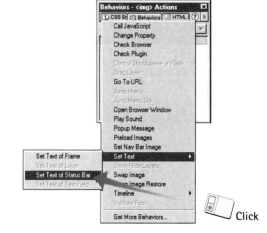

Click

4 Set the Text to Appear

In the **Set Text of Status Bar** dialog box, type the text you want to appear in the status bar when the user moves the mouse pointer over the selected page element. Click **OK** when you are happy with the text.

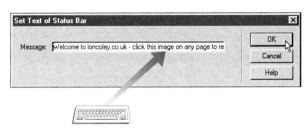

5 Look at the Event

Dreamweaver has filled in the event for you. The **Behaviors** panel shows that when the user passes the mouse over the selected page element (this event is called **onMouseOver**), the specified text will appear in the status bar. The default event is **onMouseOver**; we will look at how to edit behaviors later in this task.

6 Test the Behavior

Save the page and preview it in your browser. Move the mouse pointer over the link and look in the status bar: The specified text appears, just as expected. However, when you move the mouse away from the link, notice that the text remains in the status bar—which is not what you'd expect.

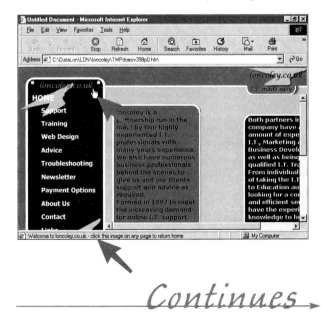

Continues

How to Attach a Behavior to a Page Element Continued

7 Solve the Behavior Problem

The problem you just discovered is a common one when people first start to use behaviors: An event has been triggered, but it has not been stopped. We have to add another action (displaying a blank status bar) that is triggered when the mouse moves away from the selected page element. Select the same element you selected in Step 3 and choose **Set Text, Set Text of Status Bar** from the **Actions** list in the **Behaviors** panel.

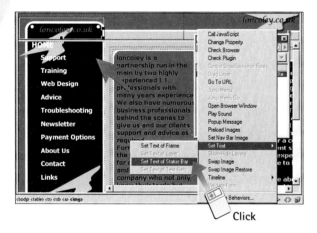

Click

8 Set the New Message

In the **Set Text of Status Bar** dialog box, type the text you want to appear in the status bar when the user moves the mouse pointer away from the selected page element. In this case, leave the **Message** field blank because you don't want any text to appear in the status bar when the user moves the mouse away from the page element. Click **OK**.

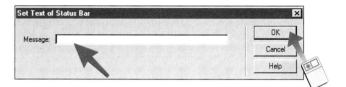

Click

9 Change the Event

By default, Dreamweaver has assigned the **onMouseOver** event to the action you just defined. To change the event for the second action, click the down arrow next to the event to display a list of other possible events. Choose **onMouseOut**—this name refers to the event of the mouse pointer moving away from the selected page element.

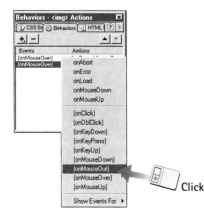

Click

10 Preview the Page Again

Open the page in the browser and move the mouse pointer over the link. Look in the status bar to see the text appear as expected. Now move the mouse pointer away from the link; the text disappears from the status bar. Problem solved!

11 Open the Code View

Now is a good time to see what is happening behind the scenes and to view the code that Dreamweaver has generated. If you don't know any JavaScript, this is a great way to start understanding it. Select the element you attached the behavior to and click the **Show Code and Design Views** button on the toolbar to open the split screen.

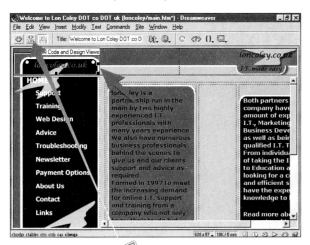

Click

12 View the JavaScript

With the page element selected, the code opens automatically to that area of the page. You can clearly see the code showing the status bar message being turned on and off in the browser. It is also worth viewing the code in the head section of the page where the script language command is inserted.

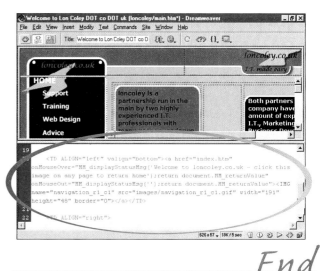

End

How-To Hints

Different Events

When you selected the **onMouseOver** event, you noticed that many other events were in the list. The names of the events give big clues about what each event does. For example, the **onClick** event is triggered when a user clicks a page element; the **onDblClick** event occurs when a user double-clicks, and so on. Other events have less obvious names. For example, **onKeyDown** is activated when a user presses any key on the keyboard, regardless of whether the key is released or not; **onKeyPress** is activated only when a key is pressed and released.

Specifying a Browser

As you know, different browsers support different JavaScript functions. The older the browser, the less options you have available. If you are designing a site and expect it to be viewed mainly by people using older browsers, you should set events that are compatible with those older browsers. To show events for a particular browser version, click the down arrow in the **Events** column of the **Behaviors** panel and click **Show Events For**. As soon as you select a browser from the list, the available **Events** list changes to reflect your selection.

How to Add a Behavior to a Page

You can attach a behavior to a whole page. You might want to attach the behavior to the page if you want to cause an action to happen as the page is loading into the visitor's browser. For example, you might want to set up an action that sends the visitor to a different URL if you have recently moved your Web site to a new server, or if the visitor is accessing a now out-of-date page. This option is also commonly used (as it is in this task) to redirect visitors to a new page if they are using older browsers that may not display your content correctly.

Begin

1 Select the <body> Tag

Open the page to which you want to attach the behavior and select the **<body>** tag at the bottom-left corner of the screen.

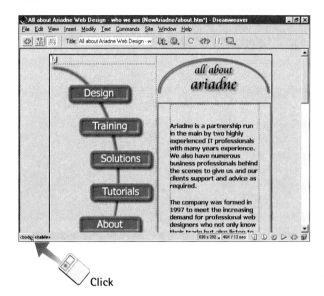

Click

2 Show the Behaviors Panel

Choose **Window, Behaviors** to show the **Behaviors** panel. Notice that the title bar of the panel shows that you have already selected the **<body>** tag.

3 Choose the Behavior

From the **Actions** drop-down menu (accessed by clicking the + button in the **Behaviors** panel), choose **Check Browser**. The **Check Browser** dialog box opens. This option creates some JavaScript code that will check the version of the browser the visitor is using before the page is loaded.

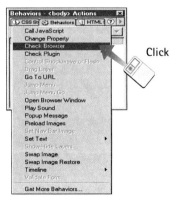

Click

4 Complete the Dialog Box

Use this dialog box to specify which page will be displayed to visitors using **Netscape Navigator 4.0** and later, **Internet Explorer 4.0** or later, and **Other Browsers**. You can specify different URLs to be displayed to visitors with browser versions earlier than 4.0 as well. For this example, select options so that visitors using browsers version 4.0 or later stay on the current page; the next step explains how to send visitors with older browsers to a different URL.

5 Set the URLs

If you selected the **Go to URL** option for any of the browsers in the top part of the dialog box, specify the URL of the page you want to display in those instances in the **URL** box. If you selected the **Go to Alt URL** option for any of the browsers, specify the URL of the page you want to display in those instances in the **Alt URL** box. If you are redirecting visitors to a remote URL (one that is not part of the current site), you must include the full **http://www** part of the address. Click **OK** to continue.

Click

6 Learn from Dreamweaver

Even if you never intend to write your own code, understanding what it is doing can help if things ever go wrong. The **Behaviors** panel now shows that you have an **onLoad** event that checks which browser is being used; the page holds all the code to accomplish this check. On the toolbar, click the **Show Code View Button** and see just what Dreamweaver has written for you.

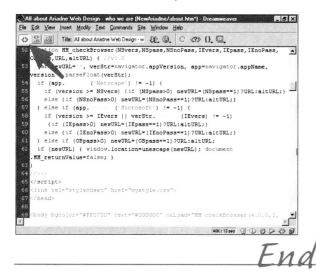

How-To Hints

Very Old Browsers

Some people still use browsers that are so old they won't even respond to the script you just set up to check browser versions and redirect browsers to other URLs. Therefore it is always a good idea to add a straightforward hyperlink on the main page that people can click to get to a simpler page that *will* display in their older browsers.

End

Task 3

How to Create a Navigation Bar

A *navigation bar* consists of a line of images used as links to other pages within the site. When you set up a navigation bar in Dreamweaver, you can make each image change when the viewer moves the mouse pointer over it or clicks it (the process of the image swapping or changing is called a *rollover*). You can use images you already have or check out the Fireworks section of this book for instructions on making your own images.

Begin

1 Name the First Element

Decide where on the page you want to insert the navigation bar. In this example, I place the navigation bar on a separate layer. Choose **Insert, Interactive Images, Navigation Bar** to open the **Insert Navigation Bar** dialog box. Each element on the navigation bar must be named. For example, you might have a set of images that link to a family page; you could call that element **Family**. A set of images linking to a catalog of products could be called **Catalog**. In the **Element Name** box, type a name for the first element you want to add to the navigation bar.

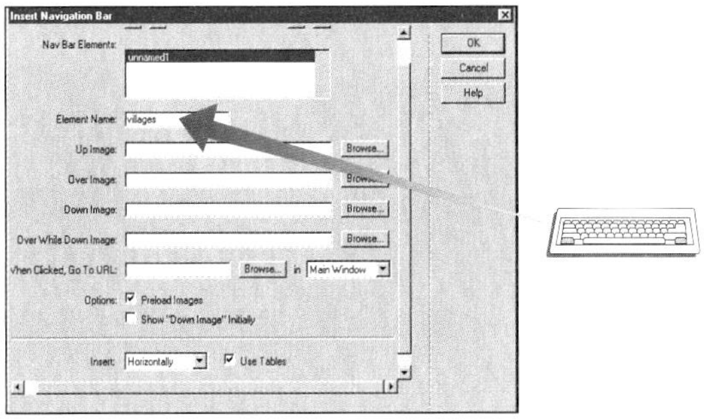

2 Select the Images to Use

For each element, you must specify at least an **Up Image**—the image visible when the mouse isn't over or clicking the image. The **Over Image** (displayed when the mouse moves over the element), the **Down Image** (displayed after the mouse clicks the element), and the **Over While Down Image** (displayed after the element is clicked and the mouse is still over it) are not required but do make the navigation bar more professional. For each of these four states, specify the folder and filename of the image you want to use.

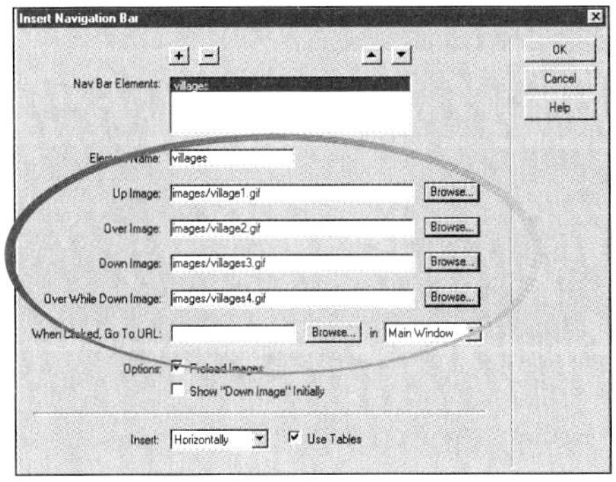

3 Insert the Link Information

In the **When Clicked Go to URL** box, either type the URL of the HTML page to link to or use the **Browse** button to navigate to the desired page. If your site uses frames, use the **in** drop-down list to specify the frame in which you want the specified page to appear. (Refer to Part 9, "Using Frames and Framesets," for more information about frames.)

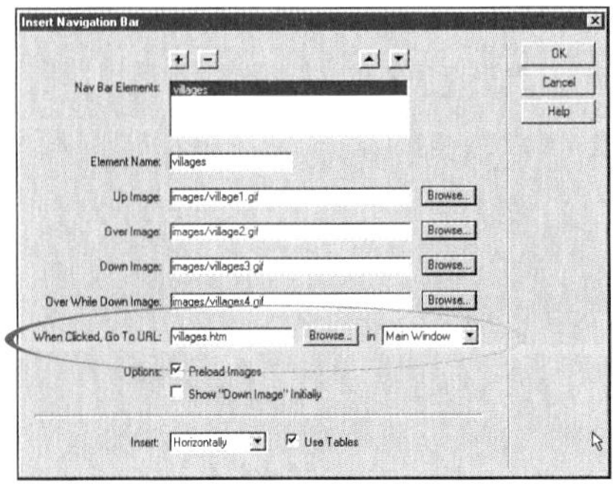

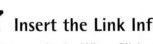

4 View and Modify

Click OK to close the Insert Navigation Bar dialog box and view the navigation bar on the page. The bar isn't very useful; it has only the one button on it. You can edit the navigation bar at any time by selecting Modify, Navigation Bar to reopen the dialog box.

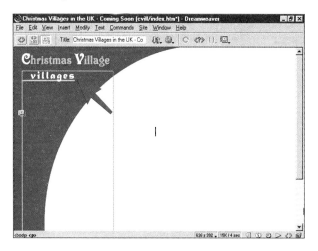

5 Add More Elements

Click the + button in the Modify Navigation Bar dialog box to add more elements to the navigation bar. Remember that you must name each button element you add to the navigation bar and you must specify an image file for at least the Up Image field before the element can appear on the page.

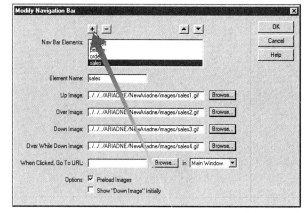

Click

6 Preview in Browser

Open the page into the browser. Move the mouse over the elements to see the rollover effect (the button image will change when you move the mouse over the element). Click an element to observe the change in the image. Make sure that the page you expect to appear when you click the navigation button is actually the page that does appear.

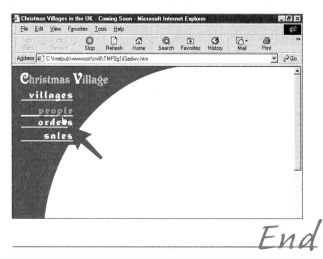

End

How-To Hints

Navigation Bar Options

The Insert/Modify Navigation Bar dialog box offers several other options you can choose from. Enable the Preload Images check box to ensure that all required files for the current element are downloaded when the page first opens. This option ensures that there is no delay in image rollover when passing the mouse over the element or when clicking the element.

Because the navigation bar includes buttons for every page in the site, you can enable the Show 'Down Image' Initially check box for each button element. When that page opens, the Down Image state of the element linked to that page is shown.

From the Insert drop-down list, you can choose to insert the navigation bar either Vertically or Horizontally. If you want the navigation bar to be created as a table, with the elements in individual cells, enable the Use Tables check box.

How to Change or Remove Behaviors

After you have attached a behavior to an element on the page, you can change or remove that behavior at any time—without affecting the page element in any other way. For example, if you have a hyperlink to which you have attached a behavior that displays a message in the status bar, removing the behavior does not affect the link itself; clicking the link still takes you to the page you expect to see.

Begin

1 Select the Page Element

Click to select the element on the page to which you have attached a behavior that you want to modify. If necessary, choose **Window, Behaviors** to display the **Behaviors** panel.

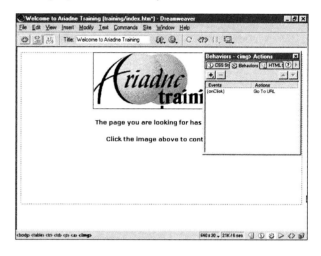

2 Change the Behavior

In the **Behaviors** panel, double-click the action you want to modify. A dialog box appropriate to the specific action opens. In this example, the action being modified is **Go to URL**; when this action is double-clicked, a dialog box opens to allow you to change the URL and the frame in which that page opens. Note that every action has a different dialog box. Make your adjustments to the action and click **OK**.

3 Change the Event

You can also change the event that triggers the action. In this example, the **onClick** event triggers the **Go To URL** action. You can change this event to **onDblClick** (the action occurs when the user double-clicks the page element) simply by clicking the arrow next to the event and choosing a different event.

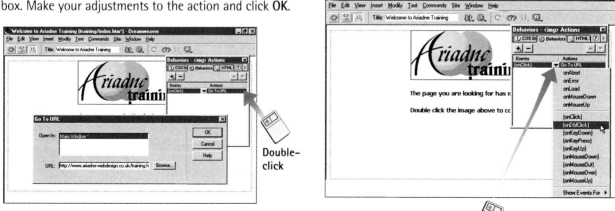

Double-click

Click

4 Delete a Behavior

You can delete a behavior completely. In the **Behaviors** panel for the selected page element, click to select the behavior you want to delete. Then click the – button to remove the event and its associated action.

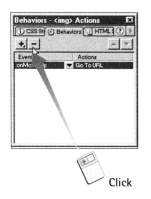

Click

5 Open a New Browser Window

Behaviors can be used to open a link in a new browser window. Select an element on the page that you want to use as the trigger for the event. Choose **Open Browser Window** as the event. The **Open Browser Window** dialog box opens.

6 Complete the Dialog Box

In the **URL to Display** field, type the URL to the file you want to open. In this example, I use an image file. You can also set the exact width and height of the new window to match an image size (or page content). Don't forget to name the window you want to open. (This name is then referenced in the code.)

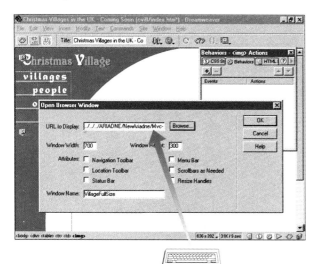

7 Specify Additional Options

The **Open Browser Window** dialog box has additional options you can complete. These options allow you to set menus and toolbars on the new window—or remove them. Enabling any of the check boxes adds that attribute to the page (such as toolbars, scrollbars, or whether the status bar is visible). These options affect only the new window. Click **OK** to continue and add the behavior to the page.

End

How to Get More Behaviors

We have looked at some of the default behaviors that come with Dreamweaver; for those of you new to Dreamweaver, these behaviors are probably enough to last for a while. After you really get into using behaviors, you might want to try new things. People who have been using Dreamweaver for a while have created some interesting behaviors for elements on their Web pages and are kind enough to share these JavaScripts with the general public. You can download these behaviors and then install them for use in your own pages.

Begin

1 Choose the Option

Make sure that you are connected to the Internet and then open the **Behaviors** panel. From the **Actions** menu, choose **Get More Behaviors**. Dreamweaver uses your default browser to open the Macromedia Exchange Web site.

2 Use the Web Site

If you have already registered with Macromedia, the Web site will recognize who you are. If you haven't registered, click the membership link at the top of the page and complete the information. If you want the Macromedia site to remember you, you must allow cookies to be enabled in your browser.

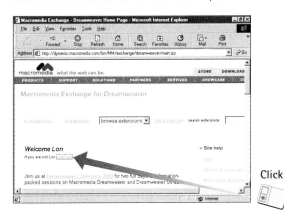

Click

3 Browse the Extensions

Open the **browse extensions** drop-down list at the top of the page and look through the list of options. Because behaviors are categorized as scripts, select the **Scripting** option to see what files are available in that category.

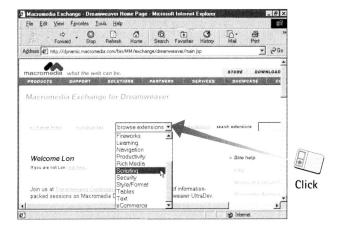

Click

4 Choose a File

Each of the files listed has information associated with it. The title of the file is a good indicator of what the script actually does. Click the title of the script to open the details page for that script. You might also see rating information along with the number of people who have downloaded the file. In this example, you see the details for a script entitled **Always on Top**.

5 Download the Script File

To download a script file you have decided to try for yourself, click the download button for your operating system (generally either **Windows** or **Macintosh**). The file is downloaded to the location you specify.

Click

6 Install and Use the Script

After you have downloaded the file, double-click it to install it into the Package Manager. After it is installed, you can access full instructions about where and how to use the script by choosing **Commands, Manage Extensions**. You learn more about managing and downloading extensions in Part 14, "Dreamweaver and Beyond."

How-To Hints

Don't Get Carried Away

The Macromedia site provides many files you can download for use with Dreamweaver. Before you start downloading everything in sight, spend a little time getting used to the behaviors that Dreamweaver has already. A word of caution: Some of the files you can download might have bugs or problems. Become familiar with the scripts that Dreamweaver comes with and then move on. By the time we look at Part 14, "Dreamweaver and Beyond," with the purpose of extending Dreamweaver, you should be more than ready to download selectively.

End

Task

Using Timelines and Animations

ou can create animations in Dreamweaver by positioning layers on your page at different points in a timeline. The moving layers create the effect of an animation. At the same time as they move around the screen, layers can also be made to change size, visibility, position, and depth (in relation to other layers).

The layers that you animate can contain text, images, or other objects (such as a Flash movie). Because the timeline only controls layers, you can animate only objects that are in layers. For more information about layers, check out Part 8, "Working with Layers and Cascading Style Sheets."

Because Dreamweaver uses JavaScript and DHTML to animate the layers, remember that your animated pages will be viewable only in browsers of version 4.0 or later. This restriction might limit your potential audience.

How to Create a Simple Animation

Creating a timeline animation is easy. The hard part comes later when you have to test, edit, and amend it to look how you really want. This task gets things moving on screen; after we have an animation in place, we can look at making changes to it. For this example, I use a simple page that contains a single layer with an image of a bicycle. You can put animations on pages with as much content as you want, but to ensure that you can see what is happening, I will keep it simple for now.

Begin

1 Open a Page and Create a Layer

Either open an existing page with content, or create a new page. To the page, add a layer and insert an image into the layer. In this example, the page contains a single layer; that layer sports the image of a bicycle.

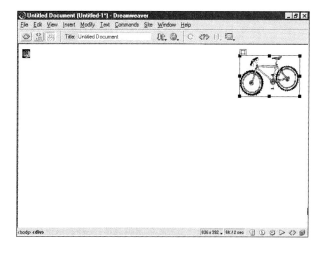

2 Show the Timeline Panel

Choose **Window, Timelines** to display the **Timelines** panel. You can shrink the size of the panel by dragging one of its corners.

Click

3 Record a Path for the Animation

Select the layer you want to animate and then choose **Modify, Timeline, Record Path of Layer**. This command allows you to define a path along which the bicycle will travel. Recording the path puts it into Dreamweaver's memory.

Click

4 Draw the Path

Select the layer and drag the layer handle around the screen to create the path of movement that you want to use. Let's start with a simple, short path. As you move the layer, a dotted line appears on the screen.

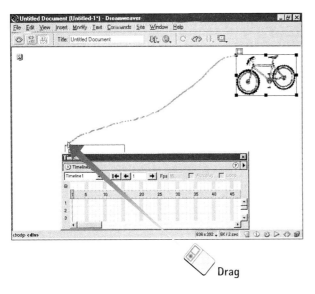

Drag

6 See the Animation in Action

Click the **Play** button on the **Timelines** panel to see the animation move through each frame in turn. Hold down the **Play** button to see a smoother movement.

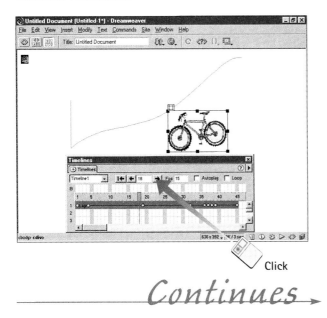

Click

Continues

5 Let Go of the Layer

When you release the mouse button to let go of the layer, a dialog box appears, telling you that Dreamweaver can animate the layer. Click **OK** to continue. The dotted line created by dragging the layer now becomes solid.

Click

7 Set a Trigger

As the name implies, a *trigger* tells the animation when to start. Let's make this animation start when the page loads. On the **Timelines** panel, enable the **Autoplay** check box. An alert box appears, telling you that the timeline is being added to the **onLoad** event. Click **OK** to continue.

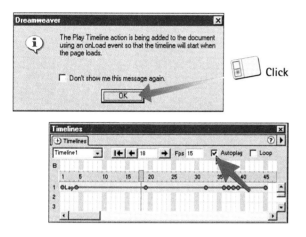

8 Set the Animation to Loop

Setting the animation to loop causes it to restart when it reaches the end of the timeline. To make the animation play continuously, enable the **Loop** check box in the **Timelines** panel. Dreamweaver displays an alert box telling you how to edit this effect.

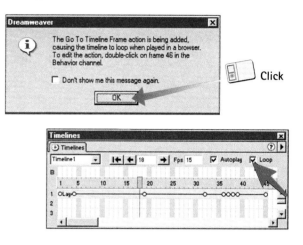

9 Save the Page

Save the page into your Web site folder by choosing **File, Save**. In the **Save As** dialog box, give the file a name, navigate to the appropriate folder, and click **Save**.

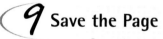

10 Preview the Page

Because you have added a trigger to the animation (the **onLoad** event), the animation should start as soon as the page loads. Choose **File, Preview in Browser** to see how the animation looks in a browser window. Notice that the bicycle animation keeps looping.

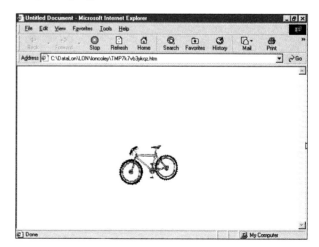

11 Remove the Loop

If you don't like the way the animation loops, disable the **Loop** check box in the **Timelines** panel. Save the file and preview the page again. Notice that the animation stops when it reaches the end of the timeline, and the object remains in its end position.

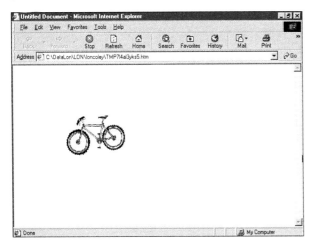

12 Name the Timeline

Because we are going to continue working with this animation in the next tasks, we must name the timeline for future use. On the **Timelines** panel, select the name **Timeline1** and type a new name in the text box. For this example, I named the timeline **bicycle**. Although this simple example doesn't require a name other than the default, you should get into the habit of naming your timelines so that you can later create more complicated animations that use many timelines.

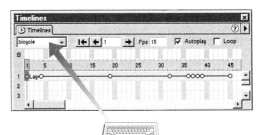

13 Name the Layer

Open the **Layers** panel by choosing **Window, Layers**. Select the layer you have been working with as an animation. By default, Dreamweaver calls this layer **Layer 1**. Because the following tasks continue working with this animation, now is a good time to provide a meaningful name for the layer. Double-click the layer name and type a new name for it.

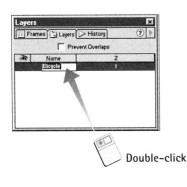

Double-click

How-To Hints

Language Issues

Creating timeline animations can be confusing, so let's try to dispel some of that confusion now. Dynamic Hypertext Markup Language (DHTML) is the language used to position layers on a screen. When you are creating timeline animations, DHTML gives you the control over where and when the layers appear using JavaScript. When you create a timeline animation, Dreamweaver creates the code for you and places it all inside a `<script>` tag so that the browser knows how to interpret it.

End

How to Add a Layer to a Timeline

The last task explained how to create a simple animation using a path of movement in a single layer. But what if you want to animate more than one layer, or to position a layer at a certain point on the timeline? Adding layers to your timeline lets you animate multiple objects on the same page and set the animations to do different things. Remember that you cannot animate objects in Dreamweaver; you can animate only layers. Make sure that you place the objects you want to animate in layers.

1 Create a New Layer

Open the file we worked on in the last task (or any page file that already contains one animated layer). Use the **Objects** panel to draw a new layer on the page in Dreamweaver. Add an object or some text that you want to animate to this new layer.

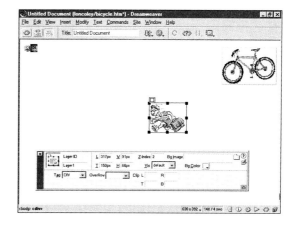

2 Drag the Layer

Make sure that the **Timelines** panel is showing. Drag the new layer using its handle and drop it into channel 2 on the **Timelines** panel. This channel is directly below channel 1, which was used for the animation of the first layer.

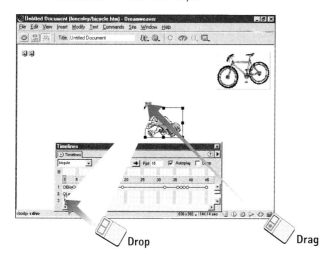

Drop   Drag

3 Position the Layer on the Timeline

Click and hold the layer marker and drag it along the channel line so that the animation for this layer starts in a different frame. Let go when it is in the position you want. Notice that the object in the first layer advances through its animation frames as you drag the second layer so that you can coordinate the activities of the two layers.

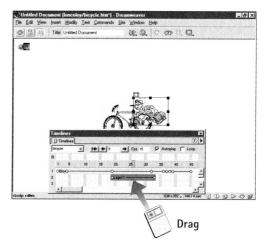

Drag

4 Set the Start Position for the Layer

Click the first keyframe for channel 2. (*Keyframes* are the white circles at the start and end of the animation marker.) Then select the second layer and drag its handle to move it to where you want it to be when the animation starts.

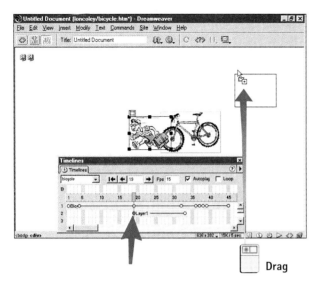

Drag

5 Set the End Position for the Layer

Click the end keyframe marker for this layer and drag the layer to the position where you want it when the animation ends.

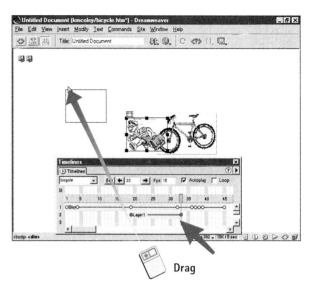

Drag

6 Preview the Animation

Save the file and preview it in the browser. Notice that the second layer moves in a straight line from its starting point to its ending point; the first layer moves along the path you drew for it when you created that animation.

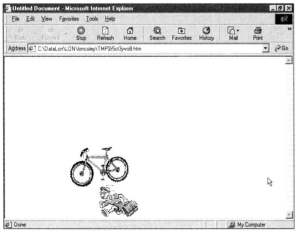

End

How-To Hints

Not Seeing the Layer?

If you see the name of the image file in the **Timelines** panel and not the name of the layer, you have made a common mistake. You must make sure that you drag the *layer* into the **Timelines** panel and not the image file. If you have inadvertently dragged the image to the **Timelines** panel, delete the image from the **Timelines** panel and drag the layer there instead.

Motion Paths

In the example in this task, we created a simple animation in which the second layer moved between two points in a straight line. When you gain more confidence, you can be creative and record a curvy motion path for the second layer as well.

How to Use the B Channel

The B channel runs across the top of the timeline. This channel is reserved for adding behaviors to your animation. The behaviors are set to trigger events that happen when the animation reaches a particular frame. For example, you can set a behavior that will play a sound or make a layer disappear in a particular frame. Note that the behaviors can activate any object on the page, not just layers in the timeline.

Begin

1 Open the Behaviors Panel

Open a page that contains at least one animation layer. Double-click any frame on the B channel in the **Timelines** panel to open the **Behaviors** panel. Dreamweaver displays an alert box, telling you how to add a behavior. Click **OK** to close the box.

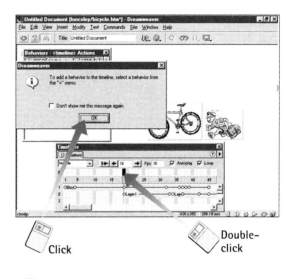

Click

Double-click

2 Add a Behavior

Click the + button at the top of the **Behaviors** panel to display a list of the available behaviors. With the timeline selected, the **Behaviors** panel displays only those behaviors appropriate to a timeline. To learn more about behaviors, check out Part 10, "Using Scripts and Behaviors in Dreamweaver."

3 Select a Behavior

From the list of behaviors for this example, choose **Popup Message**. This behavior will set up a message that will appear onscreen during the animation, beginning at the frame you selected in Step 1.

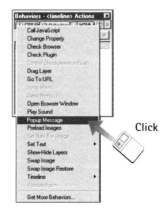

Click

4 Define the Behavior

Fill out the dialog box that opens for the behavior you selected. For the **Popup Message** behavior, type some text to appear at the appropriate moment in the timeline and click **OK** to continue.

5 Look at the Timelines and Behaviors Panels

The **Timelines** panel now displays a marker in the B channel indicating that there is a behavior that will happen in that frame. In the **Behaviors** panel, you will see the **onFrame** event set for the frame number you selected.

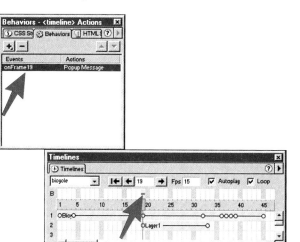

6 Save and Test

Save the file and preview the animation in the browser. You must use the **File, Preview in Browser** command to view the animation in a browser because animations will not play in the document window. Note the addition of the behavior (the appearance of the message box) to the growing number of activities on this page. The message box remains onscreen—and the animation will not continue—until the visitor clicks **OK**.

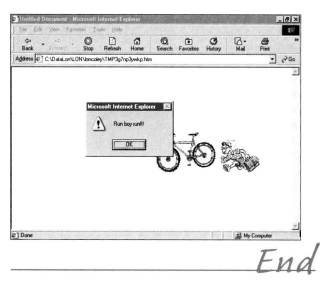

How-To Hints

More About Behaviors

So far in this part of the book, we have kept things reasonably simple and moved along one step at a time. The next tasks look more at behaviors, frames, and timelines; so sit back, relax, and get animating as we go.

End

How to Use Animation Frames

The keyframes on the **Timelines** panel are those frames in which you have specified certain properties for your object. The most obvious example of an animation property is position on the page. When you insert a layer into a timeline, two keyframes are automatically added: one at the beginning and one at the end. When you specify start and end positions for a layer in an animation, Dreamweaver uses the start and end keyframes to work out the position of that layer in all the other frames in the timeline for you. You can add keyframes to create more complicated animations.

2 Select the Layer

Select the layer handle for the layer you are working with (the one to which you added the keyframe) and move it to a new location. The animation path for the object moves accordingly. In this example, I moved the running boy so that he appears to leap over the bicycle.

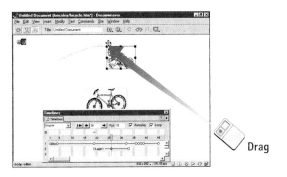

Drag

Begin

1 Add a Keyframe

Decide where you want to add a keyframe to the animation in the **Timelines** panel. Move the red playback head to the frame where you want to add the keyframe. Then highlight the animation marker in the timeline and right-click it. From the context menu that appears, choose **Add Keyframe**. In this example, I added a keyframe to the animation in channel 2 (the running boy image) so that he'll move along a curved path rather than a straight line.

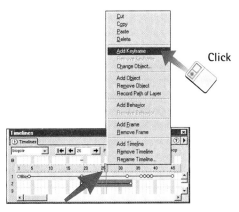

Click

3 Add More Keyframes

You can add as many keyframes to your animation as there are frames. Each time you add a keyframe, you can reposition the layer. To the running boy animation layer, I have added extra keyframes and now have an up-and-down animation path for the boy.

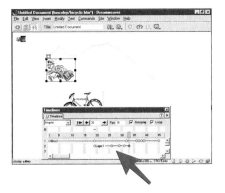

4 Delete a Frame

You can delete frames from the timeline at any point of the creation. Deleting frames shortens or condenses the length of time during which the animation executes. Simply right-click the frame you want to delete to open the context menu and choose **Remove Frame**.

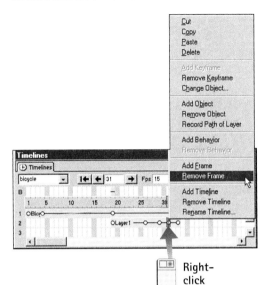

Right-click

5 Add Frames

Adding frames to the timeline to extend the duration of the animation is just as easy as removing them. On the timeline, right-click the location where you want the new frame to appear. From the context menu, choose **Add Frame**. Repeat this step to add as many frames as you want in any location you choose. Note that the default frame rate is 15 fps (frames per second); each frame you add lengthens the animation by approximately 1/15 of a second.

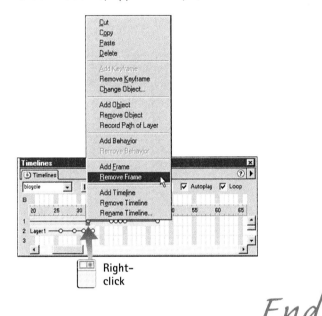

Right-click

End

How-To Hints

Take Care Deleting

When you delete a frame from the timeline, you delete it from the animations in all the channels, not just the channel you clicked in. Because Dreamweaver doesn't prompt you by asking whether you are sure you want to delete, be careful selecting the frame you want to delete.

If you accidentally delete a frame that you wanted, use the **Edit, Undo** command to bring it back.

How to Control Layers with Timelines

In the preceding tasks, you learned how to move a layer along an animation path using a timeline. But you can do much more than simply move an object when animating layers in Dreamweaver. You can make layers appear and disappear over time. This task starts with a single layer containing the image of the bicycle, with no animation path yet defined.

Begin

1 Record the Animation Path

In the document window, select the bicycle layer and record an animation path for this layer as you learned to do in Task 1 of this part.

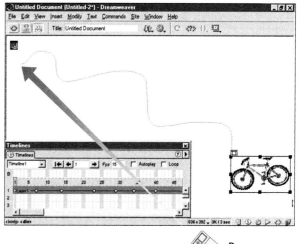

Drag

2 Create More Layers

Create four or five more layers, naming them in a logical way. For example, you could name the layers **L1**, **L2**, and so on, or name them according to the content of the layers.

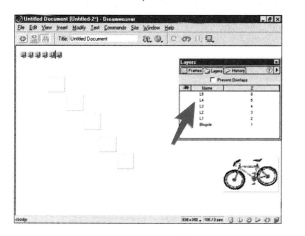

3 Add Content to the Layers

Add some content to each of the new layers. The content can be whatever you want. In this example, I use the word *UP* in different sizes in each layer.

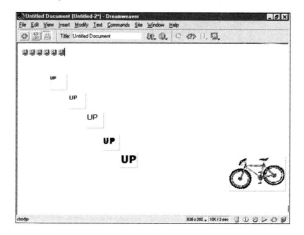

4 Set the Visibility for the Layers

Make sure that the visibility of all the layers is set to visible. A quick way to do this is to select each layer in the **Layers** panel and click the eye icon until an open eye icon appears next to each layer name. This step ensures that all the layers are visible.

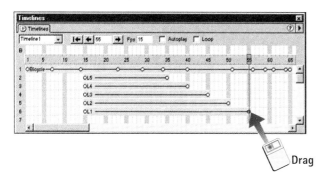

Click

5 Drag the Layers onto the Timeline

Drag each of the new layers from the document window into a new channel on the **Timelines** panel. Position the layers directly above one another, starting at whatever frame you choose. In this example, I lined up all the layers to start at frame 15.

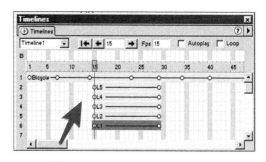

6 Extend the Length for the Layers

Select the end keyframe for the first layer and drag it to the right to lengthen its duration. Repeat this step for each of the channels so that each channel is longer than the previous one. Dragging the end keyframes in this arrangement means that each layer will be visible for a longer time than the previous one. Remember that this animation is based on time; the longer each layer is on the timeline, the longer it is visible.

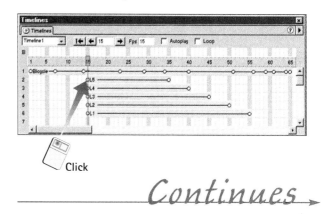

Drag

7 Select the Keyframe

Click to select the first keyframe of one of the layers you added in Step 2. The red playback marker indicates that the first keyframe is selected. You can now work with this layer from the point at which it becomes part of the animation.

Click

Continues

8 Show the Layers Panel

If it isn't already visible, show the **Layers** panel by choosing **Window, Layers**.

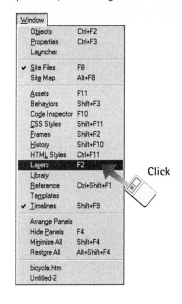

Click

9 Change the Visibility

Change the visibility for each of the layers by clicking in the eye column for each layer until the open eye icon becomes a closed eye icon. Now none of the UP layers are visible onscreen when the animation begins, but the bicycle is.

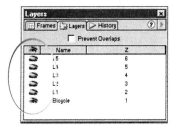

10 Select the Final Keyframe

To see what you have achieved, select the final key frame for any of the UP layers and notice that the layer is visible at that point. At that keyframe in the animation, the layer will appear; because all the layers end in a different frame, the layers will each appear at a different time.

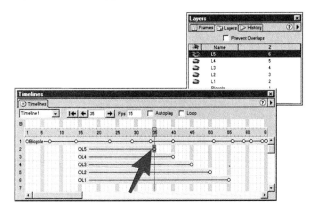

11 Select Autoplay

In the **Timelines** panel, enable the **Autoplay** check box. This option tells Dreamweaver to start the animation as soon as the page is loaded. Click **OK** in the dialog box that appears.

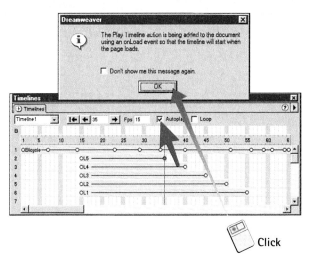

Click

12 Save the Page

Choose **File, Save** and save this page with a meaningful title (maybe **animation2** because this is the second animation you have created). If you don't want to save the page into your Web site folder, browse to a different location.

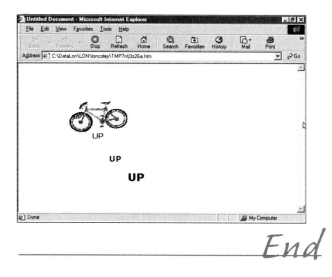

Click

13 Preview the Page

Choose **File, Preview in Browser** and test the animation in a browser. Notice how the UP layers appear in order on the screen You should test your animations in more than one browser to see how each browser handles the animation code.

End

How-To Hints

Frame Rates

As you have noticed, each frame in your animation has a number, and each frame represents a given period of time within your animation. The total number of frames in the timeline determines how long your animation lasts.

The default playback rate is 15 frames per second. Although you can change this number, it is used commonly because it works well in most browsers. Although you can change the playback rate to achieve a faster playback, this is not always a good idea. The browser always plays each frame of the animation in order; even if the frame rate is set to play faster, this will be ignored if the browser cannot handle it.

Task

Working with Forms

Forms allow you, the site owner, to receive information from your site visitors. This information can take many different formats—and usually does!! From simple feedback forms to complete surveys, a form lets you find out your visitors' thoughts and feelings on any subject you choose to ask them about. The first tasks in this part of the book look at the different options you have when creating a form in Dreamweaver; then you'll learn how to make a complete form using different form fields and layouts. Before you get too carried away with forms, check with your hosting company about what they allow you to use. Although any type of form is usually acceptable, most hosting companies are a little more restrictive when it comes to scripts. Some companies allow you lots of freedom, whereas others supply standard scripts with your hosting package. Make sure, for example, that if you want your form results to do anything other than come to you by email, you have permission from the host for the form to do so.

All forms need a handling script that tells the form what to do and where to go. Get this information from your service provider before you try anything too complicated.

All hosts accept forms in one format or another; the most basic form handlers accept user input and email the results back to you. After you get the email, you can do whatever is appropriate with the results. If you want the results of the form to go straight into a database, you will have to learn about Active Server Pages (ASP), the technology commonly used for database interaction. To find out more about ASP, go to your favorite Internet search engine and look up ASP.

Forms are contained within normal Web pages and are made up of form fields, into which the user types information or chooses from selections you offer. You can use *form validation* combined with *behaviors* to make sure that the user inputs the correct type of information. Behaviors are a combination of events and actions; in the case of a form, the act of submitting the form (an event) causes the script to check that the information is correct (an action).

How to Create a Form in Dreamweaver

Inserting a form on a page is incredibly simple—mainly because the form itself is merely a container. All the clever stuff is done when you start inserting form elements in the next task. But before you can have form elements, you must have the form. This task explains how to get the basic form on a page.

Begin

1 Open a Blank Page for the Form

Open Dreamweaver and choose **File, New** to open a blank document window. (If the **Site** window is open, choose **File, New Window** to open a new blank document.) Although you can add a form to any page, it is easier to begin work with a form in a blank page.

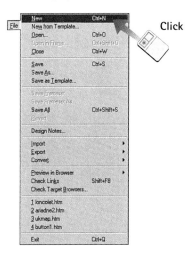

Click

2 Insert a Form Using the Menu

You can insert a form into the page by using the menu system or the **Objects** panel. To insert a form using the menu commands, choose **Insert, Form**. A default, blank form is inserted at the top of the page as shown in Step 5.

Click

3 Use the Objects Panel

To insert a form using the **Objects** panel, you must first display the **Forms** page on the **Objects** panel. From the drop-down list at the top of the panel, choose **Forms**.

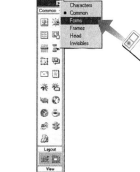

Click

4 Insert a Form Using the Objects Panel

On the **Forms** page of the **Objects** panel, click **Insert Form**. A default, blank form is inserted at the top of the page.

Click

Insert Form

5 Identify the Form

Whether you used the menu system or the **Objects** panel to insert the form, the form appears in the document window as a series of dashed red lines.

End

How-To Hints

Not Seeing Red?

If you can't see the red dashed lines that represent the form, open the **View** menu and make sure that the **Invisible Elements** option has a check mark next to it. When this option is turned on, not only is the form visible, but also any other "invisible" elements on the page will be as well. These other elements include markers for named anchors, comments, and layers.

Place Your Form

In this task, we placed a new form at the top of a blank page, but you can put a form anywhere on the page that you want. Forms can go inside tables or layers, or simply at another location on the page. When you insert a form, it appears wherever the insertion point was.

How to Insert Form Elements

Form elements are the parts of a form—the text fields, check boxes, and radio buttons—that the visitor fills in or selects. Each of the elements you can insert into a form looks and acts differently. The next task explains how to format the elements after you've inserted them into the form. This task looks at the different types of form elements and how to insert them into an existing form.

1 Insert a Text Field

Click inside the red dotted box that represents the form area to position the cursor. On the **Forms** page of the **Objects** panel, click **Insert Text Field**. A text box appears inside the form. *Text boxes* are used on a form to allow visitors to type free-form responses. After the text field exists in the form, add a text label telling the visitor what type of information to add such as **Please enter your First Name**.

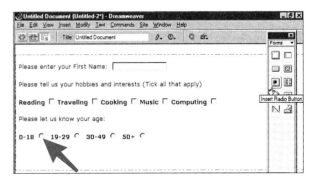

2 Insert a Check Box

Click again inside the red dotted box to position the cursor (if necessary, press **Enter** to insert additional space between existing elements and the one you want to insert). Click **Insert Checkbox** on the **Objects** panel. A small square appears in the form. Forms typically use multiple *check boxes* when more than one answer is acceptable; a single check box is often used when a site owner wants you to sign up for a newsletter or sales materials. The user clicks the check box to place a tick mark in the box. When you have inserted your check boxes, add a text label to make sure that visitors know what they need to do.

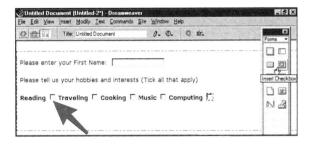

3 Insert Radio Buttons

Click inside the form box to position the cursor. Click **Insert Radio Button** in the **Objects** panel to insert a single radio button into the form. *Radio buttons* (sometimes called option buttons) are used on a form when the visitor must choose only one of several options (as when choosing an age category on a personal information form). When you build a form that includes radio buttons, you must group the associated radio buttons together, as explained in Task 5, "How to Format Radio Buttons." Don't forget to add text labels to identify the radio buttons.

4 Insert a List or Menu Field

Click inside the form box to position the cursor. In the **Objects** panel, click **Insert List/Menu** to insert a menu or list field in the form. Whether the element you insert becomes a menu or a list depends on the settings you make in the **Properties Inspector**, as explained in Task 4, "How to Format a Menu or List."

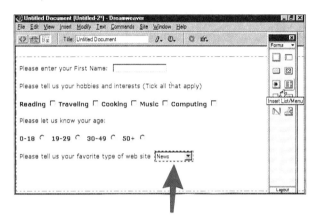

5 Insert a File Field

Click inside the form box to position the cursor. In the **Objects** panel, click **Insert File Field**. A *file field* is a specific kind of text box that accepts the pathname to a file or folder. A file field comes with a **Browse** button that the user can click to locate files or folders on the local machine. Forms use file fields so that users can specify the location from which they want to upload files. Before you use a file field on a form, check with your hosting company to make sure that your server can accept a file attached to a form.

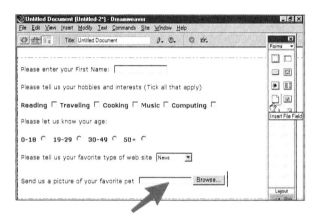

6 Insert a Button

Click inside the form box to position the cursor. In the **Objects** panel, click **Insert Button**. Buttons are used on forms to perform actions such as activating a search, resetting the form, or submitting the completed form to the server. You can change the text on the button face to make it clear what the action of the button is. By default, the inserted button is a **Submit** button that sends the completed form to a server. The button properties determine what happens when the button is clicked.

7 Insert an Image Field

Instead of the standard gray buttons that Dreamweaver creates, you can use any appropriate graphic as a button for your form. On the **Objects** panel, click **Insert Image Field**. Use the dialog box that opens to browse to the image file you want to use. Image fields can be used to perform other events if you attach a behavior to them; you learn about behaviors in Part 10, "Using Scripts and Behaviors in Dreamweaver."

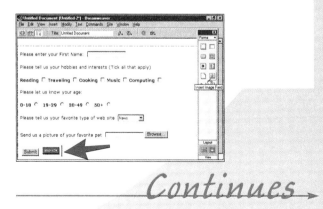

Continues

HOW TO INSERT FORM ELEMENTS **193**

How to Insert Form Elements Continued

8 Insert a Hidden Field

Hidden fields usually contain information used by or saved by the server when it processes the form. The user cannot see or change this information. To insert a hidden field, click **Insert Hidden Field** in the **Objects** panel. A common use of hidden fields is to input the email address to which the form is to be sent. We will look at hidden fields further in Task 7, "How to Collect Data from a Form."

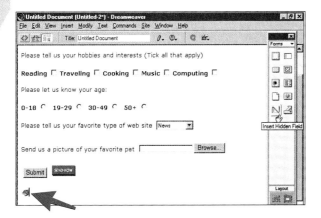

9 Insert a Jump Menu

A *jump menu* is a list of hyperlinks presented on the form as a drop-down menu. When the user makes a choice from the drop-down menu, a hyperlink is activated. Click **Insert Jump Menu** in the **Objects** panel to open the **Insert Jump Menu** dialog box.

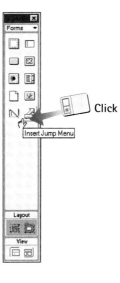

10 Specify the Menu Options

In the **Text** box in the **Insert Jump Menu** dialog box, type a description for the first link to be created. The items you place in the jump menu can be links to files within your own site or to external pages elsewhere on the Internet.

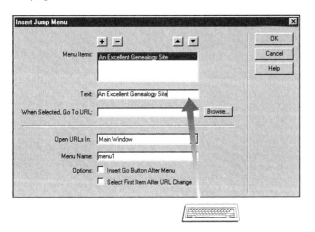

11 Browse to the Linked File

Use the **Browse** button to navigate to a file in the current Web site to which you want this menu item to link. Alternatively, type a complete Web site address in the **When Selected, Go to URL** text box.

12 Add More Items

Click the + button to add the item you have just defined to the list of jump menu options. (Alternatively, select an option in the **Menu Items** list and click the – button to remove that option from the menu.) Repeat Steps 10 through 12 to add all the options and their links to the jump menu.

13 Put the Menu Items in Order

You can change the order in which the items appear in the jump menu. In the **Menu Items** list, select the entry you want to reposition. Click the up or down arrow button to move that entry in the list.

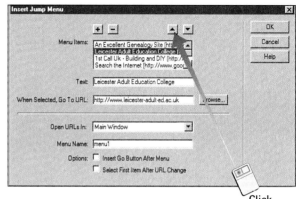

Click

14 Target the Items

Use the **Open URLs In** list to choose where you want the linked pages to open. This option is handy if the page on which your form appears makes use of frames and framesets (as described in Part 9, "Using Frames and Framesets").

15 Set Other Jump Menu Options

The **Insert Jump Menu** dialog box offers two other options: If you want, you can insert a **Go** button on the form that the user clicks to trigger the selected link. The **Select First Item After URL Change** option means that the menu reverts to the first item in the list after a hyperlink has been activated. If you turn on this feature, you should make the first item in the list of jump menu options say something like **Please Select One**. Click **OK** to close the dialog box and insert the jump menu into your form.

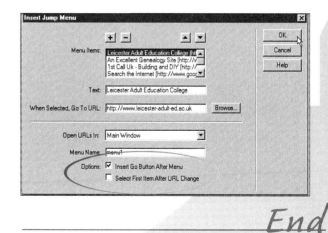

End

How to Format a Text Field

All the form elements you learned to insert in the preceding task have their own properties and features that should be formatted. You can control many of the properties of the form elements you've inserted, from the size of the element to what type of data is allowed in the element. This task focuses on the **Properties Inspector** options for the text box element; other form elements have similar property options.

Begin

1 Format Text Fields

Click the form element you want to format. In this example, click the text box you inserted in the last task. The properties of the selected element are displayed in the **Properties Inspector**. (If the **Properties Inspector** isn't displayed, choose **Window, Properties** to access it.)

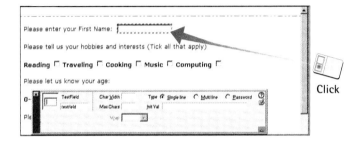

Click

2 Edit the Properties

If you are planning to add the data you retrieve from this form to a database, the name you assign to the text field must be the same as the corresponding field name in the database. If your form has more than one text field, each text field must have a unique name. The **Char Width** field controls how wide the text box is in the browser; the **Max Char** field determines how many characters the visitor can type into the text field. If the user types in more than 15 characters, the text scrolls inside the text box.

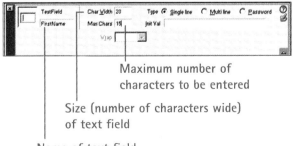

Maximum number of characters to be entered

Size (number of characters wide) of text field

Name of text field

3 Change to a Multi-line Scrolling Box

You can change the text field into a multi-line box by selecting the **Multi-line** radio button. A multi-line box appears larger onscreen and allows the user to enter multiple lines of information. Use the **Num Lines** field to specify the number of lines deep the box will be. (Note that this value specifies the number of lines shown onscreen; the actual number of lines the user can enter is limited only by her ability and desire to type into your form!)

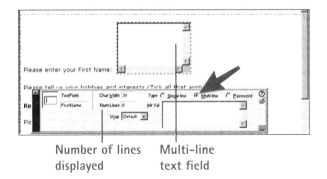

Number of lines displayed

Multi-line text field

4 Change to a Password Field

If you enable the **Password** radio button in the **Properties Inspector**, anything the visitor types in this text field will appear as asterisks when the form is viewed in a browser.

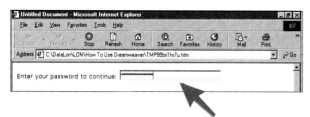

5 Set an Initial Value

The **Init Val** option allows you to specify some text or a message that will appear in the text field when the page is first displayed. The text you specify in this field can act as a prompt for information, as it does in this example. Visitors can select and delete the text before typing in their own response.

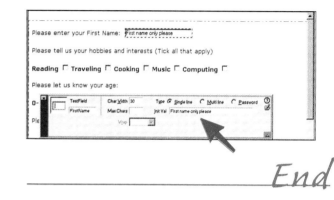

End

How-To Hints

Text Fields Galore

Although this task used only one text field to demonstrate the concept of text fields, your forms can use as many text fields as you like. Most forms have many text fields, each designed to contain specific information such as first name, last name, and the numerous fields typically used to accept different parts of an address. Splitting information in this way makes it much easier to use the information after you receive it.

Looking Good

Don't forget to use the skills you just learned. Not all text fields have to be the same size: If you have only a little space to display the field, make the width smaller—the text will scroll inside the field if it has to.

4

How to Format a Menu or List

Menus and lists have similar physical appearances, so let's first establish the differences between them. A *menu* appears as a drop-down list from which only one option can be selected. A *list* does not have a drop-down arrow and can be set to allow the visitor to select more than one item. Although this task focuses on the creation of a list, you can follow the same steps to create a menu if you first select the **Menu** option in the **Properties Inspector**.

Begin

1 Look at the Properties

Click to select the menu or list element you want to format. The properties of the selected menu are displayed in the **Properties Inspector**. Give the element a unique name by typing in the **Menu/List** box.

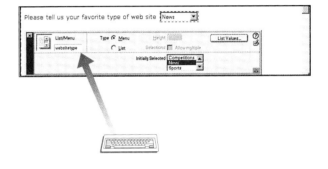

2 Decide on the Type

The two **Type** radio buttons determine whether you are creating a list or a menu. For this task, we create a list. Click the **List** button. As soon as you do, the **Height** and **Selections** options are enabled. You will see no immediate changes to the field onscreen when you click one of these radio buttons; the changes occur onscreen in the next two steps.

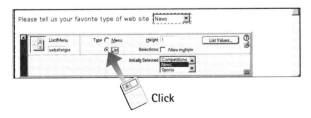

Click

3 Choose Selection Options

Because we are formatting a list, we can decide how many lines will appear in the list box, and we can allow visitors to select more than one option from the list. To specify the number of lines that will appear in the list box, type a number greater than 1 in the **Height** box; to allow visitors to select more than one option from the list, enable the **Allow Multiple** check box. The changes are reflected immediately onscreen: The drop-down arrow disappears, more options become visible, and scrollbars appear at the side of the list.

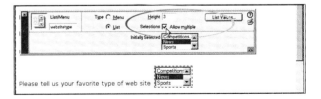

4 Add List Items

Click the **List Values** button to open the **List Values** dialog box. Click in the **Item Label** column and type the text for the first entry in the list. Press **Tab** to move to the **Value** column and type a label for that entry. (This **Value** can be abbreviated but must remain relevant to the **Item Label**.) The entries in the **Item Label** column appear in the list box displayed to the visitor, and the entries in the **Value** column are submitted with the form. If you are gathering the data from the form into a database, make sure that the value you specify here is the type of value your database is expecting to store.

5 Look at the List

You can use the **+** and **–** buttons in the **List Values** dialog box to rearrange the items in the list. When you are done adding items, click **OK** to close the **List Values** dialog box. The list element in the document window reflects the changes you have made. Bascd on the selections made in the **Properties Inspector**, the list element in this example appears with three visible lines and scrollbars you can use to see other items in the list.

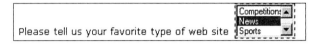

6 Choose a Default List Item

To choose which item in the list is displayed when the page first loads, select that item in the **Initially Selected** list in the **Properties Inspector**. If the user doesn't change this selection, this is the value that will be submitted with the form.

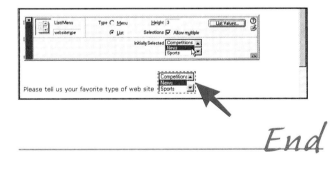

End

How-To Hints

Give the Visitor Instructions

It is not always obvious to site visitors that they can make more than one selection from this type of list. Make sure that your page clearly explains that visitors can make more than one selection and that they can **Shift+click** or **Ctrl+click** to select multiple options.

Not Wide Enough?

When you insert a menu, it automatically resizes to the width of the longest item so that the **Item Labels** you entered are always visible. Unfortunately, when you use a list, this doesn't happen, and the edge of the text disappears. You *can* cheat a little: In the **List Values** dialog box, select the longest item (in terms of characters) and hold down the spacebar until you reach the end of the typing area. Then press the period (.) key. The result is that the list box expands by about three characters, and the end of the text is visible!

How to Format Radio Buttons

Radio buttons are unique among form elements in that they come in groups of which only one at a time can be selected. In Task 2, you learned how to insert radio buttons into a form. In this task, you learn to format radio buttons and group them correctly so that only one can be selected at a time.

Begin

1 Space Out the Radio Buttons

In Task 2, you inserted some radio buttons and text on the form that asked users to input their age range. Spacing out radio buttons in a pleasing arrangement on the form isn't always easy (using the spacebar doesn't spread them out). To insert the spaces you want, position the cursor where you want the space, display the **Invisibles** page of the **Objects** panel, and click **Insert Non-breaking Space** for each space you want to insert.

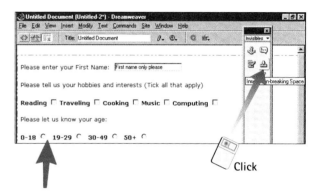

Click

2 Name the Group

Select the first radio button you want to group and open the **Properties Inspector** (choose **Window, Properties** to display it). The **RadioButton** text field must contain the same label for each radio button in the group you are creating.

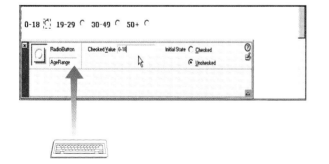

3 Give Each Button a Value

The value of the radio button is submitted with the form. Each button within the group must have a unique value. Select each button and type the value that button represents in the **Checked Value** box in the **Properties Inspector**. Logically, the value you type in this field is the same as the label identifying the button (in this example, the radio button has the label 50+, which is the same as the value in the **Checked Value** field).

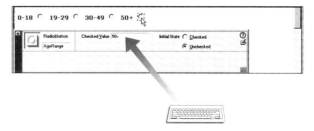

4 Decide on the Default Button

Only one radio button can be selected when the form loads (by default, Dreamweaver loads the form with all the buttons deselected). If you want a particular button to appear selected when the form loads, select that radio button in the form and enable the **Checked** option in the **Properties Inspector**.

0-18 ○ 19-29 ○ 30-49 ● 50+ ○

| RadioButton | Checked Value | 30-49 | Initial State ● Checked |
| AgeRange |

Click

5 Preview and Test the Form

Load the form page into a browser and click the different radio buttons in the group to make sure that only one can be selected at a time. If you can select more than one radio button, go back to Dreamweaver and check that the **RadioButton** text box has *exactly* the same name for each radio button in the group.

Please let us know your age:

0-18 ○   19-29 ○   30-49 ○   50+ ●

Click

End

How-To Hints

Keep It in the Family!

Using radio buttons is an easy way of getting information from your users, but make sure that the options you let them choose from are relevant to each other. For example, if you are asking about a favorite TV program or the type of newspaper they read, include a radio button with the value **Other** because your list might not be complete. It is better to let your users select some option—even if it is not a definite answer—than to frustrate them by forcing them to choose an unsatisfactory option.

How to Use Behaviors with Forms

A behavior can be set up with a form to check that the visitor has entered the right kind of information in each field and to ensure that necessary information has not been missed. This process is called form field validation. The form is checked when the visitor clicks the **Submit** button. If the site visitor attempts to submit a validated form without first entering the correct type of information, an error message displays. The validation fields must then be correctly completed before the form can be submitted successfully.

Begin

1 Select the Form

Suppose that you want to make sure that a text field on your form that asks for an email address is correctly filled out (the response must contain an @ symbol). When you work with behaviors in forms, you must first select the entire form. Click the **<form>** tag at the bottom of the document window to select the entire form.

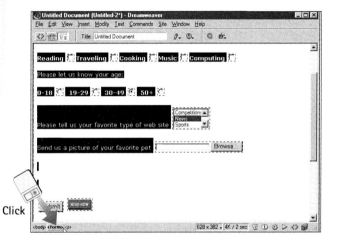

Click

2 Open the Behaviors Panel

Choose **Window, Behaviors** to open the Behaviors panel.

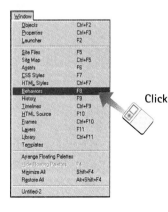

Click

3 Choose Validate

Click the + button on the **Behaviors** panel and choose **Validate Form** from the menu. The **Validate Form** dialog box opens.

Click

4 Pick the Fields to Validate

The **Named Fields** list contains a list of all the named form elements in your form. Click to select the field you want to validate (in this example, it's a text field with the name **Email**). Enable the **Required** check box if you don't want the form to be submitted unless the visitor has typed some information in this field.

Click

5 Make It an Email Field

After you have made the field required, make sure that the form handler looks for the required @ symbol in the response the visitor types into the field. Click the **Email Address** radio button; now the visitor's browser will not submit the form until the text in this field includes an @ symbol.

Click

6 Validate a Telephone Field

Using the same **Validate Form** dialog box, you can validate other form elements. Select the name of the field you want to require the visitor to complete and enable the **Required** check box for that field. For a field that asks the visitor to type a number (such as for a telephone number field), you can make sure that what the visitor types is indeed a number (and not text or other characters) by enabling the **Number** radio button.

Click

How-To Hints

Don't Go Mad with Validation!

It's all well and good to make sure that visitors to your form give you the information you want—but don't force them to tell you too much, or most people will simply ignore the form completely! Don't validate fields that might not be relevant to everyone (not everyone has a cell phone or a fax machine, for example, so don't make these required fields). Validate only the information that is vital to the success of the form.

End

How to Collect Data from a Form

When the visitor to your form clicks the **Submit** button, what happens to the data? To receive results from your form, you need a form handler. A *form handler* is a program (usually a CGI script) that tells the server what to do with the information when the visitor submits the form. The program runs on the server and is not part of an HTML page. If you're not a CGI script programmer (and don't want to learn), you can fortunately download some basic form handlers that will get the form data from the visitor to you.

Begin

1 Check with Your Service Provider

Most Internet service providers supply form-handling scripts that come with instructions on how to use them. Check the home page for your ISP to see what your hosting company says about forms. This figure shows some information about forms from the ISP I use.

2 Download a Form Handler

Although form handlers can be complicated to write, don't worry. Many places on the Internet, including most ISPs, offer free scripts you can download to use with your Dreamweaver forms. You should make sure that your ISP allows you to add these scripts to your server; many ISPs restrict you to using their own scripts. Here you can see a page that offers a free form handler—one of many hundreds out there.

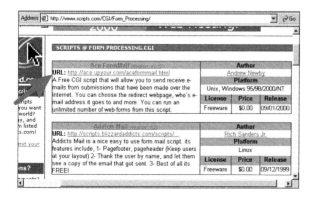

3 Configure the Script

To configure the script to work with your form, start by opening the form in Dreamweaver. Click the **<form>** tag at the bottom of the screen to select the entire form. From the **Method** drop-down menu in the **Properties Inspector**, choose the form method. The form method states what you want the form to do when the **Submit** button is clicked. Typically, you select POST (the documentation that came with your form handler script will clarify what you should select).

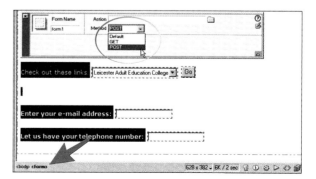

4 Set the Action

When the **Method** field is set to **POST**, the **Action** field typically contains the URL that was supplied with the script to which the form should be sent (usually the location of the handling script). Type this URL in the **Action** field in the **Properties Inspector** so that the form knows where to look for the script.

5 Customize the Form

Normally, you must customize the script to add in the email address which the handling script uses to send the form results back to you. To do this, click **Insert Hidden Fields** from the **Objects** panel and complete these fields with the information required by the script (the documentation that came with your form handler script will specify the information you must include).

This hidden field contains information necessary to the operation of the handling script

End

How-To Hints

Test It Yourself

Make sure that you follow the instructions that came with your form-handling script. Otherwise, you might never see results from your form and might think that no one is filling it out. Test your form fully before you tell others it even exists.

Capitalization Is Important

When you add hidden fields that contain email addresses and specify URLs in the **Action** field of the **Properties Inspector**, make sure that you use uppercase and lowercase letters very carefully. If you mistype one letter, your form probably won't work.

Form Buttons

Every form must have a **Submit** button that the user can click to send the contents of the form to you. By default, clicking **Insert Button** on the **Objects** panel inserts a **Submit** button. You may want your form to contain a **Reset Form** button that the user can click to clear the form and start again. Insert a second button and use the **Properties Inspector** to format the button accordingly.

Task

Reusing Information

*M*ost likely, you are coming to appreciate that Dreamweaver is a wonderful application. As you work to develop meaningful information for your Web sites, you'll appreciate that Dreamweaver lets you use that information more than once. Dreamweaver 4 makes reusing information even easier than ever before with the introduction of the **Assets** panel.

The **Assets** panel allows you to organize and display all the different elements in your site. You can drag images, URLs, colors, and other elements contained by your site from the **Assets** panel directly onto the page where you are working. This resource center complements the existing libraries and templates and will benefit both new and experienced users.

In Dreamweaver, *assets* refer to all the elements that make up a Web site. Images, movies, and animations are all assets of your site, as are the colors and URLs that you used in your site's creation. Dreamweaver stores all the element information in the **Assets** panel, giving you a single resource for locating and reusing them in your site.

By using the site cache feature, Dreamweaver knows where all the files are within your site. They are categorized based on either the HTML code (in the case of a URL or color) or the file extension (such as `.gif`) in order to know which category to place the asset in.

Templates and libraries make reusing information a simple and straightforward process. The library facility is ideal for reusing single images, tables, or layers that you want to use in more than one page but only want to create once. Templates allow you to create a complete page layout and use it for as many pages as you want, with a minimum of fuss.

All the Dreamweaver elements discussed in the following tasks are designed to make your life easier when creating both single pages and multiple-page sites. ●

How to Use the Assets Panel

When the **Assets** panel is open, it appears on top of the document on which you are currently working. The panel displays different categories of elements included in your site: images, URLs, colors, and so on. You can display elements in the different categories independently (for example, you can show a list of all the images you have used in your site). Being able to arrange and display the elements used by your Web site is the first step in reusing that information.

Begin

1 Show the Assets Panel

If the **Assets** panel is not already visible, choose **Window, Assets** to display it. Alternatively, click the **Assets** button in the **Launcher**.

Click

2 Create a Cache

For the **Assets** panel to work, you must have the site cache enabled. If it has not been enabled, Dreamweaver prompts you to refresh the local files before the assets can be displayed. Click OK to continue and see the assets for the site.

Click

3 Refresh the Site Catalog

After you have opened the **Assets** panel, it is a good idea to refresh its contents. When you make changes to your site (deleting an image for example), Dreamweaver doesn't automatically update the elements displayed in the **Assets** panel. To do that, you must choose **Refresh Site List** from the **Assets** panel menu or click the **Refresh Site List** button at the bottom of the panel.

Click

4 Look at the Category Types

Dreamweaver defines assets as the different elements that make up the site. Images, movies, and so on are all assets. The **Assets** panel categorizes all the assets for your site by type: Each category has an icon to identify it. The type icons are displayed on the right side of the **Assets** panel. Click an icon to display assets in that category.

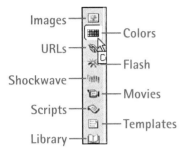

Images — Colors
URLs — Flash
Shockwave — Movies
Scripts — Templates
Library

5 Show Assets in a Category

To see the assets in your site for any of the categories, click the appropriate category icon. You can reorganize the list alphabetically by name or according to size, file type, or value. Click the **Images** category icon and then click the **Type** heading to reorganize the list according to image types. To preview an asset, select it and look in the preview pane at the top of the **Assets** panel.

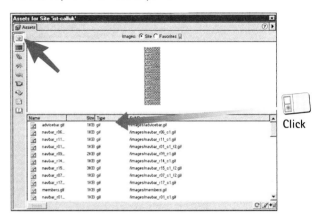

Click

6 Find an Asset You Have Used

Dreamweaver can display a particular asset in the **Site** Files window, showing you which folder contains the asset file. Right-click (**Ctrl+click** on a Macintosh) the asset name in the **Assets** panel to display the context menu. Choose **Locate in Site** from the menu to open the **Site** window and highlight the selected asset file. Note that this feature does not find a file containing the asset.

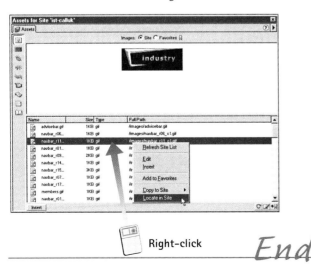

Right-click

End

How-To Hints

Can't Find Colors?

You cannot use the **Locate in Site** option to find either colors or Web site addresses. These items are simply HTML references and do not exist as objects in their own right.

Embedded or Linked?

When you insert an image into a Web page, it is *embedded* into the page. The HTML code tells you the name and source of the file, which is then called into your page from that location. Updating or modifying the image changes the page without your having to re-edit or save the page at all.

Linked assets, on the other hand, are Library items and templates. This means that the completed page shows the actual contents of the asset rather than calling it in by a reference.

How to Use Assets

After you create them, you can use assets in as many different sites as you want. To use the current site's assets in another site, you just copy them to the other site. (Of course, the other site must be defined already.) Inserting assets into your current document is as easy as selecting them from the **Assets** panel and clicking to insert them.

2 Copy Multiple Assets

To select a series of assets to copy to another site, click to select the first asset and then press and hold the **Shift** key as you click other contiguous entries. (Press and hold the **Ctrl** key as you click to select separate entries; Macintosh users have just the **Shift** key option.) Right-click any of the selected entries and choose **Copy to Site** from the context menu. Then select the site to which you want to copy the selected assets.

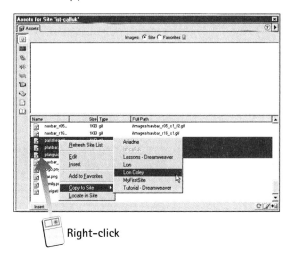

Right-click

Begin

1 Copy an Asset to Another Site

If an asset exists in the current site that you want to use in another site, you can copy that asset to the other site. In the **Assets** panel, select the asset you want to use in the other site and right-click it (**Ctrl+click** on a Macintosh) to open the context menu. Choose **Copy to Site** and then choose the site to which you want to copy the asset from the submenu that appears.

Right-click

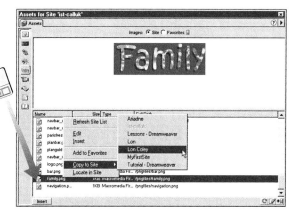

3 Choose an Asset to Insert

To insert an asset on the current page, first click to position the insertion point in the document window. In the **Assets** panel, click the icon for the category of the asset you want to use. Select the asset you want to insert and preview it in the window at the top of the panel.

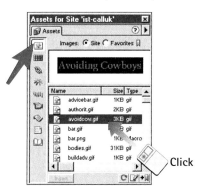

Click

4 Insert the Asset

Click the **Insert** button at the bottom of the **Assets** panel. The selected asset appears in the document window at the insertion point.

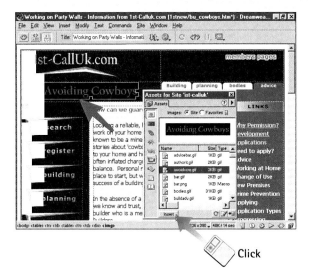

Click

5 Choose a Template

You can use a *template* to format an entire page. In this example, we will apply a template to a new blank page. (You learn more about templates later in this part.) Click the **Templates** category icon in the **Assets** panel and choose the template you want to use for the current document. Click **Apply** to change the formatting of the current page.

Click

6 Apply a Color to Text

Your site's assets include all the colors you have already used in your site. You can apply these colors to text and other elements on the page. In the document window, select the text for which you want to change the color. In the **Assets** panel, click the **Colors** category icon, select the desired color from the list, and click **Apply**.

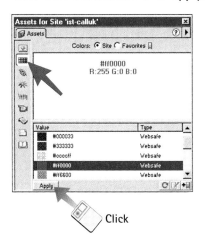

Click

7 Insert a Link

Your site's assets include all the hyperlinks within the current site. This includes internal, external, and mailto: hyperlinks. In the document window, select the text or image you want to use as a link. In the **Assets** panel, click the **URL Link** category icon and then choose the URL to which you want to link. Click **Apply** to add this link to the selected text or image.

Click

End

How to Reuse Favorite Assets

Some of the assets you create for your site might be things you'll reuse. You can save some of your favorite assets into a special group so that they're easy to locate and use. Each category in the **Assets** panel can be further divided into lists of **Site** assets and **Favorites.** (The radio buttons at the top of the panel determine which list you are viewing.) You can even give your favorite assets nicknames to make sure that you can find them.

Begin

1 Choose the Asset

In the **Assets** panel, click the category icon and select the asset you want to save as a favorite.

Click

2 Add to Favorites

Click the **Add to Favorites** button in the bottom-right corner of the panel. The selected asset is saved into your **Favorites** list for the current category. A message is displayed to confirm the entry.

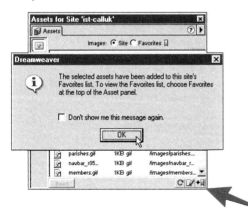

3 Look at the Favorites

The message box that Dreamweaver displays tells you to switch to **Favorites** view to see the favorites for the category you are in. Click **OK** to continue and see the **Favorites** view.

Click

4 Switch Between Views

You can view the assets in a category in one of two ways: **Site** view (shows all the assets in the selected category for the entire site) or **Favorites** view (shows only the assets for the selected category you have specifically identified as favorites, as described in Steps 1 and 2). To switch between views, click the radio button at the top of the **Assets** panel for the view you want.

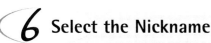

5 Give a Favorite Asset a Nickname

By default, Dreamweaver displays your assets according to their filenames. In **Favorites** view, each asset has a nickname—which by default is the filename minus the file extension. You can change this nickname to anything you want without affecting the actual filename. Click the **Favorites** radio button to switch to **Favorites** view, choose the icon for the category you want to work with, right-click the asset you want to rename to open the context menu, and choose **Edit Nickname**.

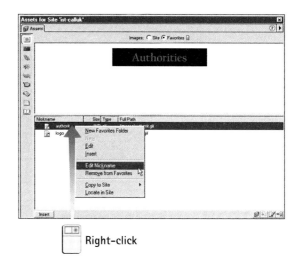

Right-click

6 Select the Nickname

Type the new nickname you want to give this asset and press **Enter**. The nickname appears in the **Nickname** column of the **Assets** panel.

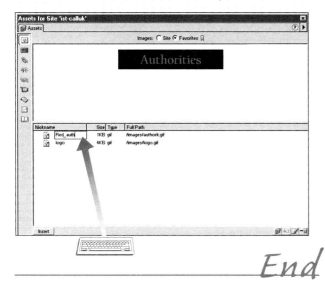

End

How-To Hints

Deleting Assets Is Easy

In previous tasks, we have looked at what assets are and how to create them. In most cases, you cannot delete assets because they are part of your site. You can, however, delete those assets that you specifically create (that is, library items and templates). Simply select the item you want to delete in the **Assets** panel and click the trash can icon at the bottom of the panel. The asset is removed—but any page already created using that asset is left intact.

How to Manage Favorite Assets

It's easy to manage the lists of favorite assets presented in the **Assets** panel. You can add and remove assets to and from the favorites categories. Managing your assets makes managing the whole site a lot easier and is a good habit to get into from the start.

Begin

1 Create a Group

You can create subgroups within the **Favorites** view for any category. For example, if your list of favorite images is getting too long or has files from different parts of your site, you can divide the list into smaller groups. To create a new group for your favorites in a particular category, switch to **Favorites** view by clicking the **Favorites** radio button.

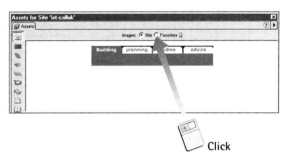

Click

2 Create a New Favorites Group

Click the **New Favorites Group** button at the bottom of the panel. A new folder icon is added; its text box is selected and ready for you to name the folder. Type a name for this folder and press the **Enter** key. Notice that the folder icon remains next to the text, telling you that this is a folder and not an individual asset.

Click

3 Add Assets to the Group

Select the assets you want to add to the new group and drag them into the group you created in Step 2. You can drag the assets individually, or select multiple assets using **Shift+click** or **Ctrl+Click**.

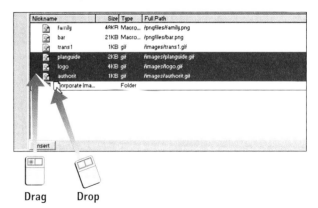

Drag   Drop

4 Remove an Asset from the Favorites

If you want to remove an asset from your **Favorites** list—or from a group you have created—first select the asset you want to remove. Second, click the **Remove from Favorites** button at the bottom of the panel. The asset is removed from your **Favorites** list but can still be found in the **Site** list for that category.

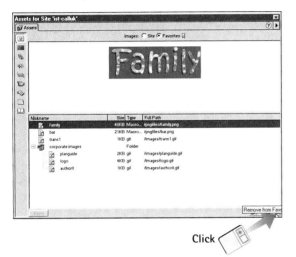

Click

5 Create a New Favorite Color

Whenever you use a color in your site, it becomes part of the assets for the site. Although you cannot add unused colors to the normal view of the **Assets** panel, you can in **Favorites** view. To add colors to your list of favorites for the site, click the **Colors** category icon and then click the **New Color** button at the bottom of the panel. Use the color picker that opens to choose a new color to add to your list of favorite colors.

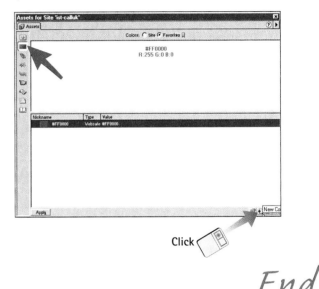

Click

End

How-To Hints

View Differences

One of the advantages of the **Favorites** view is that you can add certain elements to the list that you have not yet used in your site (such as library items, templates, colors, and URLs). You can do this only in **Favorites** view because the **Site** view is created from the cache and contains only those elements that Dreamweaver finds in your directories.

How to Use the Library

The **Library** stores elements from your Web pages (text, images, tables, or forms) that you are likely to reuse in your site. If, after you have inserted a library item onto several pages in your site, you then edit and save the original library item, all the pages that contain the library item are automatically updated. If you just used the **Assets** panel to insert an item onto your pages, you'd have to update each instance of the item when it changed. The **Library** makes the process of keeping your site up to date much simpler.

Begin

1 Select the Element to Add

In the main document window, select the page element that you want to use as a library item. In this example, I selected an image to save to the **Library**.

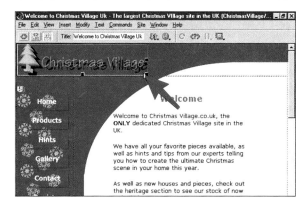

2 Open the Library

Choose **Window, Assets** to display the **Assets** panel if it isn't already onscreen. Click the **Library** category icon to open the **Library**.

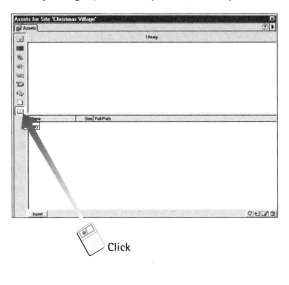

Click

3 Add the Library Item

Drag the selected element from the document window and drop it into the **Library** window. To give the element a useful name in the **Library**. right-click the entry in the **Library** list, choose **Rename** from the context menu, and type a new name for the library item.

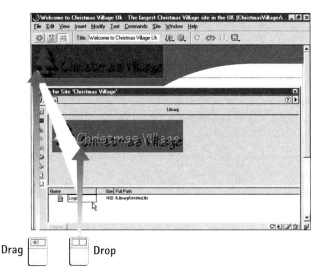

Drag   Drop

4 Choose the Location for a Library Item

When you add a library item to your page, Dreamweaver records a reference to the original library file so that it can update the item on the page if the original item is changed. To insert a library item on the page, click in the document window to position the insertion point where you want the item to appear.

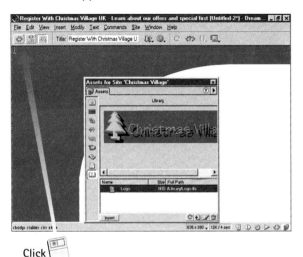

Click

5 Insert the Library Item

In the **Assets** panel, click the **Library** icon to open the **Library**. From the list of items in the **Library**, click to select the one that you want to insert. Click the **Insert** button at the bottom of the panel to place the selected item in the current document.

Click

Continues

How-To Hints

Visibility and Colors

When you use library items in your pages, Dreamweaver can highlight them on the page for you. Choose **View, Invisible Elements** to turn on this feature.

You can change the highlight color Dreamweaver uses to show the library items by opening the **Preferences** dialog box. Choose **Edit, Preferences** to open the dialog box. In the **Highlighting Options** section of the dialog box, use the color picker to select the color you want Dreamweaver to use to highlight your library items.

6 Rename a Library Item

You can rename any item in the **Library**. Select the item you want to rename by clicking it, wait a moment, and click the item a second time. (Note that this is *not* a double-click.) The name is surrounded by a box, indicating that you can edit it. Type a new name for the library item and press **Enter** (or click away from the panel). The new name is accepted.

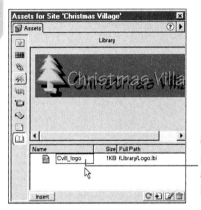

Click, wait a moment, and click again to edit the item's name

7 Select a Library Item to Edit

You can edit any library item whenever you choose. To open the item in a window appropriate for editing, simply double-click the item in the **Library**. Alternatively, right-click the item in the **Library** and choose an edit option. The item opens on a blank screen as an **.lbi** file. From this screen, you can either edit the item as an **.lbi** file (if it is text or a table) or choose how to edit the image file: Right-click the item to open the context menu. If the item was originally created with Fireworks, you can select the **Edit with Fireworks 4** option. If the element was created with some other application, choose **Edit With**. From the submenu that opens, choose the application you want to use to edit the element.

Right-click

8 Edit a Library Item

In this example, we see the file from the previous step opened in Fireworks 4, ready to be edited. Make changes to the file using all the editing powers of the application you have invoked.

9 Save the Changes

When you have finished editing the library item, save the changes you have made. To update all documents that use the library item, right-click the item in the **Library** and choose **Update Site** from the context menu. If you want to update only the file you are currently working on, select **Update Current Page**.

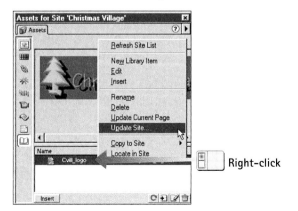

Right-click

10 Delete an Item from the Library

You can remove an item from the **Library** at any time. Note that deleting the item from the **Library** does not remove the element from any page on which you have inserted it. In the **Library** category of the **Assets** panel, choose the item you want to delete and right-click it (**Ctrl+click** on a Macintosh) to open the context menu. Choose **Delete** from the context menu.

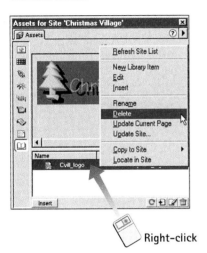

Right-click

11 Are You Sure?

Dreamweaver prompts you to confirm that you want to delete this item. Click **Yes** to delete the item from the **Library**.

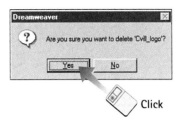

Click

End

How-To Hints

Still There?

After you delete a library item from the **Assets** panel, you will not be able to insert it from the **Library** again. However, all pages that use the item are unaffected by the removal of the entry from the **Library**. Removing an item from the **Library** does not delete that item from your existing pages.

How to Create a Template

Templates are great tools when you want a number of pages to have the same look and feel without having to create the same content over and over again. You can create a template from scratch or save an existing page as a template. A template file has the extension **.dwt**. When you create a template, you specify locked regions (areas that will remain static) and editable regions (areas that will change from page to page). When you create a new page from a template, you can alter only the content marked as editable. If you edit the actual template file, you can change anything you want. When you change the underlying template, you can update all the pages you created from that template in one easy step.

Begin

1 Create a New Template

If it isn't onscreen already, display the **Assets** panel by clicking the **Assets** button in the **Launcher**. Click the **Templates** category icon to see a list of all the templates in your site. (Your list will probably be empty if this is your first time working with templates.) Click the **New Template** button at the bottom of the panel.

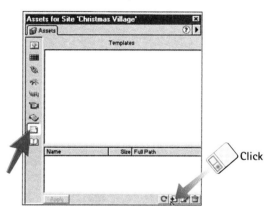

Click

2 Name the Template

The new template appears in the panel. While it is still selected, type a meaningful name for this new template.

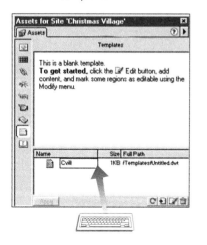

3 Open the Template to Add Content

In the **Assets** panel, double-click the template you just created. The **.dwt** file opens so that you can add content to it. Initially, the page is completely blank.

④ Add Content to Be Locked

Create the page as you would any other page, inserting a background, navigation bar, and so on. At this stage, add only the content that you want to be the same on all pages; leave the other areas of the page blank.

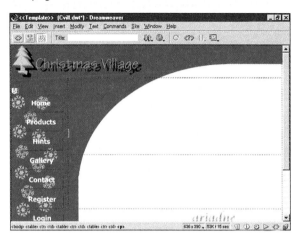

⑤ Add Editable Content

Complete the page by adding content or placeholders that will be changed on each page using the template. These areas will become the editable regions. For now, the text and images you insert here can be anything at all; they are merely placeholders. In this example, I have added a title image and some irrelevant text.

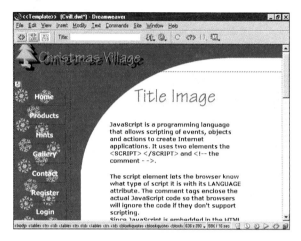

⑥ Create Editable Regions

Decide which areas of the template page will be editable. (In this example, these areas are the title image and the text.) Select the first editable region and choose **Modify, Templates, New Editable Region** to open the **New Editable Region** dialog box.

Click

Continues

7 Name the Editable Region

In the dialog box, type a name that will identify this particular region. In this example, I made the title image the editable region, so I have assigned it the name *Title Image*. Click **OK** to continue.

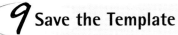

Click

8 Create and Name the Other Regions

Repeat Step 7 to identify all other editable regions in the template. Each editable region is outlined in blue on the page, and its name appears as a title tag.

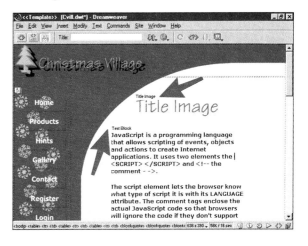

9 Save the Template

Choose **File, Save** to save the file with the editable regions in place. Give a meaningful name to the template file.

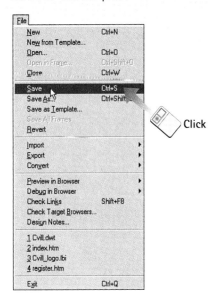

Click

10 Use the Template

To use the template as the basis for a new page in your site, choose **File, New from Template**. The **Select Template** dialog box opens. Choose the template you want to use to create the new page and click **Select**. Leave the **Update Page when Template Changes** check box enabled to ensure that if you edit the template, your page will reflect the changes.

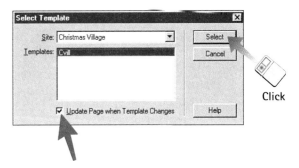

Click

11 Add the Real Content

When the new page opens, it looks exactly as the template did when you saved it. The new page file is called **untitled-***, and has a black bar with the template name visible in the upper-right corner of the page. Notice that you can change only the regions marked as editable; the rest of the page is locked. When the page is complete, save it as you normally would, remembering to add a page title.

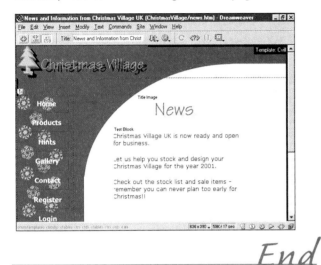

End

How-To Hints

Using Existing Pages as Templates

If you have a page or pages with the main content in place, you can save these pages as templates without affecting the original page at all. Simply follow Steps 6 and 7 of this task to create the editable regions and then choose **File, Save As Template** to save the file as a template into the current (or any other) site. The file will then appear in your list of templates, and you can use it to create new pages as described in Steps 10 and 11.

Setting Preferences

You can use the **Preferences** dialog box to change the way Dreamweaver highlights the editable regions on your templates. These editable regions are visible only in Dreamweaver and are highlighted to make them obvious to you when you are working. They are not visible to site visitors when the page is saved as an HTML file.

Choose **Edit, Preferences** to open the **Preferences** dialog box. In the **Highlighting** area, choose **Editable Regions.** Use the color picker to set the color you want Dreamweaver to use to highlight the editable regions on your templates.

How to Edit a Template

When you create a page based on a template, you can change only the editable regions. If you want to change any other areas of the page, you have to edit the template itself. Doing this allows you to remove and add editable regions as well as to change static areas if that is what you want to do. When you create a new page from a template, Dreamweaver provides the **Update Page when Template Changes** option. If this option was enabled when you created the page, the changes you make to the template (a new background, navigation buttons, and so on) are all transferred into the existing pages.

Begin

1 Open the Template

Open the **Assets** panel and click the **Templates** category icon to see a list of all the templates for your site. Locate the template you want to edit and double-click it to open the template into a new document window with the **.dwt** filename visible in the title bar.

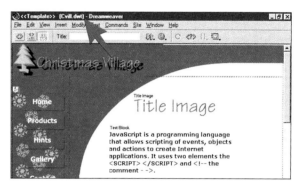

2 Select Existing Page Content

Select the text or other page element you want to make editable. In this example, I added a new image that I want to appear on all pages. (We will make this image an editable area in the next step.) Place the insertion point where you want the new page element to appear and insert it in the normal way.

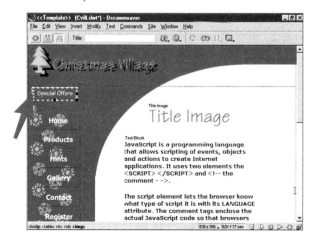

3 Make a New Editable Region

Choose **Modify, Templates, New Editable Region** to open the **New Editable Region** dialog box. In the **Name** field, type a name for this new editable region. Note that every editable region you create must have a unique name. Click **OK** to name the region. When working on a template, you can create new editable regions anywhere on the page. In this example, I made the picture we just added an editable region so that I can change or delete this image on pages created from the template.

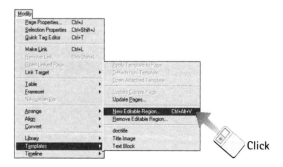

Click

4 Identify the Region

The new editable region should be highlighted onscreen. If you do not see the highlighted area, make sure that the **Invisible Elements** option is enabled. (Choose **View, Visual Aids, Invisible Elements** to turn on this feature.)

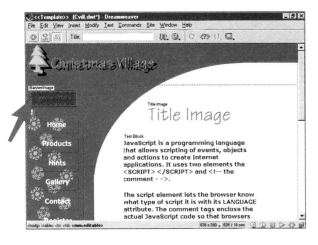

5 Delete an Editable Region

Removing an editable region from a template is as easy as creating one. When you remove an editable region from the template, that part of the page becomes "locked," and you will not be able to change that content on pages based on this template. Select the editable region you want to remove by clicking once on the name tag for the region. Then choose **Modify, Templates, Remove Editable Region** to open a dialog box.

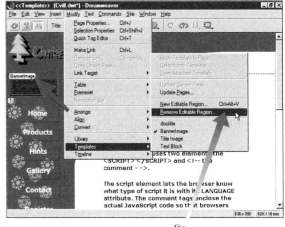

Click

6 Select the Region to Remove

In the **Remove Editable Region** dialog box, select the editable region you want to remove from the list and click **OK**. The content previously marked as editable is still present on the page, but it can no longer be edited on pages based on this template.

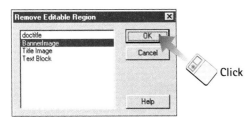

Click

7 Save the Template

Choose **File, Save** to save the template with the changes you have made. You are prompted to update all pages based on the template. You can choose either **Update** or **Don't Update**. Choosing **Update** changes all the pages you have already created using this template so that they all reflect the changes you just made.

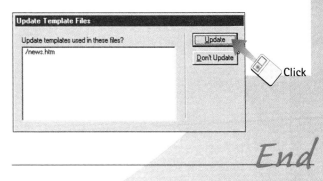

Click

End

How to Manage Templates

As you have seen, creating a template is not difficult; all you do is create the bare bones of a page. This task explains how to apply the templates you have created and use them to create document pages for your Web site. You can use a template to create a brand-new page (just start typing and inserting images into the already created editable regions, or you can use a template to reformat an existing page. Applying a template to an existing page does have inherent risks and can produce some strange results until you fully understand the options.

1 Create a New Document from a Template

The easiest way to use a template is to start building pages from scratch with it. To create a new page from an existing template, choose **File, New from Template** to open the **Select Template** dialog box.

2 Choose the Template

The **Select Template** dialog box lists all the templates available in the current site. Select which of your existing templates that you want to use to create the new document and then click the **Select** button. The template opens as an untitled, unsaved page into a new document window. You can change and insert text and images into any of the editable regions of the template. Notice that the rest of the page is locked.

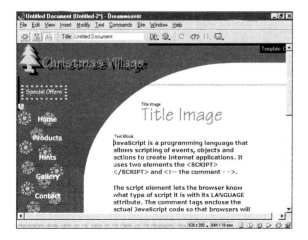

3 Apply a Template to an Existing Document

In addition to creating a document from a template, you can apply a template to a document that you have already started to create. This is not the ideal way to use templates, and it can be tricky to get it right. Open the document to which you would like to apply a template. In this example, I have opened a page with a little text, a background, and a logo. Notice that there is no navigation bar on the page.

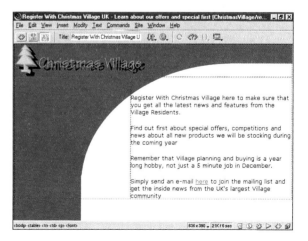

4 Apply the Template

Choose **Modify, Templates, Apply Template to Page** to open the **Select Template** dialog box.

Select Template	×
Site: Christmas Village ▼	Select
Templates: Cvill	Cancel
☑ Update Page when Template Changes	Help

5 Choose a Template

From the list of templates, choose the template you want to apply to the open document. Click **Select** to continue. The **Choose Editable Region for Orphaned Content** dialog box opens.

Choose Editable Region for Orphaned Content	×
Some of the content in this document doesn't have a place to go in the new template. Please select an editable region to receive this content, or choose (none) if it is ok to throw this content away.	OK
	Cancel
(none)	
Title Image	
Text Block	Help

6 Decide What to Do with Current Content

This is where things get a little complicated! Dreamweaver knows that you already have content on the page and that you have to decide what to do with it. Select **(none)** to delete the existing content completely and apply the template with its placeholder. Choose one of the named editable regions to place the entire contents of the current page into the chosen region. In this example, I placed the existing content in the **Text Block** region.

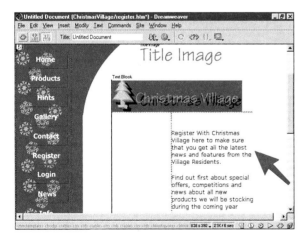

7 Edit as Required

The result from the previous step might not be what you expected, but it is still better than having to retype the content you wanted to use. In this example, I fixed up the page by deleting the duplicate logo and the unnecessary table cells, leaving the template elements in place along with the content I wanted to keep.

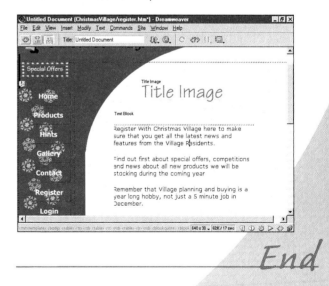

End

Task

Dreamweaver and Beyond

*B*y now you should have a reasonable understanding of Dreamweaver as well as a Web site that is ready for public consumption. In this part, you will learn how to transfer files from your computer onto the Internet. When the files are uploaded, it's time to move on, learning more about Dreamweaver and how it can help you develop and maintain your Web site.

All the built-in functionality is within your control, from working with the different views available and changing them, to moving panels, to adding items to the **Launcher**, and all the other topics we have covered so far in this book.

Dreamweaver also allows you to manipulate the generated HTML code, enabling you to change the colors of different sections of the code, and even get add-ons for the software from the Macromedia Web site. The new Reference feature allows you to view the information for a specific tag or to scroll through a complete alphabetical list and choose the tags about which you want more information.

The tasks in this part of the book show you how to make the code that Dreamweaver creates for your Web pages look the way you want it to when you view it onscreen. You also learn how to assign editors to nonHTML documents that you might want to open in Dreamweaver, and how to download and install new behaviors, or *extensions*, from the Macromedia Web site. This book proves that you don't have to be an HTML programmer to make great Web pages, but you will have seen references to code view throughout the book when I felt that looking at the code could be important. Learning a little about the code will help you understand what is happening in your pages and prepare you for the time when you decide that you want to manipulate the code on your own.

How to Upload Files

After you have fine-tuned all the pages for your Web site on your local computer, you must upload the files to the remote server so that they are accessible to others on the Internet. Initially, you will probably up-load all the files for your site; later you will want to upload selected files to update the site. Although it is not a requirement, I recommend that you save and close any open files to ensure that the files you upload are as complete as possible. Dreamweaver identifies dependant files—that is, files required to make the HTML page complete. If Dreamweaver detects that you are uploading a page with dependant files, it asks whether you want to upload these files as well. If you are uploading the site for the first time, you should upload all the dependent files also. However, if you have changed only the text in an HTML page and nothing else, you do not have to upload the depen-dant files. If you have edited an actual image file within the page, you must upload both the image file and the HTML page file.

2 Select the Remote Directory

If the connection does not automatically show the remote folder in which you want to put the files you're uploading, double-click the folder icon in the **Remote Site** pane to select the desired folder.

Double-click

Begin

1 Show the Site Window

Open the Site window by choosing **Window, Site Files**. In the toolbar, click the **Connect to Remote Host** button. (Note that you should be connected to the Internet before attempting to connect to the remote host.)

Click

3 Select the Files to Upload

In the **Local Folder** pane, select the files and directories you want to upload to the remote server. To select multiple files, press and hold the **Shift** key as you click. Click the **Put File(s)** button on the toolbar to begin the process of uploading the files. As the files are being transferred, the status bar shows the progress. For each file being transferred, the status bar indicates the filename, file size, and percent com-plete. Dreamweaver continues uploading all the select-ed files until all your pages are live on the Internet.

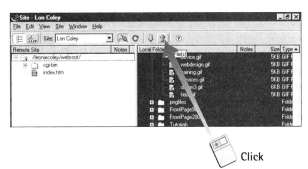

Click

4 Open the Home Page

After all your hard work, now is the moment of truth. Open your home page live on the Internet and check to make sure that it exists! You should know your home page address, so type it into the address bar in your browser and wait for your page to appear.

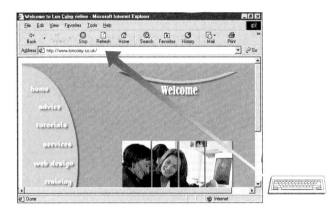

5 View the Page in Another Browser

Open the home page in a second browser and compare it with the page you saw in Step 4. Hopefully, the page will look the same in both browsers. If not, identify the problem, think about the page content, and determine what could cause the differences. Review earlier tasks in this book to determine how to correct these browser issues.

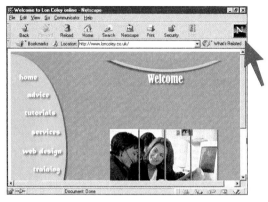

6 Check for Errors

Work through all the pages in your site and make sure that any Alt text you specified for your images appears when appropriate. (Here you see the text before the image itself appears on the page.) Make sure that there are no spelling mistakes in the Alt text (or elsewhere on the page). Check that all the pages have an appropriate title in the title bar. Check all the external links in your site, taking note of any that cannot be found—and more importantly, why. You simply might have mistyped the URL when you created the link, or the site itself might have moved. In either case, you'll have to edit the links.

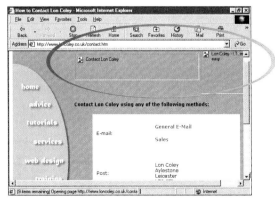

How-To Hints

Browser Compatibility

The Dreamweaver **File, Check Target Browsers** command can check your entire site against a list of browsers you specify. Regardless of any problems it finds, your documents remain intact, leaving the decision of what to do about these problems firmly in your hands. Note that this command does not check any scripts you might have included in your site. The results of this command are displayed in a new window; the pages listed are hyperlinks. Click any page name to see a detailed report about the errors found on that page.

If the errors relate only to older browsers, you might decide that those errors will not affect enough of your site visitors to be a real problem. However, if the problems appear in reports for newer browsers, you probably should address the issue and make appropriate changes to your files.

Continues

7 Update Files

If you have found errors on the pages you've uploaded to the Internet—or if you simply want to change the content of a page in your site—it's easy enough to edit the page. Open your local copy of the page, refer to tasks earlier in this book for information about editing files, edit the file to include the changes, and then save the file again.

8 Open the Site Window

Open the **Site** window for your local site and view the site files. Make sure that you can see the dates and times in the **Modified** column. Notice that the time at which you modified the files in Step 7 is later than the date and time at which you uploaded the files to the remote server in Step 3.

9 Connect to the Remote Server

Make sure that you have an Internet connection and click the **Connect to Remote Server** button. Now you can view the remote files as well as your local files. Here you can see that the modified time for some of the local files is later than for some of the remote files (indicating that the files have changed, or been updated, on the local computer). It is only these newer files that you will want to upload to the remote site.

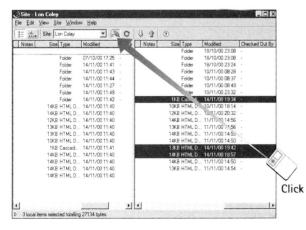

Click

10 Select Synchronize

Choose **Site, Synchronize** to open the **Synchronize Files** dialog box. Use the options in the dialog box to specify whether you want to synchronize the entire site or simply selected files. In this example, I choose to synchronize the entire site because I made a lot of changes to files in different folders. If you have changed only a few pages, you can select to synchronize only certain files or folders.

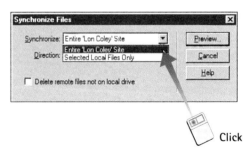

Click

11 Choose the Synchronize Direction

Use the **Direction** drop-down menu to choose which way you are going to synchronize the files. You can choose to **put** newer files onto the remote server (that is, you will upload your changed files from your local computer to the remote site). If someone else has edited files and placed the newer files on the remote server, you can **get** the files from the remote server (that is you will download files from the server to your local computer). In this example, I choose to put the newer files on my local computer onto the remote server. The third option, **Get and Put newer files**, sends and gets the newer files in both directions; it is rarely used when an individual is creating the site.

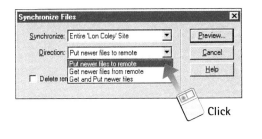

Click

12 Preview the Synchronization

Click the **Preview** button in the **Synchronize** dialog box to tell Dreamweaver to check the files on the local system against files on the remote server. When the check is completed, a **Synchronize** preview screen displays a list of files that are newer on the local server. Enable the check box next to the files you want to upload and click **OK** to start the synchronization process.

Click

End

How-To Hints

Get a Synchronize Log

When the synchronization process is complete, Dreamweaver displays a dialog box telling you so. Click the **Save Log** button to save a log file that contains a list of the files that were synchronized. Click **Close** to close the dialog box without saving a log.

Using Check In/Out and Design Notes

The **Check In/Out** feature is helpful in an environment where more than one person is working on a site. When you are working on a particular file, you "check the file out"—which means that nobody else can open or edit the file until you check it back in again. You must set up the options for Check In/Out before you can actually implement the feature. To access the options, start in the **Site** window and choose **Site, Define Site** and then select the site you are working on. Click **Edit** to open the **Site Definition** dialog box. From the **Category** list, select **Remote Info** and enable the **Check In/Out** check box.

Design Notes are optional files saved with your Web pages. Design Notes can contain information such as a few words that act as a self-reminder, a complete Web site plan, or instructions for another team member to follow. Design Notes can also be integrated with Flash and Fireworks, making your site information easily accessible to other team members. Open the **Site Definition** dialog box and select **Design Notes** from the **Category** list. Enable the **Maintain Design Notes** check box and click **OK**. Now open a file in the document window and choose **File, Design Notes** to open the **Design Notes** dialog box. Fill out the information and click **OK** to save the notes with the file.

How to Change the Code Layout

This latest version of Dreamweaver has made it easier than ever before to check the HTML code and work with it as you create your pages. You can even work in a split-screen environment so that you can see the design and code at the same time. Keeping an eye on the code might not seem important to start with, but the more code you learn, the greater your understanding will be. Let Dreamweaver's built-in facilities help as you go.

Begin

1 Open the Page in Code and Design View

Open Dreamweaver and open one of your pages. With the page open in the document window, click the **Show Code and Design Views** button on the toolbar.

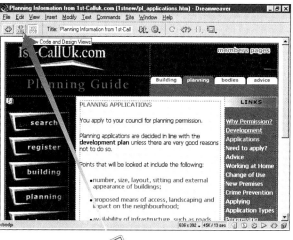

Click

2 Adjust the Split Screen

By default, the screen splits in half, with the design at the top and the code at the bottom. Click and drag the middle bar up or down to change the screen division to suit your needs.

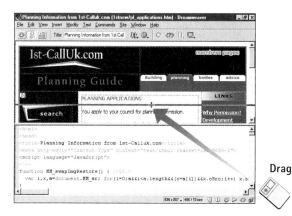

Drag

3 Open the Options for Code View

Click the **Options** button on the toolbar. The **Options** menu that appears lists several handy features you can use to arrange the code the way you want it.

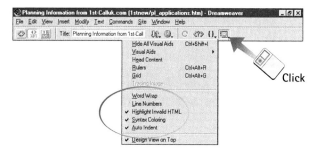

Click

4 Set the Code to Wrap

If the option is not already selected, choose **Word Wrap** from the **Options** button menu to ensure that the code is visible at all times without the annoyance of a horizontal scrollbar.

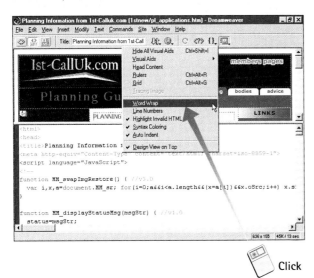

Click

5 Show the Line Numbers

Choose **Line Numbers** from the **Options** button menu to show the line numbers in the code view. This is a great feature when you're trying to deal with problem scripts that always refer back to a line number. The numbers appear on the left edge of the code window.

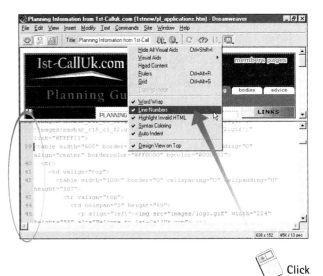

Click

6 Swap the Windows

By default, the design window appears at the top of the split screen; the **Design View on Top** option is enabled in the button menu. If you want, you can work with the design window at the bottom of the screen and the code window at the top. Choose **Design View on Top** from the **Options** button menu to disable the option; the windows are rearranged. Notice that if you do this, the menu also changes to position the code view options at the top of the list of menu options.

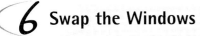

Click

7 Set Syntax Coloring

By default, the **Syntax Coloring** option should be selected. Syntax Coloring highlights the tags and code in different colors to enable you to distinguish between them more easily. If this option is not already enabled, select it now.

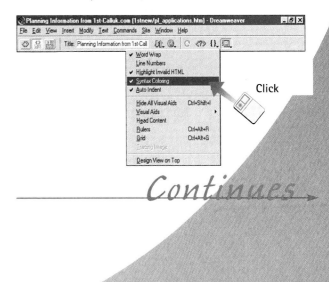

Click

Continues

8 Check for Invalid HTML

As I have mentioned before, Dreamweaver does not change any HTML that you have written in the code editor, which makes the **Highlight Invalid HTML** option such a bonus. If you enable this option in the **Options** button menu, Dreamweaver will highlight any invalid HTML that you type without actually changing it.

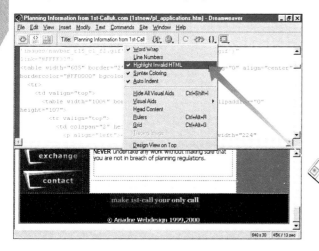

9 Change the Colors

You can change the colors used for different parts of the code with the **Preferences** dialog box. Choose **Edit, Preferences** to open the **Preferences** dialog box. From the **Category** list, choose **Code Colors**, and then select colors for each of the code elements presented.

Click

10 Select an Option to Change

By selecting the colors you want for the various options, you can quickly and easily see different page elements within the code. Use the color pickers to change the color coding for different tags and text in the code view. Click **OK** to close the dialog box when you have made your changes. Your color choices are immediately reflected in the code on the screen.

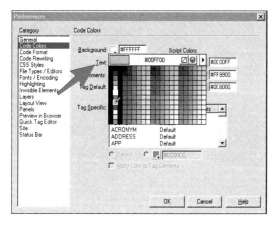

11 Format the HTML

In addition to the color coding, you can control the way that the code is displayed onscreen, including indent settings and whether the tags appear in uppercase or lowercase letters. For example, it is a good idea to have the HTML tags in uppercase letters to make them stand out when you are looking at the code. Choose **Edit, Preferences** to open the **Preferences** dialog box and choose **Code Format** from the **Category** list.

Click

12 Make Format Changes

Change the settings for the way the code is presented onscreen to suit your preferences. For example, to make all HTML tags appear in uppercase letters, choose <UPPERCASE> from the **Case for Tags** drop-down menu. Click **OK** to close the dialog box when you are done.

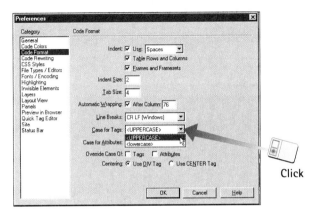

Click

13 Apply the Changes

Changing the **Code Format** options affects only new documents unless you specifically tell Dreamweaver otherwise. Choose **Commands, Apply Source Formatting** to update the current page with the changes you made to the **Code Format** page of the **Preferences** dialog box.

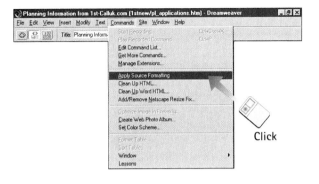

Click

14 Clean Up the HTML

Dreamweaver has a built-in feature that will tidy up the HTML code in your documents. If you have created the page entirely in Dreamweaver, there should be nothing to tidy up, but the more you work with your Web pages, the more likely you are to bring information in from other sources. Choose **Commands, Clean Up HTML** to open the **Clean Up HTML** dialog box.

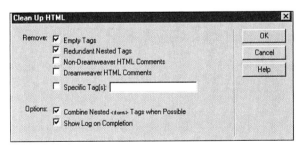

15 View the Report

Until you are more confident about working with the code, leave the default check boxes enabled. Notice that you can actually insert specific tags to remove comments from the code. For now, click **OK** to close the **Clean Up HTML** dialog box and view the report of how Dreamweaver cleaned up your code.

End

How to Use the Code Inspector

In the last task, you learned how to view the HTML code for a page by opening the code window from the toolbar. Instead of splitting the screen as you did in the last task, you can access the code in a separate panel, called the **Code Inspector**, from the **Launcher**. When you display the code for a page in a separate window, you can have the complete design view visible in the background and move the **Code Inspector** window around to whichever part of the screen you choose to display it.

Begin

1 Show the Launcher

Switch back to design view by clicking the **Show Design View** button in the toolbar. The split-screen view displayed in the last task is replaced by the more familiar full-screen design view. If it is not already visible, display the **Launcher** by choosing **Window, Launcher**.

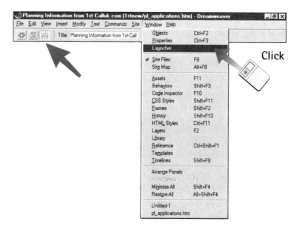

Click

2 Open the Code Inspector

From the **Launcher**, click **Code Inspector** to open that window in front of the document window. You can resize the **Code Inspector** window by dragging the edges.

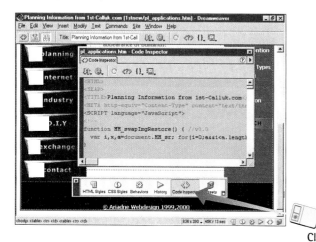

Click

3 Move the Code Inspector

You can move the **Code Inspector** window to any convenient location on the screen simply by dragging its title bar.

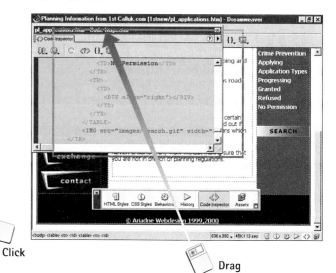

Drag

4 Check a Tag Reference

A new feature in Dreamweaver 4 allows you to check the meaning of specific tags in your pages. In the **Code Inspector** (or in the code view you opened in Task 1), select the tag you want information about. In this example, I have selected the **<IMG>** tag.

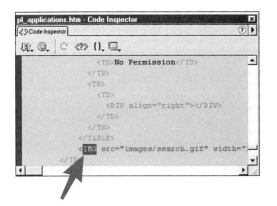

6 Use the Code Navigator

You can use the **Code Inspector** in the same way that you used code view in Task 2. The toolbar in the **Code Inspector** offers the same features as did the code view window. You can use the **Code Navigator** to find Dreamweaver-specific code: Click the **Code Navigator** button and select the code you want to find. Dreamweaver searches for and highlights that selection in the **Code Inspector** window.

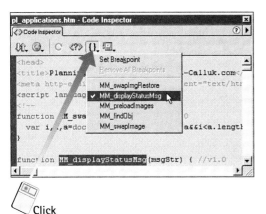

Click

5 Open the Reference Panel

On the toolbar in the **Code Inspector** window, click the **Reference** button. A **Reference** panel for the selected tag is displayed immediately. Read through the information in this panel to learn more about the selected tag. You can resize the **Reference** panel by dragging the sides of the window. Make it as large as you want so that you can read the information displayed.

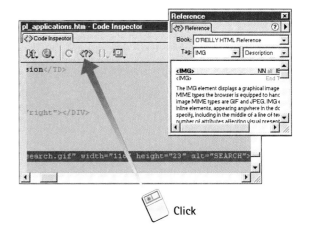

Click

How-To Hints

What's the Difference?

If the **Code Inspector** introduced in this task and the code view explained in Task 2 seem to do the same thing, it's simply because they do. Having the different ways of viewing the code is just part of the Dreamweaver way of making sure that you have control over how the code and screen look.

More References?

Task 4, "How to Use the Reference Panel," explains how to check more and different references. Never again will you struggle to know what a tag is or does. As a bonus, the **Reference** panel contains help not only for HTML, but also for CSS and JavaScript.

End

How to Use the Reference Panel

The **Reference** panel is a new feature of Dreamweaver 4 that enables you to get definitions of tags, Cascading Style Sheet (CSS), and JavaScript terms. This great built-in facility will save you hours of time scouring books and Web sites to find out exactly what something means. You can launch the **Reference** panel from the toolbar at any time, or from the code view or **Code Inspector** to immediately display the reference for a selected tag.

Begin

1 Open the Reference Panel

With a document open in the document window, either click the **Reference** button in the toolbar on the **Code Inspector** window or choose **Window, Reference** to open the **Reference** panel.

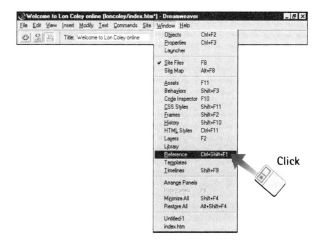

2 Select a Tag to Learn About

Use the **Tag** drop-down menu to select a tag that you want more information about. As soon as you make your selection, the information is displayed in the bottom part of the panel.

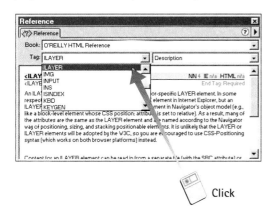

3 Learn About CSS

The options in the **Book** drop-down menu allow you to choose the reference source you want to use. You can choose **CSS Reference**, **HTML Reference**, or **JavaScript Reference**. To open the reference source for CSS terms, choose **CSS Reference** from the **Book** menu.

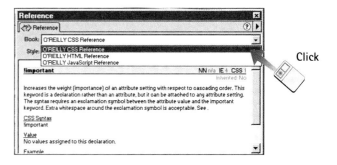

4 Choose a CSS Tag

After you have opened the **CSS Reference** book, the tag options change automatically to display an alphabetic list of all CSS styles. To learn about a specific one, choose it from the **Style** drop-down menu. The description appears in the lower part of the panel.

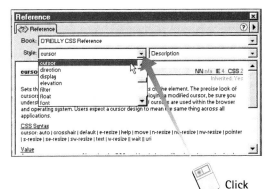

Click

5 Select a Tag in Code View

With the code showing either in the split screen or the **Code Inspector**, highlight a tag and click the **Reference** button in the toolbar. The **Reference** panel opens to display the reference for the tag you have highlighted.

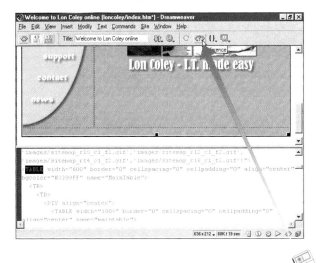

Click

End

How-To Hints

Attribute Information

Many tags are not standalone tags—they have attributes and values as well. For example, the **<FONT>** tag can have attributes such as face, color, and size. You can see the attributes for a selected tag by using the **Description** drop-down menu in the **Reference** panel. After you have displayed the information in the **Reference** panel for a given tag, you can use the **Attributes** drop-down menu to look at each of the attributes used by that tag.

Don't Want to Scroll?

Instead of having to scroll through all the tags in the drop-down list, you can type one or more letters into the **Tag** field. The index jumps straight to the first item in the list that starts with the letter you typed, making it easy to find what you want.

How to Assign Editors to NonHTML Documents

Although Dreamweaver is primarily an HTML editor, it has the capabilities to open and edit other types of code file types as well, such as JavaScript files (`.js`). Foreign files that you open in Dreamweaver automatically open in code view (design view is actually disabled for nonHTML files). After you have edited the file, you can resave it with the original extension or as an HTML file.

Begin

1 Set the Preferences

If you're planning to work with nonHTML files in Dreamweaver, you should set up your preferences for working with these foreign file types. Choose **Edit, Preferences** to open the **Preferences** dialog box. From the **Category** list, select **File Types/Editors**.

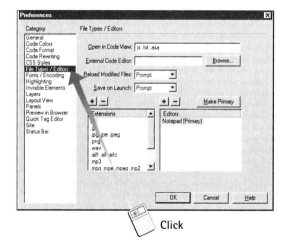

Click

2 Add a File Type

In the **Open in Code View** field, you can add the extensions for any new file types you want to open in code view. In this example, I have added the `.asp` file type to the existing list. Use a space to separate extensions in the list. Click **OK** when you are done.

Click

3 Launch an External Editor

Dreamweaver also allows you to edit files in their native environment (the application you used to create the file). When you install Dreamweaver, a large number of editors are already configured. Open the **Site** window and double-click any file to open it into its associated program. In this example, I selected a Flash movie that will open into Flash for editing.

Double-click

4 Add an Editor for a File Type

You can add new file types into the **Preferences** listings so that Dreamweaver will know what to do with new file types. In this example, we tell Dreamweaver that **.xls** files should be opened in Microsoft Excel. Open the **Preferences** dialog box and choose **File Types/Editors** from the **Category** list. Click the + button to open a text box.

Click

5 Add a File Extension

In the text box, type the file extension that you are adding to the list. Make sure that you include the period (.) with the extension, or the file type will not be recognized.

6 Add the Editor

From the **Extensions** list, select the file type you have just added and click the + button above the **Editors** list. In the **Select External Editor** dialog box that opens, browse to the application file you want to use to edit the selected file type. In this example, I selected the **.xls** file extension and have selected **Excel.exe** as the editor to use with that file type. Click **Open** to continue.

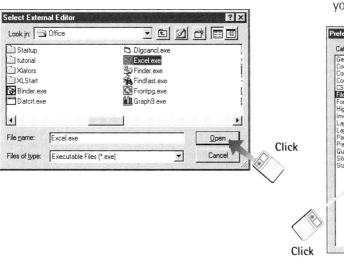

Click

7 Remove a File Type

You can easily remove a file type from the **Extensions** list at any time. Choose the file type you want to delete and click the – button above the **Extensions** list. Make sure that you really want to delete this item because Dreamweaver displays no confirmation dialog box before deleting the entry from the list. You might want to delete an extension if you uninstall the associated application from your computer.

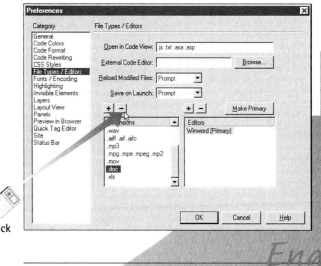

Click

End

How to Download New Extensions

As you know, the Macromedia Web site is home to some great help files; it also hosts the Macromedia Exchange, which is a great place for getting new behaviors and extensions for the software. The behaviors and extensions are written by other Dreamweaver users who post the files to the site for free download. There is no limit to the number of extensions you can download. Visit the site to discover what time-saving extensions are available: From formatting and changing text to inserting nested tables (complete with a tutorial), the Macromedia Exchange site has just about everything imaginable for you to download.

Begin

1 Open the Exchange

The Dreamweaver Exchange is full of handy information and add-ons for Dreamweaver. From this site, you can download Dreamweaver *extensions* (handy bits of script that add functionality to the software). Jump right to the Macromedia Exchange Web site by choosing **Help, Macromedia Exchange**. Click the **Browse Extensions** drop-down menu to display a list of Dreamweaver extensions that you can search the site for. Select the type of file you are looking for; select **All Categories** to see the complete listing of available files.

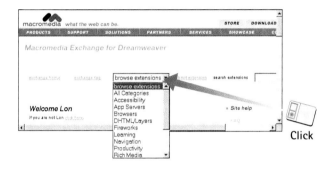

Click

2 Select an Extension

The extensions that satisfy your selection in Step 1 are displayed onscreen. You can see the name of the extension along with other relevant information such as the number of times it's been downloaded and the name of the author. Click the name of any extension to learn more about it. Note that if the extension file has the Macromedia logo next to it, Macromedia has approved the extension and found it to be stable in the working environment.

Text Extensions
Click on the column name to sort

Name	Author	Date	Version	Rating
Cent Sign	Mark Erickson	Apr 17, 2000	1.0.0	4/5
Change Case	Hava Edelstein	Apr 11, 2000	2.1	3/5
Entity Converter	Scott Richards	Apr 14, 2000	1.0.2	4/5
Get link from IE history	Tomohiro Ueki	Oct 18, 2000	1.0	No rating
Gradient Text	Ovidiu Valer HOSSU	Jun 26, 2000	1.4.3	2/5

Click

3 Read All About It

The information page for the extension you selected contains more information about the purpose of the extension as well as download information and user comments. To download the file to your computer, click the download link for the appropriate version of the file. When prompted, click the **Save this file to disk** option and choose the location on the disk to which you want to save the file.

Change Case Extension

Change the case of selected text

Features
Select text and access this command to make the selected text either all uppercase or all lowercase

Discuss

Date Started Thread
Oct 2, 2000   problem with change case
Sep 19, 2000 Proper Case
Aug 29, 2000 No updates for this great extension???

Get all the info for this extension

Download Extension
 macintosh   1.711   MX147
 windows   1.711   MX147

Author
Date
Version
Type

Click

4 Install the Extension

After you have downloaded an extension, you have to make Dreamweaver aware that it exists by installing the extension. Back in Dreamweaver, choose **Commands, Manage Extensions** to open the **Package Manager**. Click the **Install Extension** button on the toolbar to open the **Select Package to Install** dialog box. Browse to the file you downloaded and click **Install** to continue.

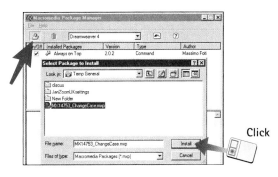

Click

5 Accept the Disclaimer

You are presented with a disclaimer screen informing you that you are about to install a third-party product. To continue, you must click **Accept** or the extension will not be installed. The extension is then installed into Dreamweaver. When the installation is complete, you'll see a confirmation screen telling you what to do next. In some cases, you might have to reboot the computer; in other cases, the extension will be installed and will require no further action.

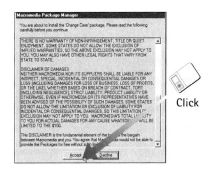

Click

6 Read the Information Screen

The next screen tells you more about the extension you have installed, such as which browsers it will work in and, more importantly, how to access it in Dreamweaver.

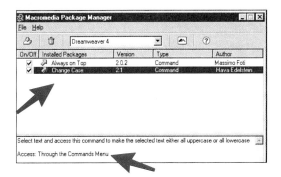

7 Close and Reopen Dreamweaver

Most extensions require you to shut down and reopen Dreamweaver before the installation takes effect. Even if the extension does not specify that you do this, it is still a good idea. Make sure that you have saved all your work before you close the program. You can immediately reopen the application to continue your work. The extension will appear in the location specified in the **Package Manager** screen.

End

How-To Hints

Remove an Extension

If you decide that you don't want an extension you have downloaded (for example, if it doesn't work the way you expected), choose **Commands, Manage Extensions** to open the **Extension Manger**. Choose the extension you want to delete and click the trash can icon.

Task

Working with Images in Fireworks

*O*kay, so what is Fireworks? Fireworks is a dedicated Web graphics solution. Unlike other graphics applications designed for paper production used for the Web, Fireworks is specifically aimed at the creation and management of Internet graphics.

The tasks in this part of the book show you how to create images in Fireworks and add them to your Web pages in Dreamweaver. Also in this part, you'll develop some expertise in Fireworks with the skills you'll need to work with images. You'll learn how to create new, "native" Fireworks files and how to work with "foreign" files created in other graphics applications.

Remember that this book is first and foremost about Dreamweaver; those aspects of Fireworks that are covered in this part are the skills you'll need to create basic graphics and buttons for use on your Dreamweaver Web pages. The tasks in this part will give you the confidence to work with images in Fireworks.

Images you create in Fireworks can be seamlessly integrated into your Dreamweaver pages. Even after an image is exported in a Web-acceptable format (primarily the GIF or JPEG format), Dreamweaver will remember the originating Fireworks file format, making editing of images easy.

Regardless of where your image files originated—in Fireworks or in some other graphics editor—the tasks in this part show you how to manipulate and fine-tune those images in Fireworks with the ultimate goal of exporting them for use in a Dreamweaver Web page.

When working with graphics, it is a good idea to save your work often—and in some cases, with many different filenames. You never know when something may need tweaking or changing. The more versions of a file you have saved during the development of an image, the easier it is to go back. When you export a PNG file from Fireworks to another format, you should keep the original PNG file—just in case.

How to Open New Files in Fireworks

Getting into the Fireworks software is easy enough. As with most applications these days, opening the program is simply a case of point and click. Creating and saving a new file in Fireworks is fairly intuitive as well. This task provides the details.

2 Examine the Menus and Toolbox

Each of the menus helps you in a different area. As with other software, the name of the menu gives you a clue about the types of commands you'll find in the list. For example, the **File** menu helps you control your files. The tools in the toolbox are grayed out (that is, they are inaccessible) until you have an active (open) document. The toolbox tools allow you to draw, change, fill, and cut areas of your document.

Menu bar

Toolbox

Begin

1 Open the Software

Assuming you have followed the default installation instructions and did not install Fireworks in a special folder, click the **Start** button and choose **Programs, Macromedia Fireworks 4, Fireworks 4**. When the software opens, you'll see a daunting array of tools at your disposal. Menus go across the top of the screen, the toolbox is down the left, and panels are stacked on the right.

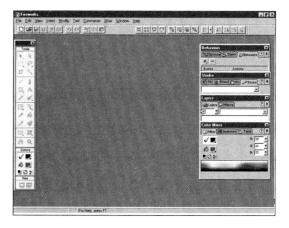

3 Open a New Document

Choose **File, New** to open the **New Document** dialog box. Alternatively, click the **New File** button in the toolbar directly below the **File** menu. In the **Width** and **Height** boxes, type values to indicate the size of the canvas you want to create (you can adjust the size of the canvas later if necessary). The units of measurement can be pixels, centimeters, or inches. The **Resolution** field defaults to 72 pixels/inch, the most suitable resolution for Web images.

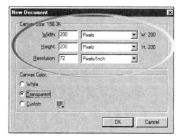

4 Set the Canvas Color

The **Canvas Color** area of the dialog box controls the background for your image. You can select the **White** or **Transparent** option or use the **Custom** drop-down button to choose a color using the color picker. Click **OK** to close the dialog box and observe the canvas on the screen.

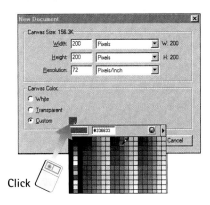

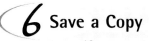

Click

5 Save the File

When you save a file in Fireworks, the default file format is PNG (Portable Network Graphic). To save the current document as a PNG file, choose **File, Save As**. The **Save As** dialog box opens. Navigate to the folder in which you want to save this file and type a meaningful filename. Notice that the **Save As Type** option lists **PNG** as the file format. Click **Save** to complete the operation.

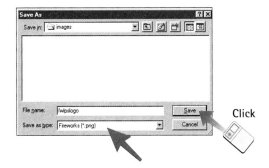

Click

6 Save a Copy

If you want, you can save versions of the same file at different stages of development. Doing so is a great idea if you know you'll want to come back to an earlier version of the file and revise it. Choose **File, Save a Copy** to open the **Save Copy As** dialog box. Navigate to the folder in which you want to save the file, type a new filename, and click **Save**.

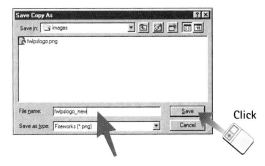

Click

7 Reopen Existing Files

Fireworks retains a record of the four files you've most recently worked on. Open the **File** menu to see these files listed at the bottom of the menu; click the filename you want to access to open it in a new document window. To open a file not in the recent list, choose **File, Open** and browse to the location of the file. Select the file and click **Open**.

End

How to Open Foreign Images in Fireworks

Fireworks supports images made in other applications. These "foreign" files can be opened in Fireworks with some of the original editability intact. These steps explain how to open most graphics files in Fireworks; you also learn how to work with an animated GIF file.

Begin

1 Open a GIF or JPG File

GIF and JPEG files are the two most common file types used in Web pages; they are the file formats you are most likely to have. Simply choose **File, Open** and navigate to the desired file to open GIF and JPEG files in Fireworks. The selected file opens in the workspace.

2 Get an Image from a Scanner

Assuming that you have a scanner or a digital camera, you can use the TWAIN options to move your images into Fireworks. Choose **File, Scan, Twain Select** and select the software you usually use to scan or import an image from the external device. The resulting image opens in Fireworks as a new document.

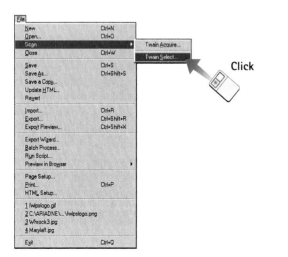

Click

3 Open Files from Other Applications

Check the Fireworks help system to see exactly which file types can be imported successfully into Fireworks. Although you might be able to open some files, you might find that you cannot edit the individual components of the image. If Fireworks cannot open a particular file (that is, if it doesn't recognize the file type), you will see an error message, and you will have to use a different application to work on the image. Fireworks supports all the file types suitable for Web pages, so you shouldn't have too many problems.

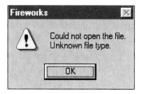

4 Open an Animated GIF File

Animated GIF files are fun to view and can add some visual excitement to your Web pages without adding megabytes of storage space to the site. As usual, choose **File, Open** and navigate to the animated GIF file you want to open. (Most such files have the file extension GIF.) The first frame of the image opens in a new document window. There are many places on the Internet from which you can download small animations to use on your sites. A simple search in any search engine will produce results.

5 Open the Frames Palette

Initially, the animated GIF file appears as a single static image. In fact, Fireworks has split the animation into frames for you. You can view and edit the individual frames just as you would separate image files. If you cannot see the **Frames** panel, choose **Window, Frames** to display it.

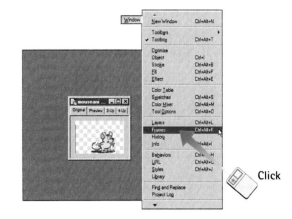

Click

6 Look at the Frames

Scroll through the list of frames in the **Frames** panel to get an idea of how many individual images make up the animation. Click each frame in the list individually and watch the document window to see the image change slightly with each new frame displayed.

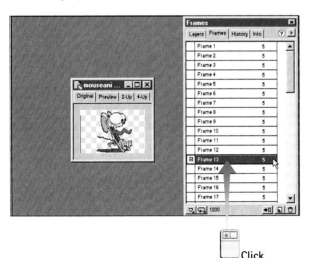

Click

7 Watch the Animation in Fireworks

Use the playback controls at the bottom of the screen to see the animation play within Fireworks. You can view the animation frame by frame (in a kind of stop-action manner) or play it as a continuous file.

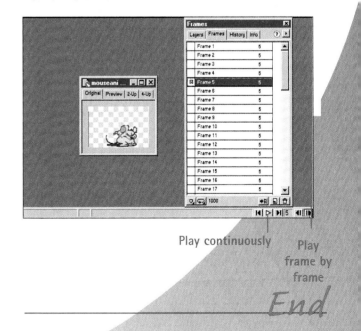

Play continuously

Play frame by frame

End

How to Use the Toolbox

Now that you know how to open a new file in Fireworks and have a blank canvas to work with, let's put some of the toolbox tools to use. We'll start with the toolbox in this task and will progress to the panels later. First, let's use some of the most common tools, starting with the **Ellipse** tool. Drawing shapes of any description is easy in Fireworks. The toolbox makes it simple by letting you choose the shape you want.

2 Draw and Select an Ellipse

Select the **Ellipse** tool from the **Shapes** menu in the toolbox. Move the mouse pointer over the open canvas and click and drag to draw an elliptical shape. After you have a shape on the canvas, you must select it before you can perform any other action on it. For example, click the **Selection** tool in the toolbox (the dark arrow in the top-left corner of the toolbox) and then click the shape you want to select. Fireworks adds a blue outline to the shape to show that it is selected.

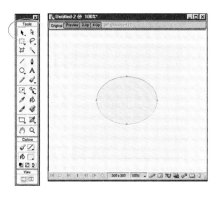

Begin

1 Choose the Tool You Want

The Fireworks toolbox has many tools (almost 40 in fact). To choose a tool, just click it. Some tools have other tools hidden in a menu; these "parent" tools have a tiny arrow in the bottom-right corner. To access the hidden tools, click the visible tool and hold the mouse button down; a menu of other related tools will pop out. Drag across the additional tools to select the one you want. When you release the mouse button, the tool you selected displays on the button in the toolbox.

Click

3 Change the Color

By default, the shape you draw is filled with the last color you used. To change the fill color for a shape, first select the shape. Then click the arrow next to the paint bucket color swatch in the toolbox to display the color picker. Click the color you want, and the selected shape changes color.

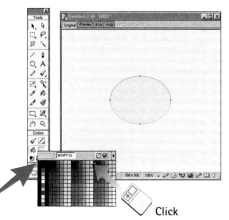

Click

4 Add a Visible Outline

Click the arrow next to the **Stroke Color** button to display the color picker. Choose the color you want to use as a visible outline around the selected shape.

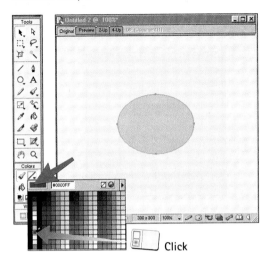

Click

5 Zoom In on the Ellipse

You can zoom in to any part of your image by using the **Magnify** tool. (Note that the tool does not increase the size of the image, merely your view of it.) Click the **Magnify** tool in the toolbox and then click inside the ellipse. The title bar for the document shows the level of magnification you are currently using to view your document.

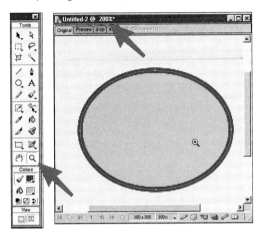

6 Move the Ellipse

Use the **Pan** tool to move the image inside the document window. This tool is very helpful when you have zoomed in on an image and want to look at a particular part of the image. Click the **Pan** tool to select it and then move the mouse over the ellipse. Drag to move the ellipse around the screen with the mouse pointer.

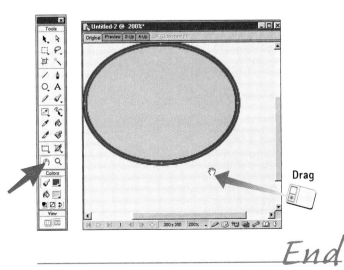

Drag

How-To Hints

Drawing in Fireworks

If you import an image in a different resolution, Fireworks asks whether you want to resample the image. A good question, but what is *resampling*? When you resample an image, Fireworks adds (or removes) pixels to try to match the original image as closely as possible. When you resample to a higher resolution, you should not have any noticeable loss of quality; however, when you resample to a lower resolution, there will always be some loss of quality.

End

How to Resize Images

Frequently, image files are simply not the size you need them to be. In Fireworks, it is easy to change the dimensions of the image file, as you learn in this task. Resizing an image in Fireworks merely changes the dimensions; it does not affect the resolution.

Begin

1 Open the Image to Resize

Open the image you want to resize. If the image file is foreign to Fireworks (that is, if it is not a PNG file), the image opens in bitmap mode. This means that you can make certain changes to the image, but not to the components that were originally created. When you are working with a file created in Fireworks, the file opens into object mode. If you are in bitmap mode, you'll see a striped line around the canvas.

2 Open the Image Size Dialog Box

You can control the size of the image down to the pixel level. Choose **Modify, Image Size** to open the **Image Size** dialog box.

Click

3 Fill Out the Dialog Box

In the **Pixel Dimensions** area at the top of the dialog box, type the new horizontal and vertical values you want the image to assume. Enable the **Constrain Proportions** check box so that you do not inadvertently distort the image. Click **OK** to close the dialog box and resize the image.

4 Transform the Image Size with Percentages

Rather than specifying exact measurements in the **Image Size** dialog box, you can resize an image to a percentage of its original size. Right-click the image and choose **Transform, Numeric Transform** from the context menu; the **Numeric Transform** dialog box opens. Specify the percentage by which you want to scale the image. Enable the **Constrain Proportions** check box to ensure that the width/height ratio of the image is maintained. Click OK to close the dialog box and resize the image.

Right-click

5 Modify the Canvas Size

When you resize an image, notice that the canvas size stays the same. Now you may have excess space around the image. To change the size of the canvas so that there is less extra space around the image, choose **Modify, Canvas Size**; the **Canvas Size** dialog box opens.

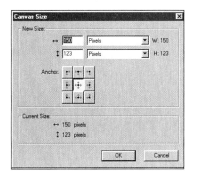

6 Enter Values

In the horizontal and vertical size fields, type new values for the size of the canvas and click OK. The canvas will shrink or enlarge around the image to your specifications. Make sure that you don't make the canvas too small, or you will lose part of the image itself.

How-To Hints

Trim the Canvas

If you don't want to play hit-or-miss with the size of the canvas, choose **Modify, Trim Canvas**. This command resizes the canvas to the same size as the image. This automatic resizing does not require any input from you, which makes it a handy tool to remember.

Using the Clipboard

If you want to work with an image from the Clipboard, choose **File, New** to create a new file with the correct canvas dimensions to fit the contents of the Clipboard. Then just paste the contents of the Clipboard onto the canvas. If there is a difference between the resolution of the image on the Clipboard and the resolution of the canvas, Fireworks asks whether you want to resample the Clipboard image to match the resolution of the canvas.

How to Crop Images

Frequently, you will have an image that could benefit from having some its background eliminated. *Cropping* is the process of cutting away that portion of the image you don't want to see (with the side benefit of shrinking the file size). Fireworks offers a simple **Crop** tool that squares up the image to your specifications. You can also produce some specially cropped shapes with the tricks you learn in this task.

Begin

1 Open the File to Be Cropped

Open in the workspace the file you want to crop. In the toolbox, click the **Crop** tool.

Click

2 Draw the Area to Keep

Move the mouse pointer over the image and drag a rectangle around the image. The portion of the image inside the rectangle is what will remain of the image; everything else will be removed. If you make a mistake drawing the rectangle, press **Esc** and drag again, or use the handles which appear around the selection when you let go of the mouse.

Drag

3 Crop the Image

Double-click inside the image to perform the crop. Note that everything outside the rectangle that you drew disappears.

Double-click

4 Crop Creatively

Consider this image of a lady and her dogs. Suppose that you want to crop the image so that just the lady and the dogs are in an oval shape. As you know, the **Crop** tool cuts away the background in a rectangular shape. If you want to crop more creatively, click the **Marquee** tool in the toolbox and choose the **Ellipse** tool.

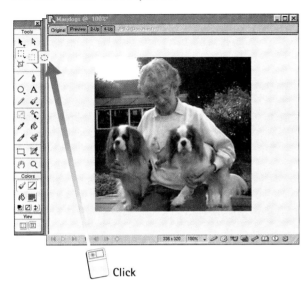

Click

6 Copy the Selection

Click the **Copy** button on the toolbar at the top of the screen to copy the area inside the marquee onto the Clipboard. Note that copying the image in this fashion saves only the area inside the marquee, not the entire image.

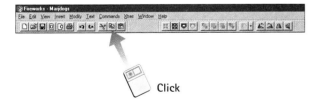

Click

5 Draw the Area You Want to Keep

Drag the mouse to draw a nice oval around the area of the image you want to keep. A dashed line appears around the area you draw.

Drag

7 Paste into a New Document

With the area you want to crop safely on the Clipboard, open a new file. Click the **Paste** button on the toolbar. Fireworks automatically suggests a canvas size that matches the copied area of the original image.

End

How to Flip, Rotate, and Distort Images

As with many things, images don't always look how you want them to when you first open them in Dreamweaver. This is especially true when you're working with files created by others or with scanned images that have come from somewhere else. Being able to make changes to the overall look of the image even in small ways will make your files look more professional.

Begin

1 Open and Select an Image

Open the image you want to work with in the workspace. If the image you loaded is not a native PNG file, click the **Stop** button in the status bar at the bottom of the screen to exit bitmap mode. Click the **Selection** tool in the toolbox and click the image to select it.

Click

2 Rotate an Image

From the **Modify** menu, choose **Transform**; from the submenu, choose one of the rotation options: **Rotate 180°**, **Rotate 90° CW** (clockwise), or **Rotate 90° CCW** (counterclockwise). When working with a single image which makes up the whole file, you can also use the **Modify, Rotate Canvas** option.

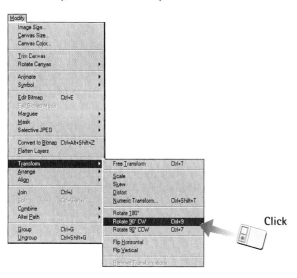

Click

3 Modify the Canvas

After you have rotated a rectangular image, you might not be able to see part of the image because it might extend off the existing canvas. Use the **Canvas Size** dialog box to increase the canvas to fit the rotated image. Because it can be difficult to guess at the proper canvas size, choose **Window, Info** to see the dimensions of the image. Use these image dimensions in the **Canvas Size** dialog box.

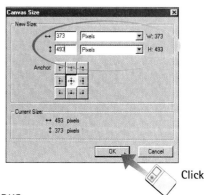

Click

4 Skew an Image

Skewing an image slants it either vertically or horizontally (or both if you like). Select the image and choose **Modify, Transform, Skew**. Handles appear on the selected image.

5 Drag to the Shape You Want

Drag any of the handles to slant the image in any direction. Drag a corner handle to give the appearance of perspective (as was done in this example). Release the mouse button when you are done.

Drag

6 Distort an Image

Distorting an image changes its dimension with no regard for ratio or appearance. Select the image and choose **Modify, Transform, Distort** to make handles appear around the image. Drag any of the handles to change the shape of the image.

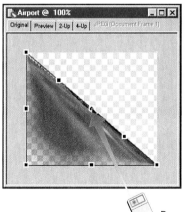

Drag

7 Flip an Image

You can flip an image vertically or horizontally within the canvas. When you flip an image, note that all the text appears mirrored, right hands will appear to be left hands, and so on. Select the image and choose **Modify, Transform, Flip Horizontal** or **Flip Vertical**. In this example, I used the image of the lady and the dogs from the last task; after being flipped horizontally, they are all facing the other way.

End

How to Add Text to an Image

Now that you know how to do some basic image manipulation in Fireworks, let's look at adding text to an existing image. In Part 17, "Using Text in Fireworks," you will learn much more about using text in and as image files. In this task, you learn a quick and easy way to add text to an image in Fireworks and save the text as part of the Fireworks file.

Begin

1 Open the Image

Open the image on which you want text to appear. Click the **Text** tool in the toolbox and then click the image to open the **Text Editor** dialog box.

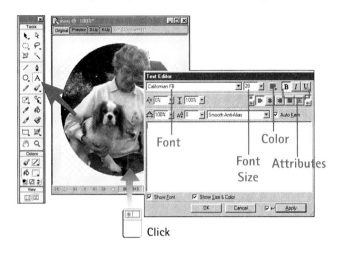

Click

2 Type the Text

In the large text box, type the text you want to show on the image. Use the **Font, Font Size,** and **Color** menus at the top of the dialog box to set the type and the color of the text; click the **Attributes** buttons to make the text bold, italic, or underlined. When you're done, click **OK** to close the **Text Editor.** The specified text appears on the image.

3 Move the Text

The text may not appear where you expected and might not even be totally visable. Click the **Selection** tool in the toolbox and drag the text to the location on the image where you want it to appear.

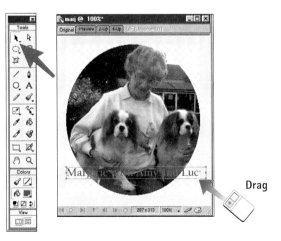

Drag

4 Edit the Text

Double-click the text at any time to reopen the **Text Editor** dialog box. Edit the text itself by retyping or changing the font, size, or color of the type. Click **Apply** to keep the dialog box open so that you can view the changes on the image; click **OK** to close the dialog box and return to the image.

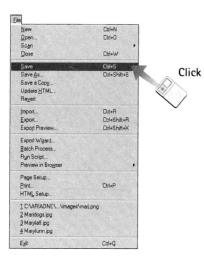

Double-click

5 Split Text over Lines

If you want, you can split the text over multiple lines. (By default, Fireworks places all the text horizontally across the image, regardless of whether it actually fits on the image.) Open the **Text Editor** and position the cursor between the words where you want the line break to occur; press **Enter**.

6 Save the Image and Text

When you save an image file in Fireworks, any text you've added to the image is saved as part of the file, with no special treatment afforded to the text. (When you save text with a graphics file in Dreamweaver, on the other hand, the text is saved on a special *layer*.) To save your Fireworks image, choose **File, Save**.

Click

How-To Hints

Making Text Go Vertical

Although we will look further in Part 17 at using text in Fireworks, it is worth mentioning here that you can have vertical text as well as horizontal text. In the **Text Editor**, click the **Vertical Text** button to make the text change direction. Note that the text appears vertical only in the document window and not in the **Text Editor**.

End

How to Export a Document to Dreamweaver

Even though some browsers support the PNG format used by Fireworks, many don't. Until the rest of the world catches up with Fireworks, you'll have to do some work to make the graphics images you develop in Fireworks accessible by most people. To do that, you'll have to export your image files from Fireworks into Dreamweaver using the traditional GIF or JPEG format. Although Fireworks has many other format options to optimize your graphics files, this task looks at the easy ones.

Begin

1 Check the File

When you are happy with the graphics file you have created in Fireworks, click the **Preview** tab on the document window to make sure that the image looks as you expect it to look. For the ellipse and text sample graphic we developed in the preceding tasks, the only difference between the original image and the preview is the white background Fireworks provides by default.

2 Select the Export Option

Choose **File, Export Wizard**. The **Export Wizard** opens; select **Continue** and then select **the Web** as your intended destination. Fireworks then analyzes your image. Click **Exit** to see the **Export Preview** window shown here.

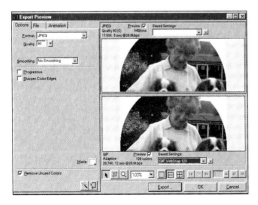

3 Select the File Type

The **Export Preview** window shows you the image in both GIF and JPEG formats. The window also presents the file size and amount of time it will take the image to download. The photo in this example has many colors, so I decided to export the file as a JPEG file. To select this format, click the JPEG preview.

Click

4 Export the Image

Click the **Export** button in the **Export Preview** window to open the **Export** dialog box. Name the file and specify a location within your Web site directory structure. Click **Save** to continue. We will look in more depth at the topic of optimizing images as we work through the next few parts of the book.

Click

5 Insert Image in Dreamweaver

Back in Dreamweaver, open the page on which you want to use the exported image. Click to position the insertion point where you want the image to appear on the page. From the **Objects** panel, click **Insert Image** and browse to the location where you saved the image. Click **Select** to insert the image at the insertion point.

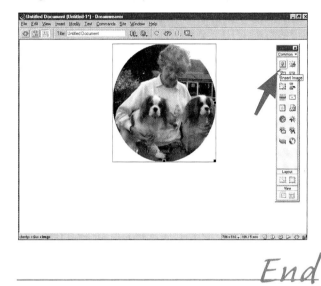

End

How-To Hints

Still Struggling?

It's very easy to look around the Internet and be in awe of some of the images you find there. Don't despair that you'll never achieve that level of graphic artistry—just start with the basics and build. The more you use Fireworks, the easier it is to turn out good graphics.

Task

Using the Library in Fireworks

*I*n Fireworks, reusing information and keeping file sizes down is made easy through the use of symbols and instances. A *symbol* is an object that is stored in the Library. An *instance* is a copy of the symbol that can be used over and over again.

In Fireworks, any object can be converted into a symbol, which is then stored in the Library. You can use this Library item to insert instances of the symbol into your document as many times as you want. After you save a symbol in the Library, you can use it in multiple documents. For example, if you have a company logo that you want to use in various files, you create the symbol once, store it in the Library, and then have it to use as many times as you want.

Using symbols reduces the size of the PNG files that Fireworks creates. Unlike in the Flash application, symbols used in PNG files do not reduce the file size of the image when it is exported to either GIF or JPEG format for use in Dreamweaver pages.

Using symbols makes editing easy: No matter how many times you use an instance of a symbol, you only have to edit the original, and all the instances are updated automatically. This great time-saving feature also means that you cannot forget to update the logo in all the files in which it appears.

How to Create a Symbol

You can create a symbol from scratch using Fireworks's **Insert, New Symbol** command. You can also start with any existing object and convert it into a symbol at any time. Being able to convert an existing object into a symbol gives you the ability to stock your **Library** with complex images (such as logos) that you use frequently.

Begin

1 Open a Blank Document

If you're going to create a symbol from scratch, start by opening a new, blank Fireworks file that will contain the symbol. The canvas for the symbol can be any size that is large enough to fit the symbol.

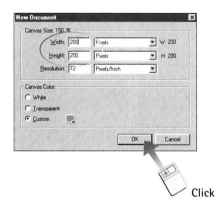

Click

2 Insert a New Symbol

Choose **Insert, New Symbol**. In the **Symbol Properties** dialog box that opens, type a name for the symbol you are going to create. Choose whether the symbol will be a graphic, animation, or a button (most symbols are graphics). Graphic symbols are those such as a company logo—a single image, however complex. Button symbols have additional properties called *states* (the different ways a button can appear in a Web browser, such as up, over, down, and over while down). In this task, create a **Graphic** symbol. Click **OK** to continue.

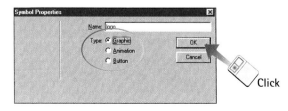

Click

3 Create the Symbol

The **Symbol** editor opens on top of your document. Create the desired object in the editor using the Fireworks skills you developed in Part 15, "Working with Images in Fireworks."

𝟰 Close the Editor

When the symbol is complete, close the editor. Your symbol will appear in the **Library**, and an instance (a copy) of the symbol will appear in the new document. You can tell that you're working with an instance of a symbol rather than the original symbol because the instance is surrounded by a dotted rectangle and has an arrow in the bottom-left corner. If it is not already visible, display the **Library** by choosing **Window, Library**.

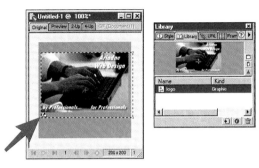

𝟱 Select an Existing Object

If you have an existing object that you want to save in the **Library** so that you can reuse it, select that object now. If you want to save multiple objects as a single symbol, select all the objects by holding **Shift** as you click each object.

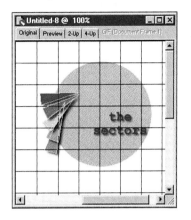

𝟲 Convert the Object to a Symbol

Choose **Insert, Convert to Symbol** to open the **Symbol Properties** dialog box. As you did in Step 2, type a name for the symbol you are creating and enable the appropriate radio button. Click **OK** to complete the conversion of the object to a symbol. The selected object or objects are converted to a single symbol and added to the **Library**.

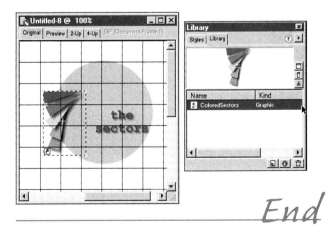

End

How-To Hints

Button, Animation, or Graphic Symbol?

Fireworks gives you three choices of symbols. Buttons are covered in Part 19, "Creating Buttons and Navigation Tools in Fireworks." Animation symbols are explained in Part 20, "Working with Layers and Frames in Fireworks."

How to Use Library Symbols

If you want to use the same graphic several times in one image file, you can minimize the size of the file by using items from the **Library**. Although using symbols keeps the size of your original PNG file small, note that when you export the file to GIF or JPEG formats, the symbols do not reduce the file size. You can use the library symbols you created for one document in another document simply by importing the symbol into the new document.

2 Drag the Symbol

You will already have an instance of the library symbol in the document window—the one created when you made your symbol or converted previous objects. To add another instance of this symbol to the document window, drag the desired symbol from the **Library** to the document window. You can drag as many instances of the symbol as you need into the document.

Drop 🖵   🖵 Drag

Begin

1 Open the Library Panel

Choose **Window, Library** to open the **Library** panel. All the symbols for the current document appear in the **Library**; use the scrollbars to move through the symbols until you find the one you want.

3 Choose the Export Option

After you have created a symbol in one document, you can use it in any other Fireworks document. By using the **Import Symbols** and **Export Symbols** commands, you can update the symbol in all the documents in which it appears just by modifying the original symbol. To export a symbol from the current document to another document, choose **Export Symbols** from the **Library** panel menu. The **Export Symbols** dialog box opens.

4 Choose the Symbols to Export

In the **Export Symbols** dialog box, select the symbol or symbols you want to export and click the **Export** button. (You can select multiple symbols by holding the **Shift** key as you click the various items; you can select all the symbols by clicking the **Select All** button.) In the **Save As** dialog box that opens, give the symbol file you are creating an appropriate name and navigate to the site folder in which you want to use these symbols. Click **Save** to save the selected symbols into a single PNG file in the chosen location.

Click

5 Choose the Import Option

Open the image file in which you want to use the symbols you just exported, or create a new file. (This image file will probably be in another folder and be part of another Web site.) Open the **Library** panel for that document and choose **Import Symbols** from the **Library** panel menu. In the **Open** dialog box, browse to locate the symbol file you created in Step 4 and click **Open**.

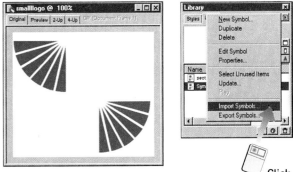

Click

6 Select the Symbols to Import

In the **Import Symbols** dialog box that appears, all the symbols in the file you selected in Step 5 are listed. Select the symbols you want to import into the current document and click **Open**. The selected symbols now appear in the **Library** panel of the document window with the word **imported** next to them. You can now drag these imported symbols into the document just as you can with symbols originally created in the document.

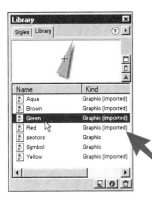

How-To Hints

Native and Imported Symbols

The symbols you create in a document and save as library symbols are native to the current document. When you export those symbols to another document, the symbols are actually linked back to the native document. If you change the original symbol in its native document, all the linked instances of that symbol in other documents are updated to show the modifications.

If you edit a symbol in any document to which the symbol has been imported, you will break the link with the original symbol. Although you will still be able to edit the symbol, it will no longer be updated when you make changes to the original. This ability to edit remains intact as long as you are working with Fireworks PNG files. After you export the file as a GIF or JPEG, you lose the ability to edit the symbol because it becomes part of the exported file.

End

How to Modify Symbols

You can modify library symbols at any time by using the symbol editor. If you want to modify symbols you have exported to other documents, you must modify the symbol in its native document and then update the symbol in the document to which it has been linked.

Begin

1 Open the Symbol Editor

Double-click any symbol in the **Library** panel to open it in the symbol editor. If you want to modify a symbol that was imported into the current document's library, you must edit the symbol in the document in which the symbol was created. If you want to modify just a single instance of the symbol, refer to the How-To Hints at the end of this task.

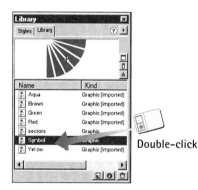

Double-click

2 Edit the Symbol

Use the normal drawing tools and the skills you learned in Part 15 to make all required edits to the symbol. In this example, we add a word to the quadrant-shaped symbol. When you close the symbol editor, the document is updated to reflect the changes you made. Notice that all instances of the symbol change in the document—not always producing the result you might want. In this example, notice that text is reversed on one of the instances because the original instance was flipped to position it correctly on the canvas.

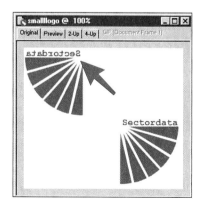

3 Duplicate or Delete a Symbol

You can duplicate a library symbol and then modify the copy. In the **Library** panel, select the symbol you want to duplicate and then choose **Duplicate** from the panel menu. A copy of the symbol appears in the **Library** with the same name as the original but with a number 1 appended to it. You can make any changes that you want without affecting the original. To delete a symbol from the library—and from all documents in which instances of the symbol appear—select the symbol and choose **Delete** from the panel menu. Note that deleting an imported symbol does not affect the original.

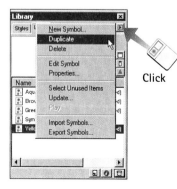

Click

4 Open the Other Document

If the symbol you just modified is used in another document (that is, if you exported the symbol to another document), you must update the symbol in the other document so that those instances contain the changes you made to the original symbol. Open the document containing an imported version of the symbol you just modified.

5 Update the Symbol

In the **Library** panel of the other document, select the imported symbol you want to update. Choose **Update** from the **Library** panel menu; the changes you made to the original symbol are now reflected in the new document.

End

How-To Hints

Look at Unused Symbols

If you want to see a list of the symbols in the **Library** that have not been used in the document, choose **Select Unused Items** from the **Library** panel menu. All used symbols disappear from the screen temporarily. You might wonder how you can have unused symbols in the **Library**. Although Fireworks always places an instance of the symbol in the file when it is created, these can be selected and deleted from the file by pressing the **Delete** key on the keyboard. This action removes the symbols from the screen but not from the **Library**. It is often handy to create all the symbols you want before assembling them into the end result, so you can have many symbols created that are not yet in use.

Breaking Links

If you want to change only a single instance of a symbol, you can. To do so, you must first break the link between the instance and the original symbol. Select the symbol in the document and choose **Modify, Symbol, Break Link**. The selected instance of the symbol becomes a single item or group and again can be edited on its own. Obviously, breaking the link to a symbol means that the image will not be updated if you modify the original symbol.

How to Work with Instances

If you want to edit the underlying properties of a single instance (for example, to make major changes to the shape or to add text into the symbol), you must first break the link between the original and the instance as explained in the How-To Hints in the last task. However, if you want to change the properties of a single instance—to change the opacity or to add a shadow, for example—you don't have to break the link. This task starts by opening a file that has more than one instance of the same symbol. We'll leave one instance unchanged and work with the other. Although this task changes only one instance, you can make changes to as many instances as exist in the document.

Begin

1 Select the Instance to Work With

In the file you have opened, decide which of the instances of the symbol you want to work with. Select that instance.

2 Transform the Instance

Choose **Modify, Transform**, and then choose from the transform options available for the instance. In this example, I chose **Flip Vertical**, but **Scale**, **Skew**, and other options are all possibilities.

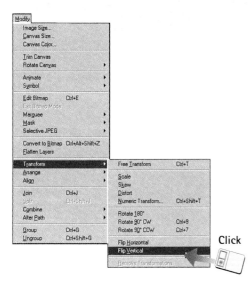

Click

3 Apply an Effect

With the now-transformed instance still selected, choose **Window, Effect** to display the **Effect** panel. Use the panel menu to apply an effect to the instance. Note that you cannot remove any effects that were in place when the symbol was created.

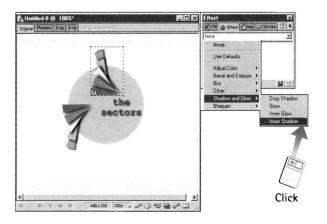

Click

4 Show the Objects Panel

By default, the opacity for the instance is set to 100%, but you can change this setting so that the instance appears as a faded version of the original. Start by choosing **Window, Layers** to display the **Layers** panel.

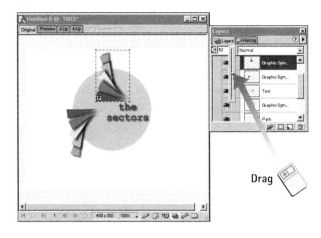

Click

5 Change the Opacity of the Instance

Select the instance you want to change. Use the **Opacity** slider to reduce the opacity for the selected instance. The lower the number you slide to, the more faded and translucent the instance will appear in the document window.

Drag

6 Change the Blending Mode

You can use the **Layers** panel to change the blending mode for the opacity. As you saw in Step 5, the default **Normal** setting fades the image into the color behind it, but you can choose any of the other settings in the panel menu to set how the instance blends into the background. In this example, I selected the **Erase** option; see how it affects the image.

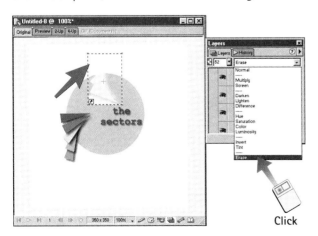

Click

7 View the Result

Look at your original image. The one instance remains as it appeared originally, but the second instance has been changed. All this came from a single symbol and shows exactly why symbols are such great things to use in Fireworks.

End

Task

Using Text in Fireworks

In addition to working with images, Fireworks lets you easily and quickly work with text. Many features in Fireworks are more commonly associated with a desktop publishing application than with a Web graphics application. For example, Fireworks allows you to continually edit and modify your text, even after you have applied effects to the text. You can create some wonderful effects by combining the basic text effects with the fill features, as you'll see in the tasks that follow. You can make your text glow, outline the characters, fill the characters with gradients, and many more combined effects. In fact, the only limitation is your own imagination.

You might be wondering why you would want to use text in a graphics application. If you are creating a company logo, for example, that logo will usually be a combination of graphics and some text; Fireworks is the ideal application to use to achieve this combination.

Another very important reason for using text in a graphics application is that many restrictions still exist on the fonts you can use within your Web pages. Creating small image files that contain the required text allows you to be more creative with text than having to stick to Web-safe fonts. Of course, using a graphics file to display text is appropriate only for small amounts of text, such as titles or buttons. But the option of presenting text in this way gives you the control and facility to be creative.

How to Work with Text

Working with text—entering and editing characters—is a simple process in Fireworks. It's very much a case of what you type is what you get. You can add text to an existing image (for example, if you want to add a fancy heading), or you can create a new file that uses the text as its basic element (such as a button graphic). Remember that when you use text in a graphic, you are not limited to the narrow range of Web-safe fonts required of most regular text.

Begin

1 Open a New Fireworks Document

Choose **File, New** to open a blank document. The **New Document** dialog box opens. Type the dimensions you want for the new document. Because this document will contain text only, let's keep it reasonably small. (In this example, the document is 150 pixels by 150 pixels.) Click **OK** when you are done.

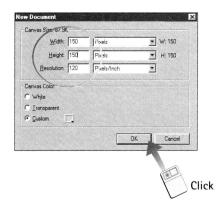

Click

2 Select the Text Tool

In the toolbox, click the **Text** tool to select it.

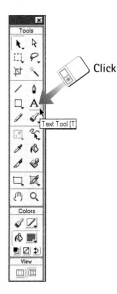

Click

Text Tool (T)

3 Activate the Text Tool

Click once inside the document window to open the **Text Editor**. Fireworks inserts the outline of a text box in the document window.

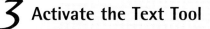

Click

4 Select the Font and Size

Use the **Font** drop-down menu to select the font you want to use and select the size for your text using the **Size** slider.

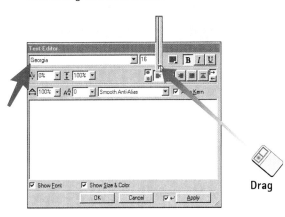

Drag

5 Start Typing

Type several words in the editor window: The text appears onscreen in both the text editor and the document window as you type.

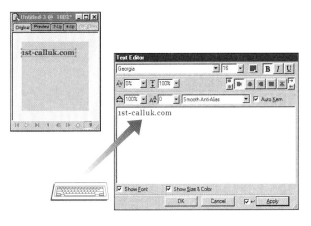

6 Apply the Text

Click **OK** to apply the text to the document and close the **Text Editor**. By default, the **Auto Apply** check box is enabled, meaning that you do not have to click **Apply** to apply the text to the document; clicking **OK** is enough.

Click

End

How-To Hints

Format the Text You Added

After you create the text, it remains a separate object that you can change simply by double-clicking it to reopen the **Text Editor** window. You can change the text characters, reformat the text, and even change the color of the text. To reformat the text, select new fonts, sizes, and attributes such as bold, italics, and underlining (click the **B**, **I**, or **U** toolbar button). To move text you have created, click to select it in the document window and then drag the text box wherever you want.

Problems Reading in the Text Editor?

If you have trouble reading the text font, size, or color in the **Text Editor** window, you can view your work in the default system fonts instead. To do this, simply open the text into the editor and disable the **Show Size & Color** and **Show Font** check boxes. You can enable these options again at any time to show the text as it will appear in the document.

How to Set Text Properties

In Fireworks, setting the size, font, and color of your text as you learned to do in Task 1 is merely the start of your options. You can set other text properties such as kerning, leading, and the baseline shift by using the **Text Editor** window. The more you use text in an imaging environment, the more you will probably want to. Fireworks gives you control over the flow of the text—even vertical and right-to-left text is possible.

Begin

1 Set the Baseline Shift

The *baseline shift* field in the **Text Editor** window allows you to move selected letters to positions above or below the baseline (the line on which the letters rest) to create subscript and superscript characters within your text. Select the character or characters you want to shift and use the **Baseline Shift** slider to reposition the characters. Note that these changes show only in the document window, not in the **Text Editor**.

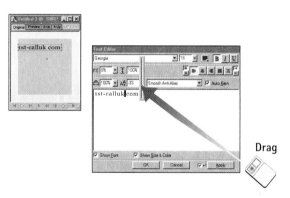

Drag

2 Specify the Leading

The *leading* value controls the amount of space between the lines of text (in other words, leading is the line spacing). Use the **Leading** slider to change the amount of space between the lines of text on the screen.

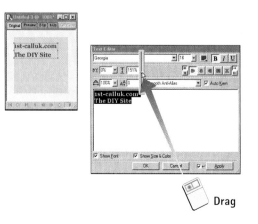

Drag

3 Set the Kerning for the Text

The *kerning* value changes the amount of space between two or more letters. Kerning is especially handy when you're working with large fonts and letters that don't fit well together (such as *AW* or *To*). Leave the **Auto Kern** check box enabled, and Fireworks improves the kerning of your characters automatically. Even if you leave the **Auto Kern** check box enabled, you can manually change the kerning between selected letters. Position the flashing cursor between two letters and then use the **Kerning** slider to adjust the percentage to bring the letters closer together or spread them out.

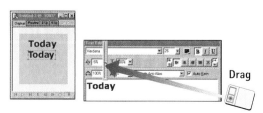

Drag

4 Align the Text

You can change the alignment of the text in a paragraph. In addition to making the text centered, left or right aligned, or fully justified, you can make the text appear vertically. Select your text (or position the cursor in the paragraph) and click any of the alignment buttons to effect the change.

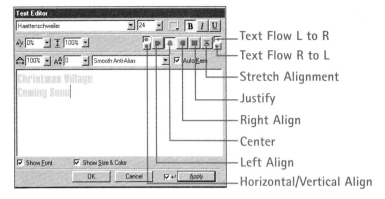

Text Flow L to R
Text Flow R to L
Stretch Alignment
Justify
Right Align
Center
Left Align
Horizontal/Vertical Align

5 Change the Text Color

When you create text, it automatically appears on the screen in whatever color is currently selected. To change the color, select the text and use the color picker to select the color you want.

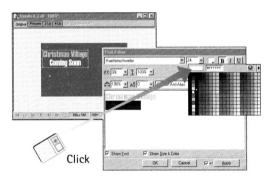

Click

6 Allow Anti-Aliased Text

Anti-aliased text has a nice, smooth edge that blends into the background: **Smooth Anti-Alias** is Fireworks's default setting. To change the anti-alias level, use the drop-down menu in the Text Editor window. Highlight your text and experiment with the settings to see which you prefer.

Click

End

How-To Hints

Alignment Options

The alignment options in Fireworks allow you to lay out your text the way you want it to appear. Just remember that some of the alignment options will be displayed only in the document window and not in the **Text Editor** (for example, vertical text appears only in the document window). Fireworks remembers the alignment settings you have enabled; the next time you use the **Text Editor**, it will use the alignment settings from the time before. Remember to check these settings before you start typing, or you might get some strange results.

How to Apply Fills and Effects to Text

In the preceding tasks, you created plain solid text and looked at how to change it in basic ways. Nothing you have done so far has really affected the overall view of the text. This task considers ways of changing the look of the text and how to enhance it. Text can be filled and have effects applied to it in the same way as any other object. Filled text can create some great effects for titles and other text-based graphics in Dreamweaver. This task explains the options and shows you how to set effects. The next task shows you what to do to make your text file into a graphics file.

Begin

1 Create a New File with Text

In Fireworks, choose **File, New** to create a blank document. Use the **Text** tool to add a single word to the document window. For this task, we'll work with the single word *Family*. If you have an existing text file, open it and select the text you want to work with.

2 Choose a Shadow Effect

Choose **Window, Effect** to open the Effect panel. From the drop-down menu at the top of the panel, choose **Shadow and Glow** and then choose the shadow effect you want from the sub-menu. For this example, I selected **Drop Shadow** to set the shadow.

3 Set the Properties for the Shadow

In the **Effect** panel, double click the **Drop Shadow** tile to display the properties for the shadow you just applied. Change the color and angle of the shadow using these options. You work more with shadow effects in Fireworks in Part 18, "Applying Effects to Objects in Fireworks."

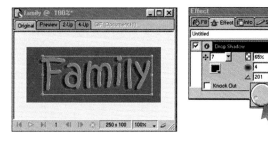

Drag

4 Set a Fill Category

By default, Fireworks fills objects with a solid color, but you can do much more. Fireworks offers a series of preset patterns in the **Fill** panel such as leaves and bark; you can also choose from other fill options such as linear, radial, and so on that fill your object with color diffused in a variety of ways. In this example, I filled the text with a **Cone** fill. You can drag the markers around the document window to change the angle and position of the fill.

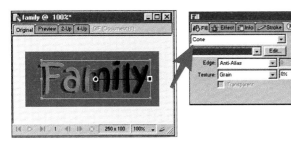

5 Choose a Fill Name

From the second drop-down menu in the **Fill** panel, select the specific effect from the category you chose in Step 4. If you chose the **Pattern** option in Step 4, you can now choose from fill names such as **Aggregate** and **Red Goo**; if you chose one of the color fill options, you can now choose from a list of preset colors. Choose the option that best fits the text image you're creating.

Click

6 Set a Texture and Amount

Use the **Texture** drop-down menu to apply a texture to the fill you just selected. To see the texture, make sure that the **Amount** slider is set to a number greater than 0.

Drag

End

How-To Hints

Text Is an Object

After you have closed the **Text Editor**, the text is held in a text box on the page. This text box can be treated like any other object, and can be rotated, scaled, and skewed as such. If you select the text box, you can then change the color of solid text simply by using the color picker in the toolbar rather than opening the **Text Editor**. When you are more familiar with the software, you can draw a path and attach text to the path to create "swirly" or "bendy" text. Fireworks has the effects you want; experiment with the software to see what you can create.

Changing Gradients

Use the **Fill** panel menu and play with the options to edit the gradient fill—or even to create your own customized fills.

How to Save Text as an Image File

The last several tasks looked at making text appear the way you want it to in Fireworks. You used the built-in tools in Fireworks to create effects and styles for your text. Now let's look at saving the text file into Dreamweaver so that it fits perfectly into your Web site. The most important thing to consider when working with a text-only file is to make sure that you export it as a GIF file and that you save a copy as a PNG file in case you want to come back and make changes. Also make sure that you trim the document canvas so that it's only as big as it needs to be to hold the text. Exporting the file without trimming the canvas gives you a larger file size than necessary and also requires a larger area on the page to contain it.

Begin

1 Trim the Canvas

With your text image open and saved in Fireworks, start by trimming the canvas to fit the text. Trimming the canvas gets rid of any excess space in the canvas and helps keep the file size down. Choose **Modify, Trim Canvas**.

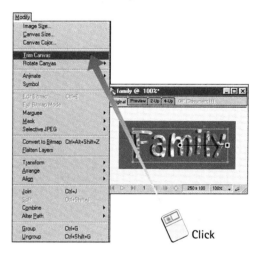

Click

2 Change the Color of the Canvas

Change the color of the canvas to match the background color of the Web page in which the image will be used. Making this change now will help the image fit smoothly onto the page without any messy edges showing. Choose **Modify, Canvas Color** to display the **Canvas Color** dialog box. Use the **Custom** color picker to select the color you want.

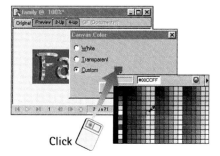

Click

3 Export the Image

Choose **File, Export** to open the **Export** dialog box. Notice that Fireworks uses the same filename as the PNG file you started with but changes the extension to GIF. Specify the location within your Web site to which you want to save the file. Click **Save** when you're finished.

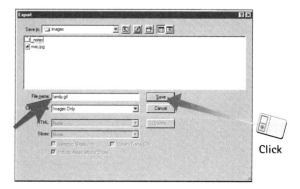

Click

4 Open Dreamweaver

In Dreamweaver, open the page onto which you want to place the image you just exported. Click to position the insertion point on the page where you want the image to appear and then click **Insert Image** from the **Objects** panel. The **Select Image File** dialog box opens.

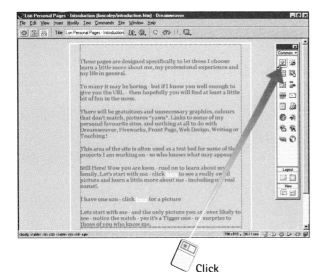

Click

5 Insert the Image

Browse to the location to which you exported the text image in Step 3 and click **Select**. The image is inserted on the page. The image should merge into the background color of your page and appear simply as text with the fills and effects you applied earlier.

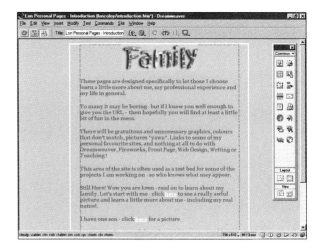

6 Optimize the Image

If the image is not the quality you had expected, you can optimize the image back in Fireworks. From the Dreamweaver **Commands** menu, choose **Optimize Image in Fireworks** to start the optimize process. This process is covered in Part 22, "Optimizing Images in Fireworks."

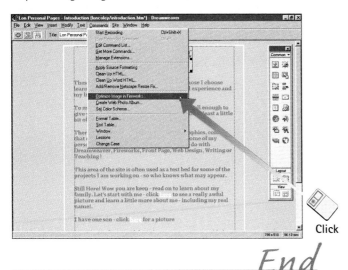

Click

End

Task

Applying Effects to Objects in Fireworks

ireworks makes it very simple to not only apply, but also edit effects. You can create your own custom effects and save them for later use. Effects are things like shadows, bevels, and glows that can be used at your discretion to make objects appear highlighted onscreen. The careful placement of a drop shadow can make an object appear to jump out of the page at the visitor.

You can let Fireworks apply the effects and then save your custom effects for use later on another document. Alternatively, you can just edit the default settings for an image each time you use an effect.

After you apply an effect to an object in Fireworks and then export that document, the effect is exported along with the image. The result is that your effects appear as you intended them to look when the image is inserted into your Dreamweaver pages.

TASK 1

How to Add Shadows

You can enhance a shape or image you have created by adding shadows to the image. You can create inner shadows that appear inside the shape or drop shadows that appear around the outside of the shape. The settings in Fireworks allow you to control the direction of the shadow as well as its color, depth, and distance from the shape.

Begin

1 Create an Object

Use the drawing tools to create a filled shape. Alternatively, open an existing image in Fireworks to which you want to add shadows. Select the image (or the portion of the image) to which you want to add the effect. Open the **Effect** panel by choosing **Window, Effect**.

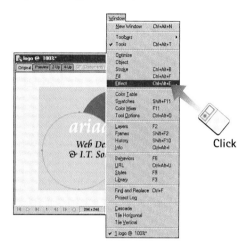

Click

2 Choose an Effect

From the list of special effects in the **Effect** panel menu, choose the **Shadow and Glow** effect. Then choose the type of shadow you want to apply. In this example, I selected the **Drop Shadow** option.

3 Edit the Settings

The **Settings** panel appears in the **Effect** panel to let you customize the options for your shadow effect. Use the distance slider to specify how far from the object the shadow will appear; the larger the number, the greater the distance.

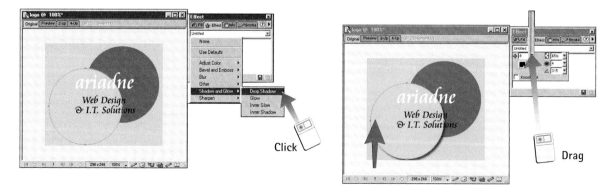

Click

Drag

286   PART 18: APPLYING EFFECTS TO OBJECTS IN FIREWORKS

4 Set the Color and Opacity

Use the **Opacity** slider to set the degree of transparency for the shadow; the lower the number, the more transparent the shadow is. Use the color picker to select a color for the shadow.

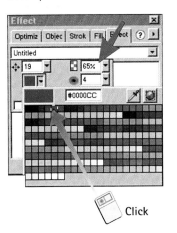

Click

5 Set the Angle and Hardness

Use the **Angle** wheel to move the shadow around the image. Drag the **Angle** wheel to select the angle at which the light appears to hit the image; watch the shadow move in the document window. Then use the **Softness** slider to set the softness of the shadow; a low number creates an almost solid shadow and a high number creates a soft, blurred one.

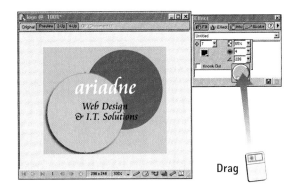
Drag

6 Knock Out the Original

Enable the **Knock Out** check box to remove the original object and show only the shadow. This feature can be used to create some really interesting effects. Notice how this appears to change the layering of the circles.

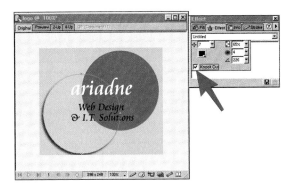

7 Apply the Effects

Click away from the **Effect** panel to close the **Settings** panel. Notice that the **Effect** panel now shows that the selected object has a drop shadow applied to it.

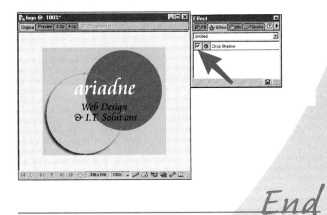

End

How to Create a Beveled Effect

Beveling the edges of an object gives it the appearance of having a sloping edge. The edge can either appear to slope upward, giving the object the impression of being raised, or the edge can slope downward, giving the object the impression of being inset. Bevels make a nice change from shadows, but like anything, don't overuse them.

Begin

1 Create or Select the Object

Create a new object or open an existing one to which you want to add a beveled edge. Select the object (or the portion of the object) to which you want to apply the bevel. From the list of special effects in the **Effect** panel menu, choose the **Bevel and Emboss** effect. Then choose the type of bevel you want to apply. In this example, I selected the **Outer Bevel** option.

Click

2 Set the Bevel Width

Use the slider to set the width of the beveled edge; the smaller the number, the smaller the width of the beveled edge.

Drag

3 Set the Contrast

Use the **Contrast** slider to control the strength of the contrast between the shadow and light sides of the beveled edge; the lower the number, the less the contrast.

Drag

4 Adjust Other Settings

The other options in the **Settings** panel for the bevel effect are the same as those for the Drop Shadow effect and are described in Task 1, "How to Add Shadows." Adjust these options to suit your needs.

Drag

5 Set the Bevel Style

The drop-down menu at the top of the **Settings** panel offers different bevel styles from which you can choose. Choose the bevel style you want.

Click

6 Imitate a Button

You can apply a bevel effect to an image you're using as a button to make it look as though it is being pushed down. Fireworks offers four settings for the Up, Over, Down, and Over While Down button states. Choose **Raised** (Up), **Highlighted** (Over), **Inset** (Down), or **Inverted** (Over While Down) from the drop-down menu at the bottom of the panel to apply one of these formats to the image.

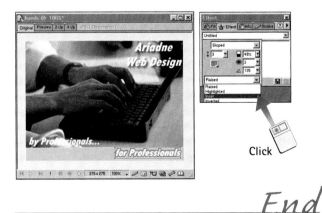

Click

How-To Hints

Beveled or Embossed?

Both the terms *beveled* and *embossed* are used constantly when working with graphics applications and can easily be confused. Applying an embossed effect makes an image appear to be raised above or pushed into the canvas. An inset emboss makes an object appear pushed into the canvas; a raised emboss gives the appearance of raising the object above the canvas.

A bevel effect adds a beveled edge to the object. An inner bevel raises the object inward from the edge; an outer bevel creates the bevel from the edge outward.

End

How to Add a Glow Effect

As its name implies, a glow effect creates a glowing halo around an object. This can be used to make objects stand out or to create an effect that radiates out from the object. Rather than a shadow that drops away from a specific part of an object, the glow effect surrounds the image completely.

Begin

1 Open or Create the Object

Open an existing object or use the drawing tools to create and select the object to which you want to add a glow effect. Choose **Window, Effect** to open the **Effect** panel if it is not already open.

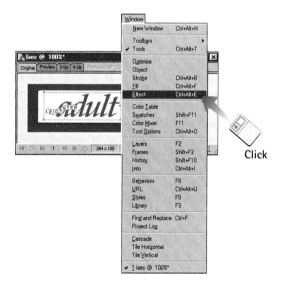

Click

2 Choose Glow

From the list of special effects in the **Effect** panel menu, choose the **Shadow and Glow** effect. Then choose the type of glow effect you want to apply. In this example, I selected the **Glow** option.

3 Set the Width of the Glow

Use the **Glow** slider to specify how wide the halo around the object will be; the bigger the number, the wider the glow ring.

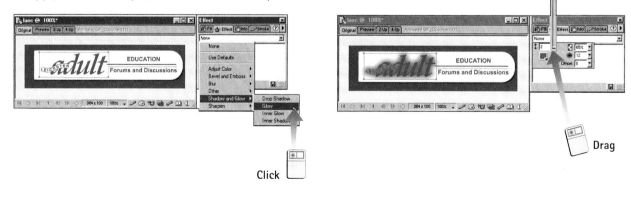

Click

Drag

4 Set the Offset

Use the **Offset** slider to determine how far from the original object the glow will appear; the larger the number, the greater the distance from the object. In general, the glow effect appears more natural when the **Offset** is set to **0**, making the glow ring begin at the edge of the object.

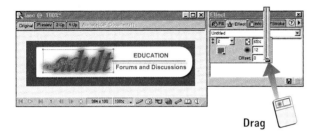

Drag

5 Set the Color

Use the color picker to set the color of the glow. You can select any color you want for the glow; the color of the glow does not need to have any connection to the color of the original object—in fact, you can achieve some other-worldly effects by selecting a poison green color for the glow!

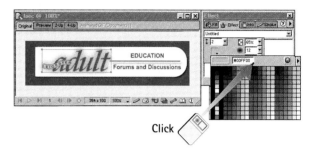

Click

6 Set the Opacity and Softness

Use the **Opacity** slider to select the degree of transparency that the glow effect will have. The higher the number, the more opaque the glow. Use the **Softness** slider to set how tight to the object the glow appears. A low number puts the glow effect close to the object; a high number sets a softer glow around the object.

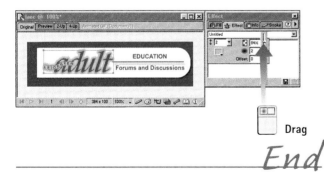

Drag

End

How-To Hints

Want to Glow Inward?

An **Inner Glow** is just as easy to set as the regular **Glow** option—the only difference is that the glow goes inside the object rather than outside. When you set an **Inner Glow** option, you can control all the same settings that are available for the normal **Glow** option.

How to Edit or Remove an Effect

After you have modified your image with some special effects, you might decide to edit those effects—or remove them altogether. Being able to change or delete special effects is a vital skill, and this task explains how to make these changes.

Begin

1 Select the Object

In the main document window, open and select the object that has the effect you want to remove or modify. Any effect that was applied to the object is listed in the **Effect** panel.

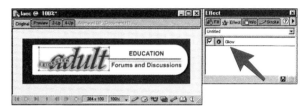

2 Select the Effect

In the **Effect** panel, click to select the effect you want to remove or modify. The entry turns black to indicate that it is selected.

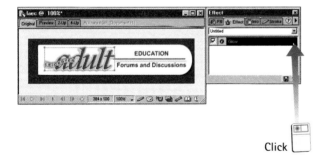

Click

3 Trash the Effect

If you want to delete the selected effect from the image—without affecting any other aspect of the original image—click the trash can icon at the bottom of the **Effect** panel. The selected effect is removed from the list in the **Effect** panel and from the image itself.

Click

4 Change an Effect

If you want to change any of the settings for an effect, double-click the selected effect in the **Effect** panel to reopen the **Settings** panel.

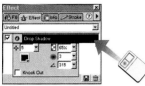

Double-click

5 Adjust the Settings

Use the options on the **Settings** panel to make adjustments to the special effect. Refer to the preceding tasks for information about these options. When you are done changing the settings options, click anywhere outside the **Settings** panel to close it.

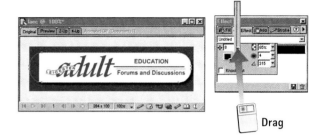

Drag

6 Bring Back the Changes

If you make adjustments to your effects and then decide you don't like them, use the **History** panel to undo the changes. To show the **History** panel, choose **Window History**.

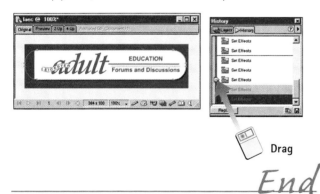

Drag

End

How-To Hints

Playtime Is Here!

The best way to come to grips with all the special effects options available in Fireworks is to play with them. Try one option and see what it does; then change the setting for that option and observe the effect the change has on the original image. Although some of the options might appear to have the same effect as other options, they all have their place. Trial and error is the best way to find out how these options can work for you!

How to Create and Save Custom Effects

If you create a specific effect, such as a drop shadow with particular color and direction settings, you can save and name that effect and apply it to other objects. Being able to apply the same effect to a group of objects makes your images more consistent and will make your Web pages more professional.

Begin

1 Create the Effect

Apply the effect or effects to an object. Make sure that all the settings are exactly as you want them. In this example, I added a drop shadow to some text. I want to save the drop shadow effect so that I can add the same effect to other text I will create.

2 Save the Effect

Click to select the effect in the **Effect** panel (the entry will turn black to indicate that it's selected) and then click the **Save** icon at the bottom of the **Effect** panel. The **Save Effect As** dialog box opens.

Click

3 Name the Effect

In the dialog box, type an appropriate name for the effect and click **OK**.

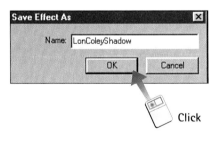

Click

④ Apply the Effect to Another Object

After you have saved an effect, you can reuse it with any other object. Open or select another object. Open the **Effect** drop-down menu and locate the name of the effect you just saved; choose it to apply that effect to the new object.

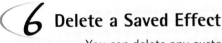

Click

⑤ Rename a Saved Effect

You can rename any effect you have saved. Select the effect you want to rename from the drop-down menu and then choose **Rename Effect** from the **Effect** panel menu. The **Rename Effect** dialog box opens. Type a new name for the effect and click **OK**.

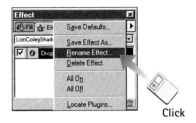

Click

⑥ Delete a Saved Effect

You can delete any custom effect you have saved to the **Effect** menu. Select the effect you want to delete from the drop-down menu and then choose **Delete Effect** from the **Effect** panel menu. That effect is no longer available for you to apply to other objects, but any objects that have had the effect applied are unaffected.

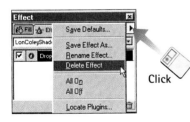

Click

End

How-To Hints

Using Photoshop Plug-Ins as Effects

If you are a Photoshop user, you can install a Photoshop plug-in so that you can use the Photoshop special effects in Fireworks as well. When installed, the Photoshop effects appear in the **Xtras** menu.

Unlike the effects you create in Fireworks, the Photoshop plug-ins cannot be edited or removed once you have applied them.

To install the plug-ins, select **Locate Plugins** from the **Effects** panel menu, locate the plug-ins, and click OK.

Task

Creating Buttons and Navigation Tools in Fireworks

aving nice buttons and a Web site that is easy to navigate can make your site more successful. Fireworks makes the creation of buttons as simple as possible, leaving anything complicated up to you.

When you use Fireworks, you can create buttons that change in appearance as the mouse moves over them or clicks them. The appearance changes exhibited by the buttons are known as *rollovers*: The image rolls over into a new one as the user moves the mouse over or clicks the button.

These effects are achieved using JavaScript; to hand-code the rollover effect is not only time consuming, but also very easy to get wrong. Letting Fireworks do all the script writing for you not only saves time but also guarantees that the code is correct.

Buttons in Fireworks have states; this is not a geographical reference but a reference to the different ways a button can look in the browser. The Up state is the way the button looks when it is simply sitting on the page with no interaction; the Over state is how the button looks when you move the mouse pointer over it. It really is very simple to create even the most complex buttons in a small amount of time. After you have mastered the creation of a single button, you'll be ready to move on to a navigation bar.

A *navigation bar* is a collection of buttons, each of which links to a different page in your site. Navigation bars give a consistent feel to your site as well as create a way of grouping your buttons together in a single image file. And just as it does for button rollovers, Fireworks writes all the navigation bar code for you.

How to Create a Simple Button

Fireworks has a built-in **Button** editor, designed specifically to make your life easier. Not only can you use it to create the button designs you want, but also Fireworks will write the script that controls the button's behavior. Start by creating a new, blank document with the canvas color and size to suit your needs.

Begin

1 Create a New Button

Choose **Insert, New Button**. The **Button** editor opens, ready to create a new button.

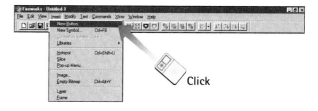
Click

2 Design the Button

Treat the **Button** editor as a canvas onto which you create the graphic you want to use as the button. You can draw shapes, import bitmaps, or drag objects from your main document into the **Button** editor. The tabs across the top of the editor window tell you that you are designing the image to be used for the button's **Up** state.

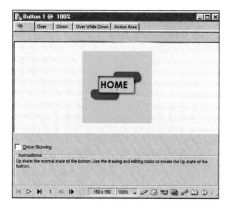

3 Set Onion Skinning for Subsequent States

Enable the **Onion Skinning** check box in the bottom-left corner of the editor window. This option displays an outline of the button you created for the **Up** state when you create the images for the other states. Click the **Over** tab to create a version of the button to be displayed when the viewer moves the mouse over the button. The **Onion Skinning** option forces the display of a ghost button as a basis for the new image.

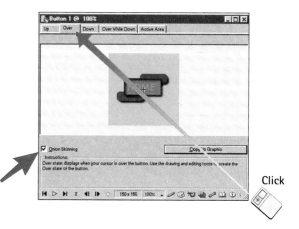
Click

4 Copy the Up Button

If you want the **Over** state of the button to be similar to that of the **Up** state (for example, you might want the images to be the same in everything but color), click the **Copy Up Graphic** button to place an editable copy of the **Up** button graphic in the **Over** tab. Edit the copied graphic to create a unique image.

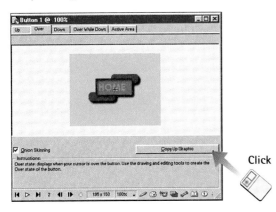

Click

5 Set the Active Area

Now that you have images for a couple of the button states, click the **Active Area** tab to establish the area of the button that will respond to the mouse. The active area is represented by a "slice" that will probably appear on your screen as a semi-opaque green rectangle. (When working with buttons, a *slice* is an area of the object that responds to a mouse movement or click.) The rectangle Fireworks creates automatically covers the entire button. You can adjust this area using the selection tools.

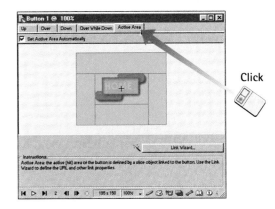

Click

6 Create a Link

Click the **Link Wizard** button to create a hyperlink from the button to a particular page. The **Link Wizard** will walk you through the steps for adding a hyperlink to the button graphic (see Task 4, "How to Link Buttons and Export the Navigation Bar," for more information). You can now close the **Button** editor and return to the main document window. Your button appears in the **Library** for this document. Save the file as a PNG file for future editing.

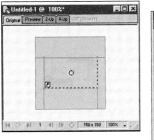 

How-To Hints

Shapes and Sizes

When you create a button with different states, you can change as much of the graphic for each state that you want. In this task, I simply changed the button colors for the different states, but you could be more adventurous and use completely different shapes for each button state. Too much change might not be good for the visitor's eyes, but there is nothing to stop you from using whatever shapes you want. Fireworks automatically sets the active area to cover the largest button.

End

How to Edit and Add Button States

In the previous task, we created a simple button that simply changes colors when the mouse moves over it. So far, that button does not change when it's clicked. After you've created a button, you can go back and add states or edit the images you've already created for the states. The single button you created in Task 1 can be used as the basis for a navigation bar, which you will learn how to create in the next task.

Begin

1 Add a Down State

Open the file you saved at the end of the previous task. The image opens as a graphic file with the active area highlighted. To open the **Button** editor so that you can further edit the image, double-click the graphic. For this task, we will add a **Down** state to the existing button: Click the **Down** tab to open the **Button** editor for the **Down** state.

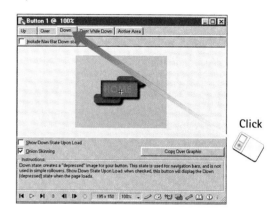

Click

2 Copy the Over State

Click the **Copy Over Graphic** button to copy the image from the **Over** tab to the **Down** tab so that you can edit the image to create the **Down** state of the button.

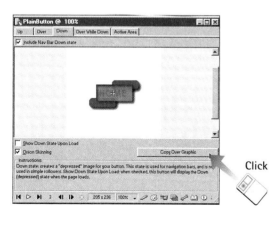

Click

3 Edit the Image

Edit the **Over** graphic to create the **Down** button. Make sure that the changes you make to the image are enough to make the **Down** graphic distinct from both the **Up** and the **Over** graphics. In this example, I am changing the colors of the bars and the text on the image.

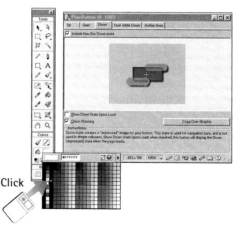

Click

4 Add an Over While Down State

Click the **Over While Down** tab and repeat Steps 2 and 3 to create the **Over While Down** state for the button. For this state, I changed the colors of the bars back to their original colors but have added a glow to the text. This example now has images for all four button states. Close the **Button** editor and resave the file. Because the graphic is a PNG file, saving the file automatically saves all the button states with the file.

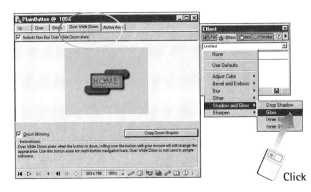

Click

5 Edit Button Text

Any text you put on the button image on the **Up** tab is copied along with the button graphic when you click the **Copy Graphic** button on the various tabs. You can edit the text just as you can any aspect of the graphic. Open the **Button** editor and click the appropriate tab; double-click the text on the button to open the **Text** editor. Change the text in any way that you want and click OK. When prompted to update the text on the other buttons, click Yes if you want the text change to appear on all the other button graphics or click **No** if you want the change to appear on only the current button state.

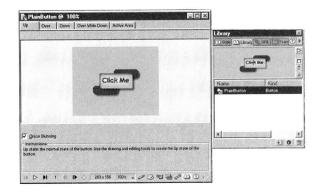

6 Edit Button Graphics

You can edit the button graphics at any time by simply opening the button in the **Button** editor and selecting the tab for the button state you want to change. Edit the graphic as you would any other object in Fireworks. Close the **Button** editor and save the file to retain your updates.

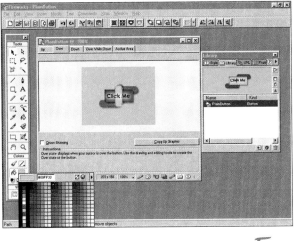

How-To Hints

Using Ready Made Buttons

Fireworks actually ships with some buttons in the **Library** that you can use in your own sites. To see the premade buttons and to insert one or more, choose Insert, Libraries and choose the button (or navigation bar) that you want to use in your site. When you have selected the button to use, click Import, and the button will be added to the Library for the current document.

End

How to Create Navigation Bars

A *navigation bar* is a collection of buttons that has been saved together as a group to create a navigation system for a Web site. In this task, we create a simple navigation bar; you can always get more complicated later. With a Fireworks navigation bar, you can create one button and then change the text and link information to create additional buttons. You can also add additional graphics to make the bar look more stylish and less like a simple collection of buttons.

Begin

1 Create a New Button

In Fireworks, choose **Insert, New Button** and create an image that uses only basic graphics—no text. Refer to Tasks 1 and 2 to copy or create images for each of the four button states (**Up, Over, Down,** and **Over While Down**). Do not add any text to the images for any of the button states. Close the **Button** editor; this action places the button into the **Library**.

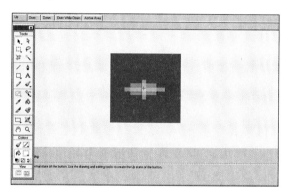

2 Create a Blank Button

In the same document, choose **Insert, New Button** to create a second button. This time, do not create any content: Leave the **Button** editor window blank.

3 Add the First Button

Choose **Window, Library** to open the **Library** panel. Drag the button you created in Step 1 from the **Library** into the new empty button window you made in Step 2.

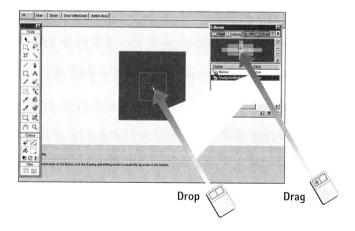

Drop   Drag

4 Open the Layers Panel

Open the **Layers** panel for the new, copied button by choosing **Window, Layers**. Select any layer that is not shared (that is, select a layer that doesn't have the ladder icon on the right). You can always double-click a layer to open the **Layer Options** dialog box to see whether the **Share Across Frames** check box is enabled.

Click 🖱️

5 Add Button Text

With the layer selected, add text to each button state. The text should be appropriate for the page to which you are linking. I used *Home* as the text for this button. Remember that, if you are using different colors for the button states, the text must also be a different color. When the text is in place, close the **Button** editor to save the button and its text.

6 Duplicate the Button

The button with its text appears in the main document window. Choose **Edit, Duplicate** to duplicate the button as many times as needed for the navigation bar. Change the text for each button by opening the **Object** panel for the selected button. Change the text displayed in the **Button Text** field. You will be asked whether you want to update all instances of the button or just the current one. Because you want the change to affect only the current button, choose **Current One**.

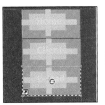

7 Save the File

Close the **Button** editor and save the file. This action saves all the instances of the button into the single file that will become your navigation bar. You can use Fireworks to add more objects or text into the file to make it look more like an image and less like a group of buttons. In this example, the collection of buttons has been made into more of a graphic that will fit the style of a Web page. You'll add the links and export the file in the following tasks.

End

How to Link Buttons and Export the Navigation Bar

After you have created a button and all its states—or a complete navigation bar with multiple buttons—you should link each button to a page within your own Web site or to an external URL. In this task, you learn to use the **Link Wizard** to add a link to a single button; to add links to multiple buttons in a navigation bar, repeat the process for each button. The **Link Wizard** can also add Alt text for each button, making your navigation bar not only look professional, but also be extremely functional.

Begin

1 Open a Button

Open the saved button graphic file (or the navigation bar graphic file) into Fireworks and double-click one of the buttons in the graphic. This action opens that instance of the button into the **Button** editor.

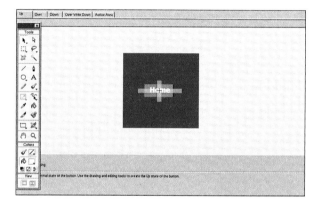

2 Open the Link Wizard

In the **Button** editor, click the **Active Area** tab and then click the **Link Wizard** button to open the **Link Wizard**.

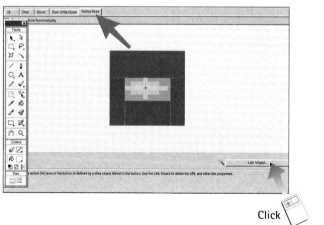

Click

3 Add a Link

Click the **Link** tab and type the path and filename to which you want this button to link.

4 Add Some Alternate Text

In the **Alt** box, type some text that will appear on the button as the mouse moves over the button. This text will also appear to a visitor whose browser cannot display the button graphic.

5 Add Status Bar Text

If you want a message to appear in the status bar when the button is activated, type that text in the **Status Bar Text** box.

6 Specify a Target Frame

If your site is frames based, use the **Target** tab of the **Links Wizard** to specify the frame in which you want the linked file to be displayed. Use the drop-down list to choose the correct frame. The text on this tab explains the meanings of the frame names. Click **OK** to close the wizard and assign the link to the selected button. To refresh yourself on frames, check out Part 9, "Using Frames and Framesets."

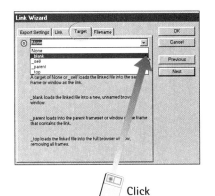
Click

How-To Hints

Let Fireworks Do the Hard Work

You can leave the settings on the other tabs in the **Link Wizard** at their defaults. Fireworks will do all the hard work for you when you export the file. Fireworks will carefully slice all the buttons and any other graphics and name them individually in a logical numbered manner, saving you hours of hard work. Remember that all the individual buttons are unique graphics as well, so each button state will have its own file and link information saved with it.

End

How to Export Buttons to Dreamweaver

After you have created a button or a navigation bar in Fireworks, it's relatively easy to export the file so that you can use the graphics and all their links in a Dreamweaver page. This task explains how to use the **Export Wizard** to send the buttons into Dreamweaver or any other HTML application. When you export the file, Fireworks exports all the required files for the buttons, states, and link information so that you can simply place the file into your Dreamweaver page and have the navigation bar or buttons work straight away.

2 View the Analysis

Fireworks analyzes your document and makes export suggestions. Click **Exit** to progress through this screen.

Click

Begin

1 Open the Export Wizard

In the main document window, choose **File, Export Wizard** to open the **Export Wizard** to the splash screen; click **Continue** to move on to the **Choose Destination** page. Enable the appropriate export option—in this case, **Dreamweaver**—and click **Continue**.

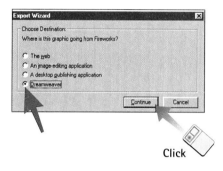

Click

3 Choose a File Format

From the **Export Preview** dialog box that opens, choose a file format for the button or navigation bar you are exporting. In most cases, a GIF file is appropriate because buttons contain only small numbers of colors and download time is vital. Leave the remaining settings as Fireworks suggests and click **Export** to open the **Export** dialog box.

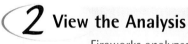

Click

4 Set Slicing Options

In the **File Name** field, type a base name for the button; from this base name, Fireworks names all the sliced files. Make sure that the **Slices** field is set to **Export Slices** and that the **HTML** field is set to **Export HTML File**. You want to slice the button graphic to ensure that Fireworks exports all the information for all the buttons and their states. To learn more about slices, read Part 21, "Working with Slices and HTML in Fireworks."

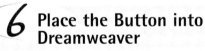

5 Browse to a Location

In the **Save In** field at the top of the dialog box, browse to the location in which you want to save the HTML file. Click the **Put images in subfolder** check box and browse to the **images** directory within your Web site folder. Click **Save** to save the files.

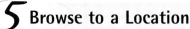

6 Place the Button into Dreamweaver

Back in Dreamweaver, open the site in which you want to use the navigation bar you created in Fireworks. Open the **Objects** panel in Dreamweaver and click the **Insert Fireworks HTML** button to open the **Insert Fireworks HTML** dialog box.

Click

7 Insert the HTML File

Click the **Browse** button and navigate to the HTML file you exported in Step 5. Click **Select** to choose the file and then click **OK** to insert it into the Dreamweaver page. The complete navigation bar—along with all its links and button states—will appear on the page.

End

Working with Layers and Frames in Fireworks

*L*ayers are used in Fireworks to give you more flexibility when working with image files; you can simply place each object in your file onto a different layer. Layers are similar to having many pieces of clear acetate, each with a part of the image on it. When the layers are stacked on top of each other, the image becomes visible as a whole. However, for editing purposes, each component or layer is totally independent of the others.

The **Layers** panel in Fireworks displays the layers in your current file, including the names of the layers and whether they are visible or invisible, locked or unlocked. The stacking order of the layers in the panel reflects the way that the layers are stacked on the canvas. It is a good idea to give each layer a unique name so that you can easily identify it.

When you change an object on your canvas, look at the **Layers** panel for the blue box that indicates which layer the object is on. When you add new objects to your image, they are placed on the layer that is selected in the **Layers** panel.

The new animation options in Fireworks 4 make it easier than ever to create great-looking animations without bothering with the technical stuff behind them. All you have to do is create the objects you want to animate and let Fireworks do the rest. In the tasks in this part, you learn how to use layers and frames; the last task shows you how to create a more complicated animation using all the skills you learned in the preceding tasks in the part.

How to Add and Work with Layers

When you create a new document in Fireworks, two layers are created: Layer 1, which is where the initial content will go, and the Web Layer. You cannot edit or delete the Web Layer; it contains information needed when you use slices or hotspots. Layer 1 is created as a starting point for you to work with. If you are creating a document without making layers, everything you do appears on Layer 1.

Begin

1 Create a New Document

Open Fireworks and create a new document. We'll use this document to build on and add layers to. The size and canvas color can be whatever you want it to be.

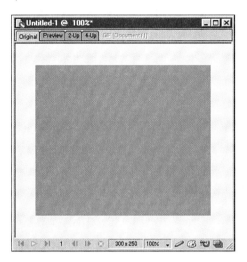

2 Show the Layers Panel

Choose **Window, Layers** to show the **Layers** panel. Notice that, even though your new document contains no real content, the **Layers** panel shows that the document has two layers: the Web Layer and Layer 1.

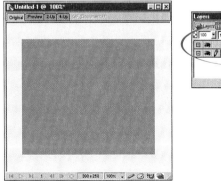
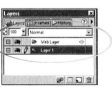

3 Add a New Layer

To add a new layer to the document, click the **Layers** panel menu and choose **New Layer**. The **New Layer** dialog box opens.

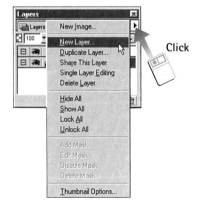

Click

4 Name the Layer

In the **New Layer** dialog box, either type a name for the layer you are adding or accept the default. In this case, the default layer name is **Layer 2**. Click **OK** to continue.

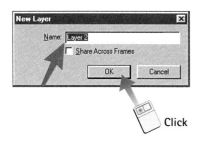

Click

5 Activate a Layer

Any objects that you add to the canvas are automatically placed on whichever layer is selected. To select the layer to which you want to add an object or with which you want to work, click the layer in the **Layers** panel. The layer becomes highlighted in the panel. Click **Layer 1** and add a circle, and then click **Layer 2** and draw a square. Notice that the **Layers** panel shows you what is contained in each layer.

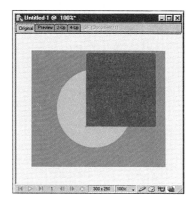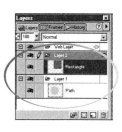

6 Rename a Layer

Layers can be renamed easily in Dreamweaver. In this example, I added a green circle to Layer 1 and want to rename the layer to identify what it contains. To rename a layer, double-click the name of the layer in the **Layers** panel to open the **Layer Options** dialog box and then rename the layer to something more appropriate. Press the **Enter** key to continue.

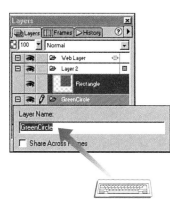

7 Delete a Layer

You can delete any layer (except for the Web Layer) just as easily as you can create a layer. To delete a layer, select it in the **Layers** panel and then click the trash can icon. Fireworks deletes the layer without prompting you to confirm the action. All the content of the selected layer is deleted.

Click

End

How to Plan a Simple Animation

Animation adds movement and life to any Web site; however, too much animation can be bad visually and actually detract from an otherwise well-presented site. Fireworks lets you create animated GIFs—a series of static images that display quickly in rotation, giving the appearance of movement. By changing the content of each frame in succession, you can create movement, resize images, change colors, create fades, and even present entire cartoons for your Web site. Fireworks can even save you some work by *tweening*, a process that creates movement between frames for you. Planning an animation before you start helps ensure that you get the results you want.

Begin

1 Create a Document and Show the Frames Panel

Create a new document that has the size you want. Choose **Window, Frames** to open the **Frames** panel. As you know, animations are made up of frames of static images that, when displayed quickly in succession, give the illusion of movement. To manage the frames for your animation, you use the **Frames** panel.

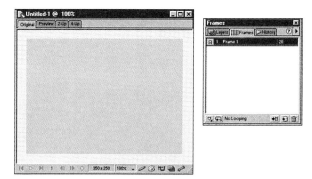

2 Add New Frames

From the **Frames** panel menu, choose **Add Frames** to add new frames to the document. In the **Add Frames** dialog box that opens, use the **Number** slider to specify the number of frames you want to add. The frame delay determines how long each frame is displayed; the frame delay is specified in one-hundredths of a second, so a setting of 150 keeps the frame on display for one and a half seconds.

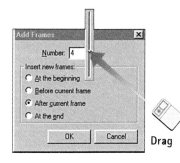

Drag

3 Position the Frames

Use the **Add Frames** dialog box to specify where the new frames will appear. When planning an animation from scratch (as we are in this task), it's easiest to add all the frames to the end of the document. However, you can add the frames to the beginning of the document or before or after the current frame. For this example, click the **At the end** radio button and click **OK** to continue.

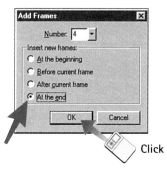

Click

4 Add Content

Select **Frame 1** in the **Frames** panel by clicking it. (The selected frame is highlighted.) Add some content to the frame. For this example, I typed the number 1 and formatted it in a large, fun font.

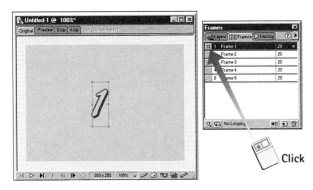

Click

5 Add Content to the Other Frames

Add some text or objects to each of the other frames. Make sure that each frame is different from the previous frame. For this example, I typed a different number in a different position in each frame.

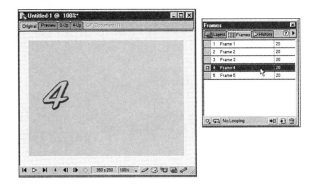

6 View the Animation

Use the play controllers at the bottom of the screen to view the animation. Notice that this simple animation will loop constantly. Refer to Task 4 for information about controlling some of the properties of an animation.

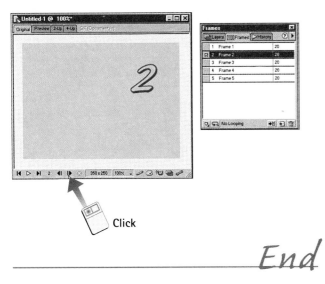

Click

End

How-To Hints

Animation Hints

In this part of the book, we are making animated GIFs (you cannot have animated JPEG files). The **Optimize** panel allows you to select the file format before you export the file to ensure that all the frames are correctly exported. If you forget to optimize the image, you will get only a single frame.

Previewing Animations

When making animations, you have to use the animation playback controls in the Fireworks document window to see the results. Previewing in a browser displays only a single frame.

Looping

The **Looping** option in the **Frames** panel lets you set how many times your animation will run. Although animated GIFs often run forever, they don't have to. Remember that if you set your animation to play only once, it might not load quickly enough to display in slow browsers; a minimum of two plays is therefore advised.

How to Export an Animation to Dreamweaver

Like any other image file, animation files should be optimized when they are exported. Fireworks lets you export your animation as a single animated GIF, as multiple files that can be edited separately, or as a Macromedia SWF file. If you choose to export an animated file as a SWF file, you will be able to edit the file in Macromedia Flash (assuming that you have the software). For more information about Flash, see the Macromedia Web site at
http://www.macromedia.com.

Begin

1 Start the Export Process

With your completed animation file open and saved in Fireworks, choose **File, Export Wizard** to launch the **Export Wizard**. Click **Continue** until you see this screen, where you will choose the type of export file you want to create. In this case, choose **Animated GIF** and click **Continue**.

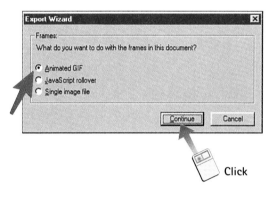

Click

2 Optimize the File

When you get to the **Export Preview** window, optimize the file in the same way as you would any other file: Remove any unnecessary colors, set the export area, and so on. Click **Export** to continue.

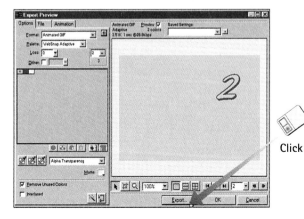

Click

3 Select a Location for the File

In the **Export** dialog box that opens, browse to the location in which you want to store your animation file (normally in the **images** folder of the site you are creating in Dreamweaver). Click **Save** to complete the export process.

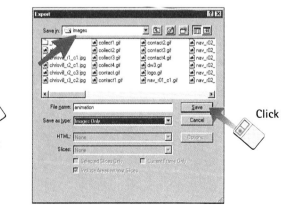

Click

$\boldsymbol{4}$ Insert the Animation into a Page

Open your site in Dreamweaver and insert the animation file on the desired page as you would any other GIF image.

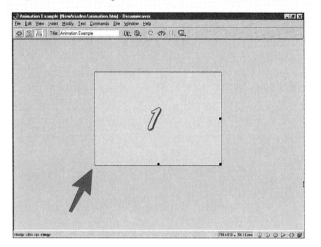

$\boldsymbol{5}$ Preview the File in the Browser

Although you can see the first frame of the animation file in the Dreamweaver window, you cannot see the actual action in Dreamweaver. To do that, you must preview the page in a browser. Choose **File, Preview in Browser** and choose a browser from your list. There you are; animation made easy using Fireworks!

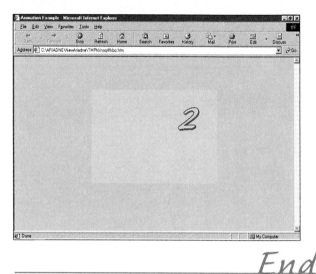

End

How-To Hints

Exporting Options

In the tasks in this book, we are concentrating on creating animated GIF files; however, Fireworks allows you to export your animation in other formats as well. You can export your animation as a series of multiple files by choosing **File, Export Special, Layer/Frames to Files**. Select **Frames** from the pop-up menu, and each frame will be saved as an individual file.

Exporting to Flash

You can export your work to the Flash application for further editing by selecting **File, Export Special, Flash SWF**. Exporting an animation to Flash causes some Fireworks formatting to be lost. It is well worth your time to check the Fireworks help files for a full list of formatting options you might lose in this transfer.

How to Control Animations

The preceding tasks explained how to create a simple animation in Fireworks and how to export it to Dreamweaver. Many factors control the way an animation looks and plays. This task looks at the panels and control options that affect those factors. Starting with a new document, let's create a series of shapes and letters that will change in the animation. You can use any topic for an animation. In this example, I used the letters in my name and a series of random shapes.

Begin

1 Create a New Document

Create a new document and draw or insert all the objects you want to use in the animation. Don't worry too much at this stage about the layers on which the elements appear in the document—we will sort this out later.

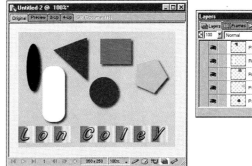

2 Save the File

Saving the animation file periodically as you work is a good idea. You don't want to risk losing all the hard work you put in to it. Choose **File, Save As** and save the file as a PNG file so that you can continue to work on it in Fireworks.

3 Create a New Layer

Create a new layer that will contain all the shapes in the image. In the **Layers** panel, click the **New/Duplicate Layer** button at the bottom of the panel. The new layer, with the default name **Layer 2**, is added to the **Layers** panel and is automatically selected.

Click

4 Select the Shapes to Add to the Layer

Select all the shapes in the document (do not select the squares with text in them). To select all the shapes at the same time, hold down the **Shift** key as you click. Each shape becomes highlighted as you select it. Notice that the items are also selected in the **Layers** panel.

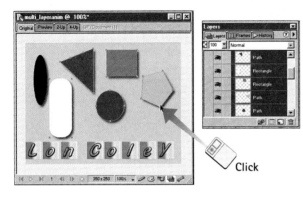

Click

5 Move the Shapes

Look at the **Layers** panel. Notice the blue square next to Layer 1. This icon indicates that the selected items are currently on that layer. Drag the square to Layer 2 to move the selected shapes to Layer 2. Now the shapes are on Layer 2, and the text remains on Layer 1.

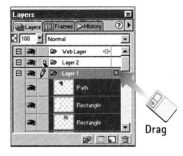

Drag

6 Make the Text Visible in All Layers

We want the text to be visible at all times in the animation. To do this, we need to share Layer 1 (the layer that contains the text) across all frames in the animation. Click Layer 1 in the **Layers** panel to select it and open the **Layers** panel menu.

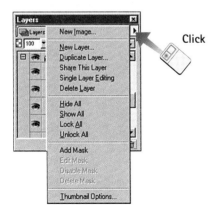

Click

7 Share the Layer

From the **Layers** panel menu, choose **Share This Layer**. Fireworks inserts a filmstrip icon next to the layer name to indicate that this layer is shared across all the frames.

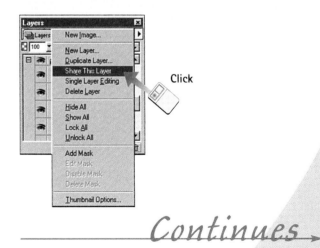

Click

Continues

8 Select and Move the Shapes

In the **Layers** panel, click the **Layer 2** tile to select the layer that contains the shapes. Select each shape in turn and move it to cover part of the text. The order doesn't matter; just cover the text with the shapes. In your own files, select the layer containing the objects you want to move and arrange them so that they appear in their initial locations.

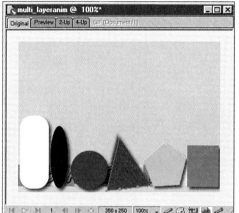

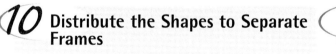

9 Select the Shapes and See the Frames

Select all the shapes by holding the **Shift** key as you click each shape in turn. Then show the **Frames** panel by clicking its tab. (If the **Frames** panel isn't showing onscreen, choose **Window, Frames** to display the panel.)

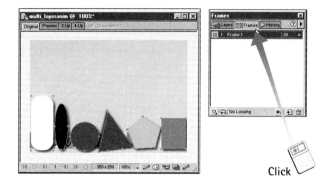

Click

10 Distribute the Shapes to Separate Frames

Click the **Distribute to Frames** button at the bottom of the **Frames** panel. This action places each of the shapes onto a different frame in the animation.

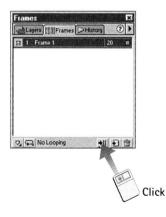

Click

11 Preview the Animation

Use the animation playback controls at the bottom of the document window to see the animation in action. Notice that, as each frame appears, one of the shapes covers a different part of the series of letters.

Click

12 Optimize the Image

Choose **Window, Optimize** to display the **Optimize** panel (alternatively, click the **Show Optimize** button at the bottom of the document window). Choose **Animated GIF** from the options. If you don't choose **Animated GIF** at this point, when you export the file for use in Dreamweaver, you will export only Frame 1.

Click

13 Set the Frame Rate

Press and hold the **Shift** key and click all the frames in the **Frames** panel. From the **Frames** panel menu, choose **Properties**. In the dialog box that opens, set the **Frame Rate** (the amount of time each frame displays). The default is 20 hundredths of a second; 50 hundredths is half a second. To make the animation play faster, make the **Frame Rate** number smaller.

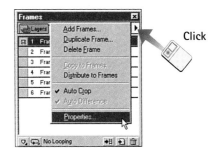

Click

14 Save the File

Now save the file and export it for use in a Dreamweaver page. Refer to the previous task for instructions on optimizing and exporting animation files.

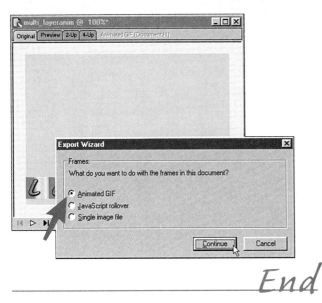

End

How to Work with Symbols and Animations

You can use many options to create and change animations in Fireworks. This task looks at some of those options and clarifies some terminology that you might have heard about. In the preceding tasks, you created the content for every frame in an animation. This task looks at how Fireworks can automatically generate the content for frames if you identify the starting and ending frames of the animation. This process is known as *tweening*.

Begin

1 Create a New Document and a Symbol

In a new document, draw a shape and convert it to a symbol by choosing **Insert, Convert to Symbol**. The **Symbol Properties** dialog box opens. Choose **Animation** from the symbol options and give the symbol a meaningful name. The symbol now resides in the **Library** for this document. To make it obvious how tweening works, I stick to a simple shape, but you can be more creative with your symbols.

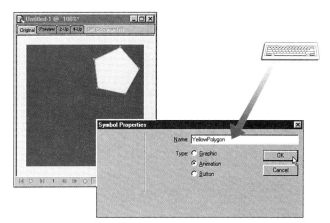

2 Insert the Symbol

Into the new document, insert two instances of the symbol you created in Step 1. Make sure that there is some noticeable space between the two objects.

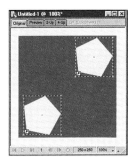

3 Tween the Symbols

Hold down the **Shift** key and click to select both instances of the symbol in the document window. Choose **Modify, Symbol, Tween Instances** to ask Fireworks to create frames to animate the selected symbols. The **Tween Instances** dialog box opens.

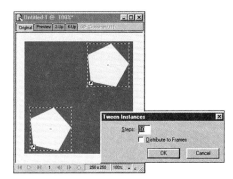

4 Distribute to Frames

Enable the **Distribute to Frames** check box. This option creates a new animation frame for each step that the polygon must take to move from the initial position of the first instance to the position of the other instance. Type the number of steps you want Fireworks to create to move the symbol from the canvas location of the first instance to the canvas location of the second instance. Click **OK** to continue.

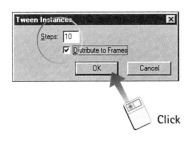

Click

5 Test the Animation

Click the Play button at the bottom of the screen to see the effects of tweening. The first instance of the symbol moves across the screen and ends up where the second instance was. The **Frames** panel now shows all the frames for the animation. Notice that, as the animation plays, the panel highlights each frame in turn to show you which is the current frame.

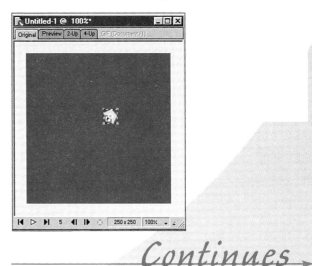

Click

6 Choose an Instance to Transform

You now have a symbol moving across the screen. Now let's change some of the instances. In the **Frames** panel, click Frame 5 to select that frame. In the document window, you can see that the symbol moved slightly. Click to select this instance of the symbol and choose **Modify, Transform** to display a submenu of transformation options that you can apply to this instance.

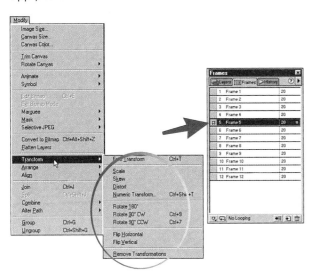

7 Apply Transformations

Choose any of the normal transformation options and apply them to this instance of the symbol. Note that this transformation effect affects only the instance in the selected frame—not all the instances in the other frames. Select other frames and adjust or transform them to create some variation in the animation you are creating. In this example, I transformed an instance to be 25% of its original size.

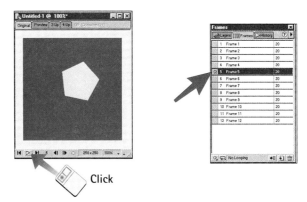

Continues

8 Set Looping Options

The **Looping** setting controls how many times the animation will play. Most animated GIF files play forever, but you can control this by clicking the **Looping** button at the bottom of the **Frames** panel.

Click

9 Pick a Number

From the menu that opens, choose the number of times you want the animation to play. If you select **3**, the animation will play once and then three more times before stopping. Choose **Forever** to cause the animation to play constantly, as long as the page on which it is displayed is open.

Click

10 Fading

By changing the **Opacity** setting during the animation, you can give the impression of a symbol fading in at the start of the animation. From the **Frames** panel, select the instance of the symbol in Frame 1. Choose **Window, Object** to display the **Object** panel. Use the **Opacity** slider to reduce the opacity for this instance of the symbol. By changing the **Opacity** setting across all frames, you can set objects to fade in at the beginning of the animation and then fade away at the end. Work through the instances frame by frame to adjust the opacity to achieve this effect.

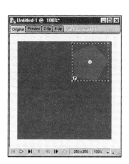

11 Rotate an Instance

Use the **Rotation** setting in the **Object** panel to rotate a symbol in a frame or frames. Use the **Rotation** slider to select the angle of rotation; select the **CW** (clockwise) or **CCW** (counterclockwise) radio button to specify the direction of the rotation.

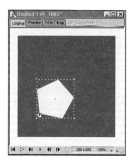

Drag

12 Scale an Instance

Use the **Scaling** slider on the **Object** panel to change the size of any or all instances of the symbol. Remember that changing the properties of an instance has no effect on the underlying, original, symbol. From the **Frames** panel, select the instance that you want to change the size of and use the **Scaling** slider to set the percentage of change. A setting of more than 100% makes the symbol larger than the original, but does not show until you preview or save the animation.

Drag

13 Preview the Animation

Use the animation playback controls at the bottom of the document window to see the effects that you have added to your animation. Do not use the **File, Preview in Browser** command because this command displays only a single frame and not the complete animation.

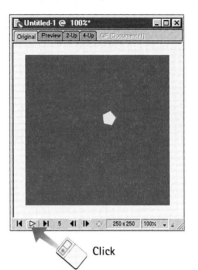

Click

14 Save the File

Save the file as a PNG file by choosing **File, Save** and naming the file. You can edit the PNG file in Fireworks at any time. After you have saved the file, choose **Window, Optimize** to display the **Optimize** panel. Select **Animated GIF** from the drop-down menu and make any other optimization settings that you want. To export the optimized version of the file, choose **File, Export** and complete the dialog box. The file is now ready to be included into any Web page.

Click

How-To Hints

Playing or Working?

Learning how to animate objects in Fireworks (or any other application) can be a time-consuming process. Even still, it should be fun! Start by playing with text, and see whether you can get your name to bounce across the screen, fading in and out. Then, you can use that knowledge to build the animations you want for your Web pages.

Getting Flash?

Remember that if you also have access to Macromedia Flash, you can save your animations as Flash files. Then you can open those files into Flash and edit them further, using some of the dedicated animation techniques in Flash to refine your animations even more. If you don't already have Flash, download a trial version from Macromedia at **http://www.macromedia.com**. Although this trial version will time out, you will have a chance to get to know the application.

End

How to Use Onion Skinning

Onion skinning is a common technique when working with animations. In simple terms, it allows you to see the contents of more than one frame at a time. Onion skinning can help you move an object a certain distance from one frame to the next; the "ghost images" of the objects in the frames before and after the current frame help you position the objects in the current frame.

Begin

1 Open the Onion Skinning Options

Open a file that contains more than one frame and make sure that the **Frames** panel is displayed. Click the **Onion Skinning** button at the bottom of the panel to display a menu of options.

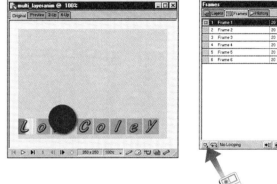

Click

2 Turn On Onion Skinning

By default, the onion skinning feature is turned off in Fireworks. To turn it on, click the option you want. In this example, I want to show the frames before and after the current frame, so I select **Before and After**.

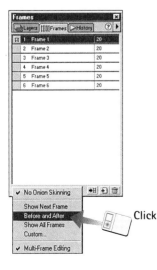

Click

3 Click Between Frames

In the **Frames** panel, click to select different frames. In the document window, you can see not only the contents of the selected frame, but also a dimmed version of the next and previous frames. Notice that the **Frames** panel shows you which frames are being displayed.

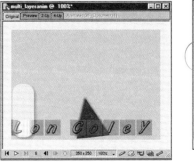

4 Use Multiframe Editing

By default, you can edit the visible contents of any frame in Fireworks, a feature called *multiframe editing*. If you have turned on the onion skinning option, you can manipulate all visible objects regardless of which frame they are on. Select objects from different frames and move them to see this feature in action.

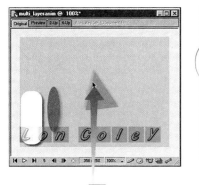 

Drag

5 Turn Off Multiframe Editing

If you don't like having the ability to change objects in frames other than the current frame, you can turn off the multiframe editing feature. Click the **Onion Skinning** button on the **Frames** panel and deselect the **Multi-Frame Editing** option. Now you can edit only those objects actually on the selected frame.

Click

End

How-To Hints

Frame Rate

The frame rate controls the playback speed of your animation. You have total control over the length of time each frame is displayed. The frame rate is specified in hundredths of a second. A value of 50 displays each frame for one-half second; a value of 300 displays each frame for three seconds. To change the frame rate, open the **Frames** panel menu and select **Properties**. Enter the desired value (in hundredths of a second).

How to Create More Complex Animations

Fireworks 4 makes it easier than ever to create more complex animations. In this task, we will use layers, frames, and tweening to create a single animation that uses different objects from the **Library** and makes them all do different things at the same time. In this task, we will create an animated advertising banner for a Web site. Before you start this task, open a new file and create all the objects (shapes, text, and so on) that you want to use in your banner and convert them to individual symbols. The total dimensions for the banner we are creating is 300 pixels by 100 pixels, so make sure that everything you want to include is the right size!

Begin

1 Save Your Work So Far

If you followed the instruction in the opening to this task, you have already done a lot of the hard work. Before we start placing items on layers and in frames, let's save what we have already. Click the **Save** icon in the toolbar and use the **Save As** dialog box to save the file as a PNG file. The file and all the library items are now safe in case our experiments fail and we have to start over again.

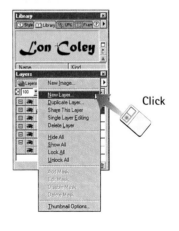

2 Add Static Items

Choose **Window, Layers** to display the **Layers** panel. Select Layer 1 and draw or insert any items, text, or symbols that you want to appear static throughout the animation. In this example, I add a Web site address that I want site visitors to see at all times. Use the **Layers** panel menu to share Layer 1 across all frames.

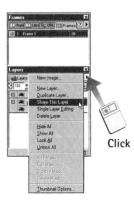

Click

3 Add More Layers

Use the **Layers** panel to add more layers. For this example, add one layer for each symbol that you intend to use in the animation. Give each layer a meaningful name.

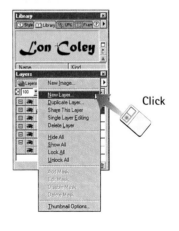

Click

4 Add Content and Animation

Select the first of the new layers that you added in Step 3 and insert the appropriate symbol from the **Library**. In this example, I add a symbol of some oversized text. As you can see, this symbol is too big for the document, but we can animate it to be the correct size. Select the instance on the screen and choose **Modify, Animate, Settings** to open the Animate dialog box.

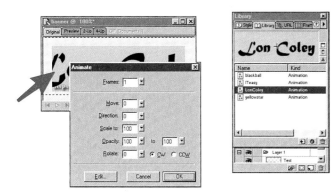

5 Set Up the Animation

Use the **Animate** dialog box to specify what will happen to the symbol (in this case, the text). Start by setting how many frames the animation for this instance will be. (I specified 10 frames in this example.) Select other options to make the symbol move to its final position. The numbers for these options are in pixels; the **Direction** dial specifies the direction in which the symbol will travel based on a 360-degree circle. Use the **Scale to** slider to set the final size of the symbol.

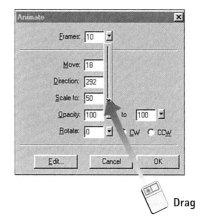

Drag

6 Preview the Animation

Use the animation playback controls at the bottom of the document window to see whether the symbol moves as you expect. If you want to make any adjustments to the final position of the symbol, simply reopen the **Animate** dialog box and make changes to the options. Keep tweaking the adjustments until you get the results you want.

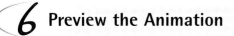

Click

Continues

7 Add the Next Content

Select the next layer and place the symbol on the canvas where you want it to be when the animation starts. In this example, I place the symbol at the edge of the canvas; we will animate it so that it moves across the screen. Open the **Animate** dialog box and specify the settings you want to apply to this symbol. Set the number of frames to 10 (to agree with the value you specified in Step 5 so that the animations run concurrently). Set the **Move** field to be the width of the document (the maximum is 250 pixels). Set the **Opacity** values to **0 to 100** so that the symbol fades in as it moves across the screen. Click **OK** to apply these settings and repeat Step 6 to preview the animation.

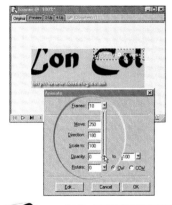

8 Add Layer 3

In the next layer, I place a yellow star that is only partly on the canvas. In the **Animate** dialog box, I specify that this symbol is to rotate 360 degrees over 10 frames and scale it to **0**. These settings will give the illusion that the star is spinning and shrinking until it disappears. Repeat Step 6 to test the animation and make adjustments as necessary.

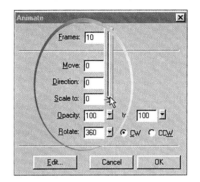

9 Add the Rest of the Symbols

Repeat Steps 4 through 6 until you have added all the symbols you created for the animation. Make any adjustments to the location of the symbols as they move through the frames. In the last layer of this example, I add a little black ball that will bounce across the text. To make sure that the ball appears exactly where I want it to, I manually place the symbol into each frame. This gives you exact control over the location of the symbol; it also gives you the option of missing a few frames if you choose.

10 Set Looping

Choose **Window, Frames** to display the **Frames** panel and set the **Looping** option for the animation. In the case of a banner advertisement, you will probably want the animation to loop forever.

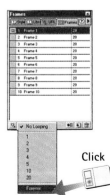

Click

_11_ Optimize the Animation

Use the **Optimize** panel to make the file an **Animated GIF** to ensure that all the required frames are exported with the image file.

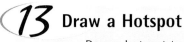

Click

_12_ Select the Hotspot Tool

There is no real point in a banner ad that does not link anywhere. To make the animation link to a particular site, select Frame 1 of the animation and then click the **Hotspot** tool in the toolbar.

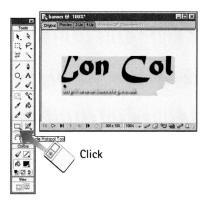

Click

_13_ Draw a Hotspot

Drag a hotspot to cover the entire document window. Then use the **Object** panel to specify the URL of the hyperlink along with any alternative text you want visitors to see when they hover the mouse pointer over the banner.

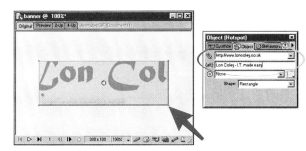

_14_ Export the File

Use the normal export procedures to export the file into your Dreamweaver site folder. Remember to save the PNG file as well so that you can come back and edit the animation in Fireworks at any time. After all, you don't want to start all over again!

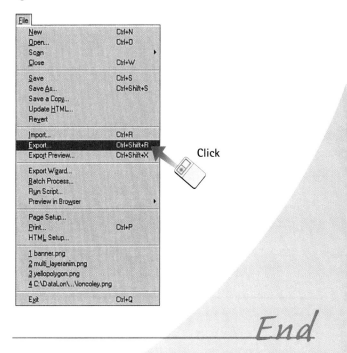

Click

End

Task

Working with Slices and HTML in Fireworks

*A*s its name suggests, a *slice* is a piece of an image. Large images can be sliced into smaller sections that are then rebuilt in the browser window into the complete file. Slices are the perfect way to download large images speedily. Slicing an image not only saves download time, but it also gives the site visitor something to see early in the browsing process.

The slicing process actually cuts the image into smaller pieces; when the file is exported, Fireworks generates a table that holds all the smaller images as well as the code required for a perfect rebuild in the browser.

You might choose to slice an image for any of several reasons: You can split a large image into pieces to enable a smooth and speedy download, you can use slices for text messages that have to be updated, and you can use slices to save different parts of an image in different formats. (For example, you can save one part of an image as a GIF file and another part as a JPEG file.)

When you create a text slice, Fireworks creates a table cell that contains none of the image—just your text. This cell can then be edited in Dreamweaver without your having to open the image file at all.

How to Split a Large Image

Fireworks allows you to split, or *slice*, an image into multiple pieces, each of which is stored in a separate file. When you slice an image in this way, Fireworks also creates an HTML document that instructs the browser how to reassemble the separate files back into the original image. Think of slices like a jigsaw puzzle: You create the pieces in the shapes and sizes you want, and Fireworks brings them together in the browser for you. You can slice the image into simple rectangles, or you can use the polygon tool to create different shaped slices. When you use polygons, remember that the code Fireworks creates is more complex and can make the end result take longer to download.

Begin

1 Open the Image to Slice

Open a large single image (such as one that has a long download time) into the Fireworks window. In the toolbox, click the **Slice** tool to select it. If necessary, reduce the size of the image on the screen so that you can see the entire image; use the toolbar to select the percentage you need. Do not resize the image to do this; simply display it at a smaller percentage.

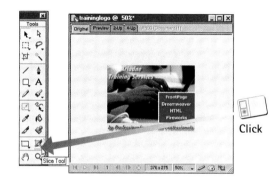

Click

2 Draw the Slices

Use the **Slice** tool to drag out rectangles over the image. Each rectangle represents an image slice. Draw as many rectangles as you need to split the image. In this example, I sliced the image into areas representing different parts of a company.

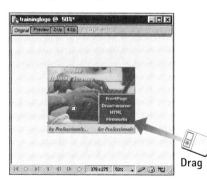

Drag

3 Look at the Export Preview

Choose **File, Export Wizard** and click through the screens until you come to the **Export Preview** window. Select either GIF or JPEG, depending on the type of file you are working with. When you are happy with the settings, click the **Export** button to continue.

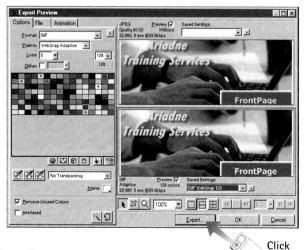

Click

4 Choose the Slicing Option

A warning dialog box pops up, telling you that you have to choose **Use Slice Objects**. Because you will do that in the next dialog box, click **OK** to acknowledge the warning. In the **Export** dialog box that opens, use the **Slicing** drop-down list to choose **Use Slice Objects**. (Note that simply exporting the file does not give you options for choosing the file type or using slice options.)

Click

5 Choose the HTML Type

Use the **Save in** field at the top of the dialog box to specify a location for the HTML file that Fireworks will create. Click the **Options** button to check that the created HTML is for Dreamweaver. Use the **Save as type** drop-down menu to select **HTML and Images**.

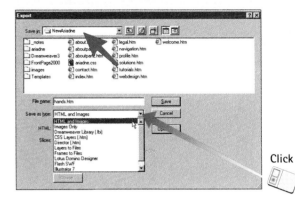

Click

6 Choose a Location for the Images

Having specified that the HTML file will be stored with your other pages, you must now tell Fireworks where to store the images that it creates. Assuming that your images are stored in a subfolder, enable the **Put Images in Subfolder** check box and browse to your **images** folder. Click **Save** to export the image as multiple image slices. The **html** page contains all the code for your image to be reassembled in a table as part of your Dreamweaver page.

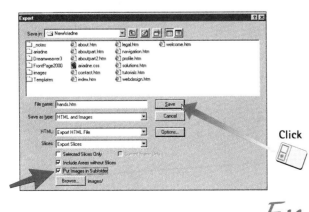

Click

How-To Hints

What Is Fireworks HTML?

Fireworks HTML is the code created when you use either slices or hotspots in an image. We will look at imagemaps and hotspots in Task 3. The HTML contains all the necessary information for the browser to rebuild your images, show links, and download correctly in the browser.

Fireworks will create a complete HTML page for you when you use hotspots and slices. As you work through the tasks in this part, you will see that you can use the page, just the code, or let Dreamweaver insert the code and then delete the Fireworks page after you have used it.

End

How to See a Rebuilt Image

If you followed the steps in Task 1, you have created several files from a single sliced image using Fireworks. You can rebuild the image by inserting the HTML file that Fireworks also created into your Dreamweaver site and viewing the page with the **File, Preview in Browser** command. If you want, you can view the **HTML** code Fireworks generates for you: Click the **Code and Design View** button on the Dreamweaver toolbar.

Begin

1 Open Dreamweaver

If Dreamweaver isn't already open on your desktop, open it now by selecting **Start, Programs, Macromedia Dreamweaver 4, Dreamweaver 4**.

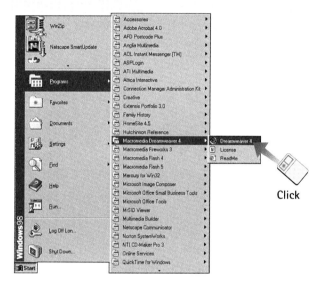

Click

2 Open the Page

Choose **File, Open** to launch the **Open** dialog box. When you exported the sliced image from Fireworks, it created an HTML page that contains the information necessary to rebuild the image (see Step 6 of Task 1). Locate this file and open it into the Dreamweaver document window. When the HTML file opens in the Dreamweaver document window, it will look almost as it did before you sliced and exported it from Fireworks.

Click

3 See the Image in Dreamweaver

Although the HTML file you loaded does not contain the image itself (the image files are stored in the **images** directory for the site), it contains references to those image files so that Dreamweaver can reassemble the slices into the original image.

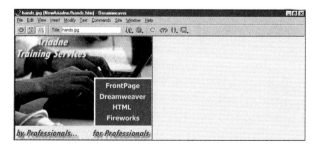

4 Choose Preview in Browser

So that you understand how the browser rebuilds the sliced image in stages, you should view the page in a browser. From the Dreamweaver **File** menu, choose **Preview in Browser** and select your preferred browser.

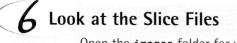

Click

5 Watch the Image Rebuild

The image rebuilds completely into the browser window. However, the time it takes to assemble the sliced image files into a whole takes less time than it would to display the original large image file.

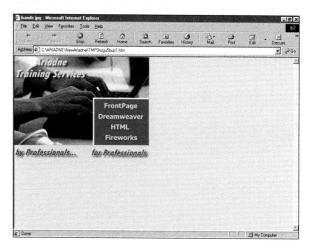

6 Look at the Slice Files

Open the **images** folder for your site to see all the separate image files that Fireworks created from the slices.

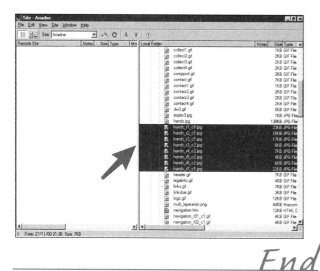

End

How-To Hints

Table Properties

By default, Fireworks creates a **shim.gif** file, which is a very small image file used to ensure that your tables and images align correctly. If you want Fireworks to create nested tables to achieve this alignment instead, check out the **HTML Properties** dialog box. Choose **File, HTML Properties**. Note that any changes you make here become the default for future exports.

Be Careful Using Nested Tables

If you choose to use the **Nested Tables** option for your sliced images, beware! Using nested tables can increase download time for your rebuilt file.

How to Create an Imagemap in Fireworks

In Task 1, we simply sliced an image, cutting it into several rectangular pieces so that it would download more quickly. You can also use a graphic image to create an *imagemap* in Fireworks. In an imagemap, you define several hotspot areas within a single image; each hotspot is a link to additional information. If you then slice the imagemap image, you have an image that will not only load quickly, but will also have any links that you want already inserted.

Begin

1 Open the Image to Edit

In Fireworks, open the image you want to transform into an imagemap. Images appropriate for imagemaps vary depending on the purpose of the site. In this example, I use a map of Great Britain and define several hotspots that link to travel information about those particular areas of the country.

2 Decide on Hotspot Areas

A geographic map like the one in this example has regions such as states, countries, or cities that are logical locations for hotspots. Decide where you want your hotspots to be and select the **Hotspot** tool from the toolbox. Choose the appropriate shape for the tool from the menu of options that appears when you click and hold the tool.

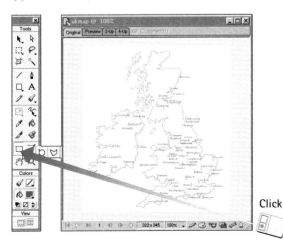

Click

3 Draw a Hotspot

Click in the image and drag out the first hotspot so that it covers the area you want to function as a link. When you release the mouse button, the area becomes highlighted in blue. You'll control the properties of the hotspot using the **Object** panel; choose **Window, Object** to display this panel.

Drag

4 Add the URL to Link

In the **Link** field of the **Object** panel for the hotspot, type the name (and path if required) to the file to which you want to link this hotspot. In the <alt> field, type some text that will appear in a pop-up box over the image when the visitor moves the mouse over the hotspot. If you are using frames, specify the target frame in which you want the linked page to open; otherwise leave the **Target** field blank.

Linked URL
Popup text
Target frame

5 Add More Hotspots

Complete the image by drawing additional hotspots. Fill out the **Object** panel to create a link for each hotspot.

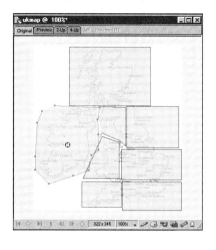

6 Export the File

Choose **File, Export Wizard** to open the wizard. Leave the settings as they are and click the **Export** button to open the **Export Preview** window. Follow the steps in Task 1 to export the file, ignoring the slicing options. You must export the image to ensure that the code containing the link information is also saved. You can export the file as a GIF or a JPEG, depending on the type of image you are working with. Note that the hotspots do not appear in the preview. Fireworks exports a complete HTML page with the image and all the code for the links.

7 Preview in Browser

Open Dreamweaver and load the file you created in Step 6. Choose **File, Preview in Browser** to test that the files have all exported correctly. Check that all the links work and that all the alternative text you added appears when you hover the mouse over the hotspots on the image.

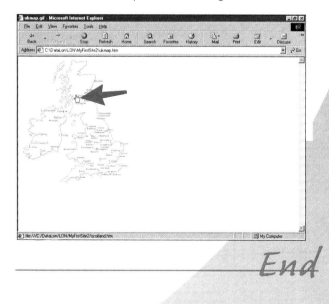

End

How to Create a Text Slice

Text slices are great! In simple terms, a *text slice* is a way to add HTML text to a section of your image. When you slice the image, Fireworks creates a table cell that contains only text, no images. If you use text slices in your images, you can change the text in Dreamweaver without having to launch Fireworks. This is a great idea if you want to advertise a particular item on sale one week and then change the text or price for the item the following week.

Begin

1 Open the Image

Open Fireworks and load the image to which you want to add a text slice.

2 Draw a Text Slice Object

In the toolbox, click the **Slice** tool to select it. Drag out a slice rectangle where you want the text to appear on the image.

Drag

3 Set the Type to Text

On the **Object** panel for the slice you just drew, set the slice **Type** to **Text**.

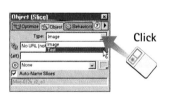

Click

4 Add the Text

In the white text box at the bottom of the **Object** panel, type the text you want to appear on the image. This should be a short message— something that can be changed or amended easily. Also remember that the text has to fit within the slice. Because you can change the text regularly, keep it short and sweet.

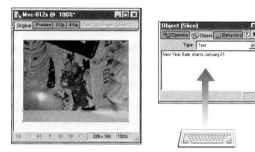

6 Format the Text

Because the text is not actually part of the image (it is located in a single cell within the Fireworks table), you can format the text in Dreamweaver just as you do any other text on the page. Open the HTML file Fireworks created into Dreamweaver. You can then use the **Properties Inspector** to format the text to match your site.

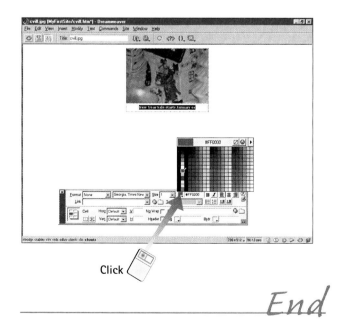

Click

5 Export the File

Use the export procedures to export the file into your Web site directory—make sure that you export the slice object as well. Use the most appropriate export options for the type of image you have used. In this example, I exported the file as a JPEG file because the base image is a photo. Select the **Export Slices** option in the dialog box to ensure that the text slice is correctly exported with the HTML. Fireworks creates a complete HTML file containing the image and text slice.

How-To Hints

Tables on Top of Images

The text slice is, in fact, a table placed on top of the image. Not only can you edit and format the text in the slice in Dreamweaver, but you can also edit the table cell itself, meaning that you can change the background of the cell to make the text stand out.

End

How to Insert Fireworks HTML into Dreamweaver

Fireworks creates a complete HTML page for you that contains not only your graphics, but also any HTML code or JavaScript needed to display your image correctly in the browser window. In the preceding tasks, we have worked on these HTML pages only as complete entities. In this task, we look at what happens when you want to use the image and code in an existing HTML page.

Begin

1 Export a Sliced Image

From Fireworks, follow the steps in Task 1 to export an image containing slices into your Web site's directory. Notice that the single image file you started with has multiplied: Now there are several image files (one for each slice) as well as an HTML file. Open the HTML file directly into Dreamweaver as a separate page.

Multiple image files for slices

The HTML file that unites all the slice files

2 View the Source Code

Click the **Show Code View** button on the toolbar to see the Fireworks-created HTML. It is clearly visible among the other code.

3 Copy the Code

Notice the instructions at the top of the file. You can copy the code created by Fireworks and paste it into another Web page of your choice. When you are working with Dreamweaver, you might never have to do this. However, if you are working with an application other than Dreamweaver, there are very clear instructions in the code for copying and pasting. The code even tells you exactly where and when to start and stop copying.

4 Insert HTML Using Dreamweaver

Dreamweaver has a built-in facility that inserts HTML code generated by Fireworks into an existing Dreamweaver page. In Dreamweaver, open the file you want to contain the exported Fireworks HTML. In the **Common** page of the **Objects** panel, click the **Insert Fireworks HTML** button to open the Insert Fireworks HTML dialog box.

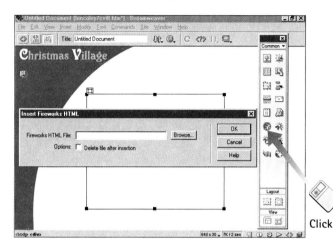

Click

5 Browse to the HTML File

Click the **Browse** button and use the **Select the Fireworks HTML File** dialog box to locate the Fireworks-generated HTML file you want to insert into the current document and click **Open**. Back in the **Insert Fireworks HTML** dialog box, click **OK** to insert the selected file into the document window.

Click

6 Place the Table

The HTML file you inserted into the current Dreamweaver document is called a "Fireworks Table" by the **Properties Inspector.** You can change the properties for this table just as you can change the properties for any other table you create in Dreamweaver, such a making it larger, centering it in a layer, or changing the padding and spacing.

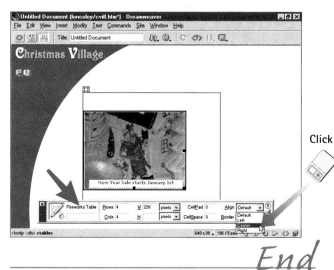

Click

How-To Hints

Copying and Pasting the HTML

In this task, you learned how to copy the HTML, a really quick way of moving the information from Fireworks into your HTML editor. Many people use more than one editor; just because most people who use Fireworks also have Dreamweaver, it might not always be the editor that you are using.

If you select **Edit, Copy HTML Code**, a wizard opens that will guide you through exporting the image files to a specified location and copying the HTML code into the Clipboard. When you paste the code into your editor, the links to the graphics are updated.

End

Task

22

Optimizing Images in Fireworks

*T*he main idea with Web graphics is to create something that looks great in a browser and that site visitors will wait around long enough to see. There is no point in creating the perfect graphic if it takes forever to download. Fireworks has a lot of helpful tools to make your life easier in this regard. You can establish your own optimization settings to ensure that the graphics you create not only look good, but also download quickly.

One of the main features that sets Fireworks apart from other imaging applications is that various parts of the same image can be optimized in different ways. As you know, various types of images have different attributes: Photographs have millions of colors and should be saved as JPEG files; small graphics such as bullets, lines, and buttons contain very few colors, are usually small, might be transparent in parts, and should be exported as GIF files.

However, what happens if your graphic is a composition that uses different object and image types? In most applications, you have to select the best compromise you can find. In Fireworks, however, you can use slices to optimize the different parts of the image to best suit that part of the image. For more information on using slices, refer to Part 21, "Working with Slices and HTML in Fireworks." ●

How to Use the Optimize Panel

In Fireworks, you can optimize your image files as you work in the main window. You can also optimize the image when you finish manipulating it or during the export process. In this task, you get acquainted with the **Optimize** panel.

Begin

1 Open the Optimize Panel

With the image you want to optimize open, choose **Window, Optimize** in the main document window to open the **Optimize** panel. Alternatively, click the **Show Optimize** button at the bottom of the document window.

Click

2 Look at the Panel

The **Optimize** panel contains options that you can set to make the document appear how you want it to appear. Familiarize yourself with this panel before we start to use it. The panel shows the default type of file, the number of colors used, and any transparency that is in the file.

3 Choose a Preset Optimization

Fireworks comes with some built-in optimization settings that you can choose for the current image. These presets vary based on the type of file you are creating. From the **Settings** drop-down menu, choose the appropriate option for your file. The default setting is **GIF WebSnap 128**, which results in a file with a maximum of 128 colors, as close to Web-safe colors as possible. The word *snap* means that the exported image uses colors that are snapped as closely as possible to Web-safe colors. If you are working with a photographic image, choose one of the JPEG options.

Click

4 Set the File Type

Use the **Export File Format** options to select the type of file you are creating. Each of the available file types has some unique optimization settings. For example, you cannot have transparency in a JPEG file. The choice you make here should follow the selection you made in Step 3. Recall that GIF files can be up to only 8-bit color and PNG files can be up to 32-bit color. The next task looks at JPEG files in more detail.

Click

5 Set Transparency

PNG and GIF images can contain transparency when they are exported. This means that your Web page background can appear through parts of your image. Transparency does not affect the actual graphic file: The effect is visible only when the page is displayed in a browser. You can choose the color or colors to be transparent in the browser.

6 Set Color Depth and Dithering

The **Colors** option allows you to set the maximum number of colors used in the file. By keeping this number to a minimum, you can keep the file size down. *Dithering* colors is the process used when a color in the image is not in the current panel. Fireworks uses two Web-safe colors and alternates between them to create the closest match possible. The amount of dithering in the file is set using the slider.

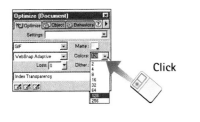

Click

End

How-To Hints

File Type Confusion?

In this task, we merely introduced the **Optimize** panel, so it is quite possible that you are still a little confused. Don't worry too much because the following tasks will help you understand the various file types—and the optimization methods that work best with each. Here are some basic things to remember at this point:

Different images work better in different formats, so make your file format choice based on the type of image you are working with. GIF files are ideal for buttons and nonphotographic logos. JPEG files are ideal for photographs, images that need a large number or colors (more than 256), and images using gradients. PNG is the default format for Fireworks images and produces high-quality images that support transparency and have no loss. However, PNG is not yet fully supported by Web browsers, and so should not be used for your exported images.

TASK **2**

How to Optimize JPEG Files

JPEG is a compression format designed particularly for graphics with continuous colors, such as photographs. Images in the JPEG format cannot have transparency. You can adjust the amount by which the JPEG file is compressed. Remember that the more the file is compressed, the smaller the file is—and the lower the quality of the image. This task looks at the optimization settings available for a JPEG file.

Begin

1 Reduce the Quality

Open a JPEG file in Fireworks. Click the **4-Up** tab to preview the image with four different sets of options. Click one of the previews to select it; all the changes you make are applied to this preview. You can select another preview and apply different options to that preview and then check the differences in the download time and file size. Start the optimization process by dragging the **Quality** slider on the **Optimize** panel to reduce the quality to **50** percent. In this example, I set a different quality for each image.

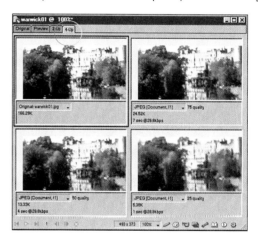

2 Check and Adjust

As you can see, reducing the quality reduced the download time and the file size, but the previews show that the image quality is diminished. Adjust the **Quality** slider until you reach an acceptable compromise between file size and image quality.

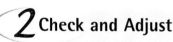

Drag

3 Smooth or Sharpen the Edges

You can reduce the size of a JPEG file by smoothing the hard edges in your file. Do this by adjusting the **Smoothing** setting in the **Optimize** panel. However, you might decide that smoothing the edges blurs your picture too much, even on a low setting. If you want, you can sharpen the edges in the JPEG image to ensure a nice break between color and text or two colors. (Note that sharpening edges can bloat the file size.) To sharpen edges, you must access the export options: Choose **File**, **Export Wizard**.

4 Work Through the Wizard

Click **Continue** on the first page of the **Export Wizard**. When prompted for the destination of the file you are working on, choose **Dreamweaver** and click **Continue**. Fireworks presents an **Analysis Results** window; click **Exit** in this window to view the **Export Preview** window.

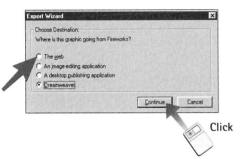

Click

5 Choose the JPEG Preview

The **Export Preview** window presents your image as both a JPEG (the top image) and a GIF (the bottom image). Click the top image area to select the JPEG file format as the one you want to work with. The **Format** drop-down menu at the top-left of the window now displays the **JPEG** option.

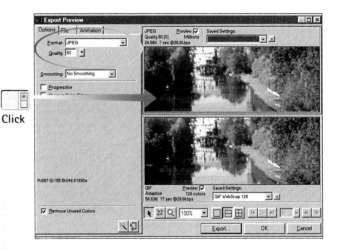

Click

6 Experiment with Options

Enable the **Sharpen Color Edges** check box to enhance the breaks between colors and around text. If you don't like the results you see in the preview, click the check box again to disable the option. Enable the **Progressive** check box to make your image act like an interlaced GIF file. You can also adjust the quality of the image using the **Quality** drop-down menu. To export the file with these settings, click the **Export** button and save the file to your Web site. The graphic is now ready to use on your Web page.

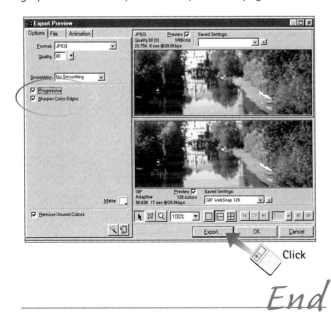

Click

How-To Hints

Progressive Problems?

If other people are working on your files, you should be aware that not all image editing applications can open a progressive JPEG file. In most cases, if you are the only person working on the file, this is not likely to present a problem. If you are working in a group environment, check which applications your co-workers are using. In addition, not all Web browsers can display progressive JPEG images; they simply show the finished image, which gives the illusion of a longer download time.

End

TASK 3

How to Optimize GIF and PNG Files

GIF and PNG files have similar properties except that PNG files can contain more than the 256 colors that GIF files are limited to. You will generally find that GIF and PNG file formats are more effective at compressing files with large areas of solid color (those images without the graduating colors common to JPEG files). This task explains how to optimize GIF and PNG files for Web use.

Begin

1 Choose the Export Wizard

Using an image that is appropriate to export as a GIF, follow the instructions in Task 2 to open the **Export Wizard**. When you get to the **Export Preview** window, click the GIF image area at the bottom of the window to select this format.

Click

2 Choose a Color Depth

The *color depth* of an image is the maximum number of colors available for the image. You can change the number of colors used by a GIF image; the fewer the colors, the smaller the file. Note, however, that you might lose image quality by deleting too many colors. A GIF file can use a maximum of 256 colors, but you can choose a different number from the drop-down menu.

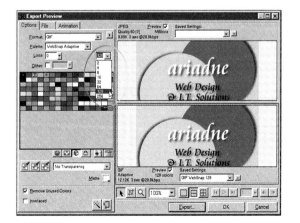

3 Dither Colors

Adjust the **Dither** slider to determine the extent to which the browser can dither colors it can't display. The greater the percentage of dither, the closer the end result will be to the original. If the browser can't display a particular color in the image, it *dithers* (that is, it tries to reproduce the color using alternating pixels of two other colors).

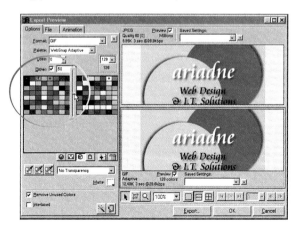

4 Enter a Loss Value

Drag the **Loss** slider to reduce file size and also quality. The higher the **Loss** value, the smaller the file is and the greater the reduction in image quality. Any value over 20 is likely to result in a serious loss of quality, but a value less than 5 probably won't show much difference in image quality.

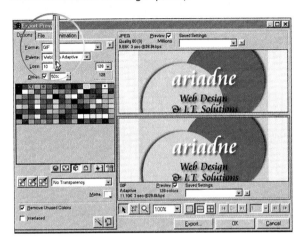

5 Remove Unused Colors

Enable the **Remove Unused Colors** check box to create a file with the smallest file size. All the colors left in the panel after reducing the color depth in Step 2 that the image does not use are removed.

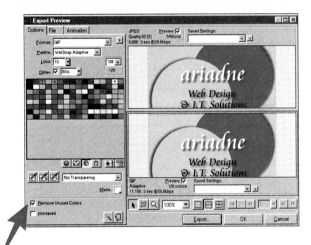

6 Interlace the Image

Interlaced images are those that appear in the browser bit by bit, the quality improving as each part of picture appears. An interlaced GIF file is always larger than a file that is not interlaced, but being able to display a complex graphic and then update the image as the file continues to download might be worth the additional file size. To create an interlaced GIF file, enable the **Interlaced** check box. Click **Export** and save the file into your Web site. The image is now ready to use in your Web pages.

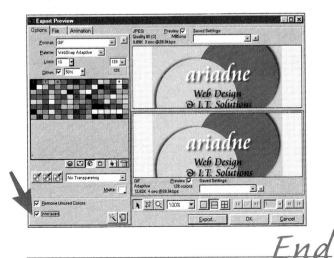

How-To Hints

Optimize a PNG File

When working with 8-bit color images, the options for GIF and PNG files are very similar. However, PNG files can be exported with greater color depth. The greater the depth of color selected, the greater the resulting file size, so use 24-bit or 32-bit PNG files only when you need to. As can GIF images, PNG images can support the use of transparency and interlacing.

Dithering

Dithering can improve the way a GIF file that contains gradients will display. If the image contains continuous-tone colors, check that it wouldn't be smaller as a JPEG file.

End

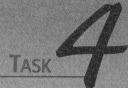

TASK

How to Optimize Colors

When you export either a GIF or a PNG file in 8-bit color or less, the file uses a color panel that contains the required information for the colors used and referenced in the image. This color panel is optimized using the **Color Table** panel.

Begin

1 Open the Optimize Panel

Open the file for which you want to optimize the color panel. Choose **Window, Optimize** to open the **Optimize** panel if it is not already open. The default color panels listed in the **Indexed Panel** drop-down menu are explained in the How-To Hints at the end of this task.

2 Set the Maximum Number of Colors

Use the **Colors** option to specify the color depth (the maximum number of colors) for the image file. The smaller the number of colors, the smaller the file size—but the more you might degrade the quality of the image. Remember that these changes affect only the image you export, not the original, so don't expect to see changes in the document window.

Click

3 Use the Color Table

If it isn't already open, choose **Window, Color Table** to open the **Colors** panel so that you can see all the colors in the panel. Change the panel option in the **Optimize** panel to change the display in the color table. Step 1 shows the **WebSnap Adaptive** panel in the **Colors** panel; here you see the **Windows** color table. Refer to the How-To Hints at the end of this task for information about each panel.

4 Lock a Color into a Panel

Locking colors into a panel ensures that even if you change panels, specific colors will be retained by the image. You might want to lock specific colors for an image if the image uses specific Pantone colors (as is true with many logos). In the **Color Table** panel, select the color you want to lock and then click the lock icon at the bottom of the panel. Select the color and click the lock icon again to unlock this color.

Click

End

How-To Hints

Color Panel Options

Fireworks ships with nine preset color panels, each of which can be selected and optimized to suit your requirements:

The **Adaptive** panel is self-created based on the colors that Fireworks detects within your file. In most circumstances, an **Adaptive** panel produces excellent results—a high-quality image with a small file size.

The **Web Adaptive** panel detects colors that are close to Web-safe colors and converts them in the exported file to the nearest Web-safe color.

The **Web 216** panel uses the 216 colors available on both Macintosh and Windows computers. It is commonly known as a Web-safe panel and produces results that are usually consistent in all browsers. This panel differs from the **Windows** or **Macintosh** panel, which uses the 256 colors available on either operating system.

The **Grayscale** panel uses a maximum of 256 shades of gray. Any image using this panel converts the exported image into shades of gray. The **Black and White** panel is different in that it uses only two colors: black and white with no shades of gray at all.

The **Uniform** panel is made up of the Red Green and Blue values of pixels in the image. The **Custom** panel is one that has been either imported from an external location or has been saved from a previous GIF image.

How to Optimize Graphics That Contain Slices

Fireworks allows you save files that contain image slices with different optimization settings. For example, if you have a graphic that contains both photographic data and solid-color objects, ideally you would want to optimize the photographic area as a JPEG and the solid colors as a GIF. Fireworks allows you to do that easily by using slices.

Begin

1 Open or Create a Graphic

Open or create a graphic that contains elements to be optimized in different ways. This file contains both a photograph and other objects. I want the photograph to remain as a JPEG; the other objects are fine as GIF images.

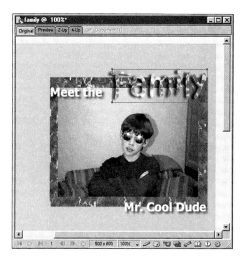

2 Create a Slice for the Photo

Select the photograph within the graphic and choose **Insert, Slice**. Fireworks draws a slice the same size as the selected area. Open the **Optimize** panel by choosing **Window, Optimize**.

3 Optimize the Slice

In the document window, click the slice to select it. In the **Optimize** panel, select **JPEG-Smaller File** from the **Settings** drop-down menu.

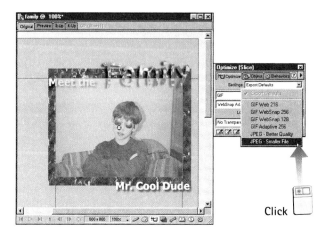

Click

4 View the Optimized Effect

Select the **2 Up** tab to see two versions of the file. The right pane shows you the optimized version of the file, with the photographic area clearly visible; the left pane shows the original image. If you cannot see the sliced area clearly, use the **Pan** tool (the hand icon) to bring it to the center of the pane.

5 Optimize the Rest of the File

When you select the slice, you can change the optimization settings that affect the slice. By clicking in any other part of the image, you can optimize those areas instead. The title bar of the **Optimize** panel clearly states which area is currently selected. In this example, we have to optimize the rest of the file as a GIF.

6 Export the Image

The settings you applied to the individual slices for the image are exported along with the image when you use the **Export Wizard**. Make sure that you select the **Export Slices** option when you export the file. As you can see, being able to apply optimization settings to individual slices gives you control over all parts of the image.

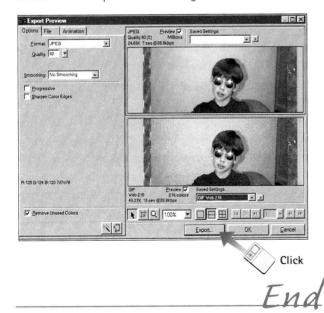

Click

How-To Hints

Save the Original File

When you export the sliced Fireworks File for use in a Web page, remember also to save the file as a Fireworks PNG to make future editing easy.

End

Glossary

A

action   JavaScript code inserted into a Web page. Actions are what happens when events are triggered.

align   The term used to specify where your page elements appear. Images can be aligned to the left, right, or center of a page, layer, or table; they also can be aligned vertically in relation to the text in a paragraph.

anchor   A specified point on a page to which you can link so that the page opens to that particular spot rather than to the top of the page.

asset   Any element that is part of a Web site. Assets are all the images, templates, library items, movies, colors, and URLs that make up the site. Dreamweaver collects all the information about your site and displays a categorized list of assets in the **Assets** panel.

authoring tool   The aspect of Dreamweaver that allows you to add scripts and animations wherever and whenever you want them.

B

background color   A color that displays while the background image is loading. Specify a background color for your pages so that your text will be visible even if the background image fails to load. If you want a solid-color background, do not specify an image.

background image   An image that tiles (repeats in a tile-like fashion) to fill the background of a page.

BASEFONT   The default size of the text you type in a document window. You can change the size of the font on the page by specifying a particular font size or by sizing the text relative to the BASEFONT size.

baseline   The imaginary line on which the base of letters rests. Descenders in letters such as *g* or *q* dip below the baseline.

baseline shift   The moving of selected letters to positions above or below the baseline (the line on which the letters rest) to create subscript and superscript characters within your text.

behavior   A JavaScript script that allows you to create interactive Web pages easily in Dreamweaver.

Behaviors Inspector   A Dreamweaver window that allows you to attach, check, and modify any behaviors you have set.

bevel   A special effect that you can apply to an object in Fireworks.

BMP   A Windows bitmap image format that features low quality and large file sizes. BMP images are used for screen backgrounds. Not suitable for display on Web pages.

button   A form element. Buttons are used to perform actions such as activating a search, resetting the form, or submitting the completed form to the server. You can change the text on the button face to make it clear what the action of the button is. The action of the button is controlled by the form handling script.

C

cache   A storage space in memory or on the hard disk that Dreamweaver uses to help manage the site and to ensure that links are kept up-to-date. When you first create a site, you can specify that a cache be created along with the site. In Dreamweaver, the **Assets** panel requires a disk cache so that it can assemble and sort pertinent data for the site.

cell padding   In a table, the amount of space between an object contained in a cell and the border of the cell.

cell spacing   The amount of space between two cells in a table.

check box   A form element. Forms typically use multiple check boxes when more than one answer is acceptable, as in a list of preferences. A single check box can be used for yes and no answers or to enable or disable an option. The user clicks the check box to place a tick mark in the box.

color depth   The maximum number of colors available for the image. A GIF file, for example, can have a maximum of 256 colors; a JPEG file can have millions of colors; and a PNG file can also have millions of colors.

command   A series of actions saved as a single named action that you can apply over and over again—to elements in a single document or to elements in multiple documents.

crop   To cut away unwanted areas of an image to focus the viewer's attention on the desired subject.

CSS (Cascading Style Sheets) styles   CSS styles are custom created for a site and are used to control the way that page elements are displayed. From formatting text to adding borders and backgrounds to tables and text, CSS can be used to guarantee consistency in your site.

D

definition list   A list in which the word being defined appears left-justified, with the definition on the following line, slightly indented.

delimiter   A character that separates information in table fields or a spreadsheet. Commas and tabs are the two most common delimiters used.

DHTML (Dynamic Hypertext Markup Language)   A programming language that gives you the flexibility to lay out and create interactive Web pages.

distort   To change an image's dimension with no regard for ratio or appearance. Distorting an image is an easy way to add interest to a simple graphic or to text.

dither   The process by which an application tries to reproduce a color that it can't otherwise display by using alternating pixels of two other colors. You can set how carefully the application tries to produce the missing color by setting a dither percentage. The greater the percentage, the closer the result is to the missing color.

docking   The process of combining panels into a single floating panel. Each panel is represented by tabs at the top of the floating panel; click a tab to display that panel.

E

editable region   On a template, this is a region that has been designated specifically as an area that can be changed. If the area on the template has not been designated as an editable region, that area cannot be changed.

element   An item on a page, such as a graphic or text.

emboss   A special effect that you can apply to an object in Fireworks.

event   In a script, the incident that triggers the action. For example, you might want a particular action to occur when the user clicks a button; the button click is the event that triggers the scripted action.

Exchange   The online site provided by Macromedia where you can go to get easy-to-install extensions that add new features to Dreamweaver. You can access the Exchange from the main screen of the Dreamweaver Support Center site.

export   To take a file from its native application and prepare it for use in another application. For example, you can create a graphics file in Fireworks, save it in the Fireworks native PNG format, and then export the file to Dreamweaver as a GIF file.

extension   Sometimes called an "add-in" or a "plug-in." Extensions provide additional features for your Dreamweaver software. Many extensions can be downloaded from the Macromedia Exchange at **http://www.macromedia.com/ exchange/dreamweaver/**. These downloadable extensions are categorized by type and cover everything from DHTML effects to the latest browser profiles. Make sure that you download extensions for Dreamweaver version 4. The site will tell you which version of Dreamweaver the extensions work with.

external hyperlink   A hyperlink that links to a page within a different site.

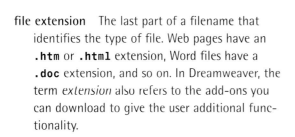

file extension   The last part of a filename that identifies the type of file. Web pages have an **.htm** or **.html** extension, Word files have a **.doc** extension, and so on. In Dreamweaver, the term *extension* also refers to the add-ons you can download to give the user additional functionality.

file field   A form element. A file field is a specific kind of text box that accepts the pathname to a file or folder. A file field comes with a Browse button that the user can click to locate files or folders on the local machine. Forms use file fields so that users can specify the location to which they want to download files or from which they want to upload files. Before you use a file field on a form, check with your hosting company to make sure that your server can accept a file attached to a form.

font family   A generic name for a group of similar fonts. Most computers acknowledge these font families: cursive, fantasy, monospace, sans serif, and serif. If a browser cannot display any of the specific fonts you have chosen, the browser will display the text using the default font associated with the font family.

form   A container object that holds all your form elements (text boxes, radio buttons, and so on). Forms are used to collect data and information from site visitors.

form elements   The parts of a form—the text fields, check boxes, and radio buttons—that the visitor fills in or selects.

form field validation   A behavior that checks whether the visitor to a form has entered the right kind of information in the form fields and ensures that necessary information has not been omitted. The validation behavior is executed when the visitor clicks the Submit button on the form.

frames   Individual Web pages held together in sets. When the browser sees them, it draws the frames together to give the impression of a single page.

frameset   An HTML page that holds all the information for all the frames you want to appear together. When you create a frameset, you must also create the individual pages to be displayed as frames.

GIF (graphics image format)   An image format that is ideal for small files using minimal colors. The GIF format can support up to 256 colors as well as the use of transparency. GIF files are ideal for buttons, lines, and backgrounds.

GIF animation file   A single GIF file created from multiple frames. GIF animations are ideal for Web pages because they have small file sizes.

glow   A special effect you can apply to an object in Fireworks.

gridlines Lines that display on your page as squares set to a size of your choice. Gridlines can be used with or without the rulers to help you achieve exact placement of elements and layers on the page.

head content The title information about the page. The head section also contains any metatags that you add to your site and is commonly used for holding references to scripts.

hidden field A form element. Hidden fields usually contain information used by the server when it processes the form. The user cannot see or change the information contained in the hidden field.

home page The first page that visitors to your site see. The home page in your site has the filename `index.html` or `default.html`.

hosting company The company that hosts your Web site. This can be your ISP or a specific hosting company that offers the services you require. If you want to use CGI or ASP scripts, make sure that the hosting service you intend to use offers support for these technologies before signing up with it.

hotspot In a larger graphic image that functions as an imagemap or a navigational tool for the site, one of the areas that actually links to another page or site. For example, if you have an imagemap of a U.S. map, each state can be a hotspot that, when clicked, links to a page or site about that particular state.

HTML editor The aspect of Dreamweaver in which you input your page content and can change the HTML code that actually creates the Web page.

HTML styles A named group of formatting elements that you can apply to text and paragraphs in a site. Styles are a way to ensure consistent formatting of the text in your site. After you create an HTML style, you can reuse it.

hyperlink An image or a clickable piece of text that takes the site visitor to another page or reference in the site, to another Web site, or to an open email application.

image field A form element. An image field can consist of any appropriately sized graphic image. When the user clicks the graphic, the action assigned to the graphic occurs, just as it does when you click a normal button.

imagemap A single image with areas that are actually links to other pages or sites. For example, you can have a graphic of a pirate ship on your site's home page. Clicking the skull and crossbones can link the visitor to a list of banner vendors; clicking the carved figurehead on the front of the pirate ship can link to a list of woodworkers; clicking the trapdoor can link to an online version of a popular dungeons-and-dragons game.

instance A copy of a symbol (located in the library) that can be used over and over again.

internal hyperlink A hyperlink that links to a page within the same site.

JPEG (Joint Photographic Expert Group) The best format for photographs because JPEG files contain millions of colors. JPEG images don't give you the option of including transparency or interlaced images, but they do allow you to specify the degree of file compression so that you can create a balance between image quality and file size.

jump menu A form element. A jump menu is a list of hyperlinks presented on the form as a drop-down menu. When the user makes a choice from the drop-down menu, a hyperlink is activated. Items on the jump menu can link to other pages within the site or to external pages elsewhere on the Internet.

K

kerning   Changing the amount of space between two or more letters to make the letters look less tight or less airy. This adjustment feature is especially handy with large fonts and for letter combinations that don't fit together well (such as *AW*).

keyboard shortcut   A keyboard equivalent for using the mouse to open a menu and select a command. For example, pressing **Ctrl+F2** ⌘**+F2** on the Mac) is the keyboard shortcut for opening the **Window** menu and selecting **Objects** (both approaches open the **Objects** panel).

keyframe   One of the white circles along the animation marker in the timelines panel. The keyframe markers indicate where the animation starts, stops, or changes direction during the course of the animation.

L

Launcher   One of the panels most commonly used in Dreamweaver. This panel contains buttons for opening and closing other panels and windows.

layer   A container or holder for page content. Layers can hold any page element, have their own properties and settings, and also have the advantage of being positioned exactly on the page. In Web design terms, layers are still an innovation, implemented quite recently into the vocabulary of Web designers and developers. The idea behind layers was to give designers complete control over the appearance of the content of the pages at all times.

leading   The amount of space between lines of text (in other words, the line spacing).

Library   A folder for a site that contains all the page elements you use or update frequently. Also the location in the **Assets** panel that permits the storage of elements you want to reuse in your site. If you insert items on your pages from the library, you can update all those pages simply by updating the element in the Library. The Library then traces the item's links to pages

in the site and updates the pages with the new version of the item.

library items   The page elements (images, text, and so on) contained in the Library folder for a site.

link   *See* hyperlink.

list   A form element. A list offers a scrollable list of options from which the user can select multiple options. *See also* menu.

local folder   How Dreamweaver refers to the location on your hard disk that contains all the files used to create the current Web site.

lossless   A compression technique that makes large graphics or audio files smaller without noticeable loss of data. The ubiquitous WinZip program, for example, compresses files without losing any of the data in the files.

lossy   A compression technique that makes large graphics or audio files smaller by actually dropping some information from the file. (For example, you can save a large color graphic file to a smaller size by removing some of the colors.) The JPEG compression technique uses the lossy method to make smaller file sizes.

M–N

menu   A form element. A menu offers a drop-down list of options from which the user can select only one. *See also* list.

metatags   The term used for keywords and descriptions used by search engines to locate sites that match a search request.

multiframe editing   A feature in Fireworks that enables you to edit the visible contents of any frame. If you have turned on the onion skinning feature, you can edit the content of any frame you see in the document window   not just the content of the currently selected frame.

navigation bar   A collection of buttons that have been saved as a group to create a navigation system for a Web site.

navigation frame   A separate frame on a page in which lists of links to other pages in the Web site can be found. Because the navigation frame remains onscreen even when other pages are displayed in the main frame, the links in the navigation frame can be accessed at any time, making the navigation frame an easy way for visitors to navigate through your site.

nested frameset   A frameset within another frameset.

nested tables   A table inserted inside another table. For example, you might use one table as a design element for your page; you might want to insert into that table another table of information. The second table is "nested" within the design table.

O

Objects panel   One of the panels most commonly used in Dreamweaver. The Objects panel has six categories, each of which offers shortcuts to menu commands and other actions.

onion skinning   A common technique when working with animations. In simple terms, it allows you to see the contents of more than one frame at a time. Onion skinning can help you move an object a certain distance from one frame to the next; the "ghost images" of the objects in the frames before and after the current frame help you position the objects in the current frame.

option button   *See* radio button.

P–Q

padding   *See* cell padding.

page properties   The default properties for the pages in a site. You can specify these properties in the **Page Properties** dialog box. Properties include the title of the page, the background color and image for the page, text and link colors, and margins.

panel   A collection of tools used for performing functions or actions. For example, the Objects panel allows you to insert various objects into your pages.

PCX   Originally developed by Zsoft for its PCpaintbrush program, PCX is a graphics file format for graphics programs running on PCs. This format is not suitable for display on Web pages.

PNG   An image format similar to the GIF format that is the default file format for graphics files created in Fireworks. PNG files can have millions of colors and are more effective at compressing files with large areas of solid color than JPEG files are.

progressive JPEG   A version of a JPEG file that acts like an interlaced GIF file. When a progressive JPEG file loads on a Web page, a low-resolution version of the file appears first and continues to improve as the file completes the download process.

properties   The information about the currently selected page element. Image properties include the source reference, dimensions, and any Alt text. Text properties include the color, font, and size of the text.

Properties Inspector   One of the panels most commonly used in Dreamweaver. When you select an element on the page, you can view the properties for that element in the Properties Inspector.

R

radio button   A form element. Radio buttons are used when the visitor must choose only one of several options (as when choosing an age category on a personal information form). When you build a form that includes radio buttons, you must group the associated radio buttons together.

resample   To change the resolution. Resampling an image object adds or removes pixels as required to make the image larger or smaller. Resampling a path object causes it to be redrawn at a larger size with minimum loss of quality.

rollover   The effect caused by moving a mouse pointer over a Web-page button. The original button might be red, but hovering the mouse pointer over the button might change the button to green; clicking the button might cause the button to turn purple and then black as it remains in the "pressed in" position. These color changes are one example of a button rollover effect.

ruler   A convenient measurement tool that you can display in the document window to show exactly where each and every element has been placed. Rulers are particularly handy if you are not accustomed to using the pixel measurement system. Although rulers can be displayed in centimeters and inches, they appear in pixels by default.

S

script   A dedicated piece of JavaScript or other language coding that performs a task in your Web page. Scripts are usually JavaScript or CGI (common gateway interface) and are used for everything from handling and processing forms to checking which browser a site visitor is using.

site manager   The aspect of Dreamweaver that lets you see all your Web site files at a glance.

skew   To slant an image either vertically or horizontally (or both). Skewing an image is an easy way to add interest to a simple graphic or text.

slice   An individual part of an image file. Slices can be optimized individually, can have hotspots attached, and are used in the creation of rollovers. Slices can be edited individually, meaning that you can use the same images from file to file and change only the required slices.

spacing   *See* cell spacing.

style   A group of formatting options that can be applied to elements on the page to make the formatting of those elements consistent. For example, you can create a style that formats a paragraph of text in a certain way (with a certain font, size, and color). If you apply that style to all paragraphs of text on the page, the document will be formatted consistently.

symbol   An object that is stored in the Library.

T–V

tabular data   Information created in another application (such as Microsoft Excel) and saved in a delimited format (comma or tab separated).

target   A link that specifies which frame or window a page displays in when it opens.

template   Predesigned Web pages on which you can model additional Web pages. Dreamweaver does not come with templates; you can, however, make your own templates that you can use to build all the pages for your site. Templates make it easy to design a complete site with consistent elements.

text box   A form element. A text box is a bound field into which visitors to the form can type free-form responses. Text boxes can be formatted to a specific size to allow a maximum number of characters and to allow the visitor to enter a single line or multiple lines of text. Text boxes can be designated as password boxes, meaning that characters the visitor types are disguised as asterisks as they appear on the screen.

text slice   A slice of an image that contains only text. You can edit the text in the text slice in Dreamweaver, even if the image was created or modified in Fireworks.

thumbnail   A smaller version of a graphic that, when clicked, opens to a larger version of the same image. Thumbnail versions of images download quickly and allow your site visitors to decide which images they want to see enlarged. If you use thumbnail images, you actually must have two versions of the same image available: one larger and one smaller.

TIFF (Tagged Image File Format)   The only file format that can be edited on both PC and Macintosh machines. Not suitable for display on Web pages.

tracing image   A Dreamweaver feature that allows you to copy a page layout from a graphic "mock-up." Use the tracing image as a screen background and position elements and images exactly on top of it. The tracing image is only displayed in Dreamweaver.

trigger   An event that tells Dreamweaver when to begin a particular action or animation. For example, the trigger that tells an animation on a page to start can be the loading of the page.

tweening   In creating animations, a process by which Fireworks creates the movement between frames for you.

W–Z

window   A pane or special box that shows you information about a certain aspect of your page or site. For example, the **Site** window shows all the files in your current site, and the **HTML Source** window shows the code behind your current page.

Z index   A value that indicates the order in which a particular layer appears in the "stack" of layers on the page. The higher the Z index value a layer has, the higher up in the stack of layers that layer will appear.

Index

scripts, configuring for forms, 204–205. See also behaviors

scrollbars (frames), 148

Search facility (Support Center), 14

Search help (main help screen), 13

searching assets, 209

Select Image Source dialog box, 90–91

Select Template dialog box, 226–227

selecting layers, 129

Selection tool (Fireworks), 252

Set Color Scheme command (Commands menu), 43, 81

Set Color Scheme Command dialog box, 81

shadow effects
adding to objects, 286–287
applying to text (Fireworks), 280

shapes, drawing (Fireworks), 252–253

sharing layers, 317

shortcuts (File menu), 48

Show Code and Design Views button (toolbar), 22, 163

Show Me movies (help system), 15

Show Panels command (Window menu), 10

Site Definition dialog box, 38–39

Site menu, 27

Site view (assets), 213, 215

Site window, 39
links, 72
Web pages, opening, 48

sites. See Web sites

sizing
document window, 45
images, 92–93, 254–255
symbols, 323

skewing images in Fireworks, 259

slices, 331
exporting images into Dreamweaver, 340–341
large images, splitting, 332–333
optimizing images with slices, 352–353
previewing rebuilt images, 334–335
text slices, creating, 338–339

slider (History panel), 32

snapping
layers to grids, 133
panels to edge of screen, 35

source files (images), 92

spaces (images), 94

Spell check feature, 66–67

Split-screen view, 22–23

splitting frames, 152

standalone panels, 34

states, adding to buttons, 300–301

Status bars
displaying text, 160–163
document window, 8

steps, 32
reusing, 33
setting amount retained in History panel, 33
undoing, 32

style sheets
Cascading Style Sheets. See CSS
importing, 135
linking to Web pages, 135

Submit buttons, 193

Support Center, 14–15

Switching between open Web pages, 49

Symbol editor (Fireworks), 270–271

Symbol Properties dialog box (Fireworks), 266–267

symbols, 265
animating, 320–323
converting objects to symbols, 267
copying, 270
creating, 266–267
deleting, 270
editing, 270–271
exporting, 268–269
fading, 322
importing, 269
instances, 265, 272–273
library symbols, 268–269
links, breaking, 271
resizing, 323
rotating, 322
transformation effects, 321

synchronizing files (uploading files), 232–233

syntax coloring (HTML code), 235

T

tables, converting layers to, 138–139

Tag selector (document window), 8

tags (HTML)
attributes, 241
<DIV>, 133
<ILAYER>, 133
<LAYER>, 133
reference, displaying, 239–241
Reference feature, 25

target frames, 94

templates
applying to Web pages, 226–227
creating, 220–223

editable regions
creating, 221, 224
deleting, 225
highlights, setting, 223
naming, 222
editing, 224–225
managing, 226–227
Web pages
creating, 41
saving as templates, 223

testing
frameset links, 156–157
links, 82–83

text, 53, 275
adding to images (Fireworks), 260–261
aligning, 56–57, 279
alternative text
imagemaps, 101
images, 93
anti-aliased text, 279
baseline shift, 278
bold, 55
button text, editing, 301
Cascading Style Sheets (CSS), defining, 64–65
centering, 56
colors
changing, 54
selecting in Fireworks, 279
setting, 43
displaying in status bar, 160–163
editing in Fireworks, 276–277
entering, 54
fills, 281
finding and replacing, 68–69
fonts
changing, 58–59
size, 54–55
formatting, 54–55, 277
indenting, 57
italic, 55
kerning, 278
leading, 278
links
bold text, 81
colors, selecting, 80–81
creating, 72–73
properties, 31, 278–279
saving as an image file, 282–283
shadow effects, 280
textures, 281
underlined, 55
wrapping around images, 104–105

Text Editor (Fireworks), 276–279
aligning text, 279
anti-aliased text, 279
baseline shift, setting, 278
kerning, setting, 278
text colors, selecting, 279

Text Editor dialog box, 260–261

text fields
adding to forms, 192
formatting in forms, 196–197

Text menu, 27

text slices, 338-339

Text tool (Fireworks), 276

textures, 281

thumbnail images, 78

timeline animations
B channel, 180-181
behaviors, adding, 180-181
creating, 174-177
keyframes
adding, 182-183
deleting, 183
playback rate, 187
layers, 178-179, 184-187

Timelines panel
animations
creating, 174-177
layers, adding, 178-179
keyframes, 182-183

Title bar, 9

titles
documents, 23
framesets, 147
Web pages, 42

Toolbar, 4, 6, 22-25
Code Only button, 22
Copy button, 87
Design View button, 22
File Status button, 23
Options button, 22-23
Page Title text box, 23
Paste button, 88
Preview in Browser button, 24
Reference button, 25
Refresh Design View button, 25
Show Code and Design Views
button, 22, 163

Toolbox (Fireworks toolbox), 248,
252-253

transformation effects, applying to
symbols, 321

transforming instances, 272

transparency (images), setting in
Fireworks, 345

triggers (animation), 176

Tween Instances dialog box
(Fireworks), 320

tweening (animations), 312,
320-323

U - V

underlined text, 55

undoing steps, 32

Uniform panel (Fireworks), 351

updating links, 87

uploading files, 230-233

Using Dreamweaver command (Help
menu), 12

Validate Form dialog box, 202-203

validation (form fields), 202-203

vertical orientation (Launcher), 18

vertical space (images), 94

vertical splits (framesets), 142

View menu, 26, 191

viewing. See displaying

Visibility setting (layers), 132

W - Z

Web 216 panel (Fireworks), 351

Web Adaptive panel, 351

Web browsers
adding to Preview in Browser list, 24,
50-51
AOL browsers, 51
default browser, 24
event support, viewing, 163
NoFrames option, 150
removing from Preview in Browser
list, 51
windows, opening with behaviors,
169

Web Layer (Fireworks), 310

Web pages
background colors, 43
background images, 42
behaviors, 164-165
closing, 48
creating, 40-41
images, 90-91
link colors, 43
margins, 43
naming, 46-47
opening, 48-49
page view, 44-45
previewing in browsers, 50-51
properties, 42
saving, 40-43, 46-47
switching between, 49
templates
applying to Web pages, 226-227
saving pages as, 223
text colors, 43
titles, 42

Web sites
defining, 38-39
Dreamweaver Support Center, 14-15
home pages, 40
local root folders, selecting, 38
Macromedia, 12, 244-245, 323
Macromedia Exchange, 170-171
naming, 38
pages
background colors, 43
background images, 42
behaviors, 164-165
closing, 48
creating, 40-41
link colors, 43

margins, 43
naming, 46-47
opening, 48-49
page view, 44-45
previewing in browsers, 50-51
properties, 42
saving, 40-41, 43, 46-47
switching between, 49
text colors, 43
titles, 42
uploading, 230-233

What's New in Dreamweaver 4
command (Help menu), 12

What's New section (Support
Center), 15

width values
frames, 147, 153
images, 92, 95
layers, 131

Window menu, 27
Hide Panels command, 10
History command, 32
Launcher command, 18
panels, 10
Properties command, 30
Show Panels command, 10

Window Size menu (document
window), 8

windows
browser windows
opening with behaviors, 169
closing, 11, 19
displaying, 10
document window, 4-11
download time display, 9
file size display, 9
grid, 45
Launcher, 9
mini Launcher, 9
resizing, 45
rulers, 44
snapping panels to document
window, 9
status bar, 8
tag selector, 8
title bar, 9
Window Size menu, 8
hiding, 10
opening with Launcher, 19
Site window, 39
links, creating, 72
opening Web pages, 48

Word, importing HTML documents
from Word, 60-61

Word files (HTML format), 49

word wrap (HTML code), 235

wrapping text around images,
104-105

Z index (layers), 131

HOW to USE

How to Use provides easy, visual information in a proven, step-by-step format. This amazing guide uses colorful illustrations and clear explanations to get you the results you need.

All prices are subject to change.